The Irish Story

R. F. FOSTER

The Irish Story

TELLING TALES AND MAKING IT UP IN IRELAND

OXFORD

UNIVERSITY PRESS

2002

OXFORD
UNIVERSITY PRESS

Oxford   New York
Auckland Bangkok Buenos Aires
Cape Town Chennai Dar es Salaam Delhi Hong Kong Istanbul
Karachi Kolkata Kuala Lumpur Madrid Melbourne Mexico City Mumbai
Nairobi São Paulo Shanghai Singapore Taipei Tokyo Toronto

and an associated company in Berlin

First published by Allen Lane, The Penguin Press, London, 2001

Published by Oxford University Press, Inc.
198 Madison Avenue, New York, New York 10016

Library of Congress Cataloging-in-Publication Data
is available at the Library of Congress
ISBN 0-19-515902-0

1 3 5 7 9 10 8 6 4 2
Printed in the United States of America
on acid-free paper

For Tom Dunne

Contents

Acknowledgements

I should like to thank the friends and colleagues who have helped with criticisms, suggestions and inquiries: they include Toby Barnard, Brendan Barrington, Peter Conradi, Mary Daly, Jack Dunn, Owen Dudley Edwards, Marianne Elliott, Richard English, Antony Farrell, David Gilmour, Victoria Glendinning, Warwick Gould, Henry Hardy, Michael Holroyd, Paul Keegan, John Kelly, Sunil Khilnani, Hermione Lee, Mary-Lou Legg, Ian McBride, the late Angus Macintyre, Bill McCormack, Christina Hunt Mahony, William M. Murphy, Senia Paseta, Sheila Sheehan, Bruce Stewart, Robert Tobin, Deirdre Toomey and Leon Wieseltier. Valerie Kemp helped immeasurably with the production of the whole. Two people merit special mention: my wife, Aisling, for her eternal critical vigilance, and Tom Dunne, with whom I have discussed so many of the ideas in this book, and to whom it is dedicated with unreserved affection and admiration.

I should also like to thank Simon Winder, most encouraging of publishers, Gill Coleridge, most supportive of agents, and Donna Poppy, most perfectionist and perceptive of editors.

Some of these pieces have first appeared in partial or different versions elsewhere: parts of Chapters 1 and 2 as pamphlets published by Oxford University Press and Queen Mary and Westfield College in 1995 and 1997 respectively, part of Chapter 1 in G. Cubitt (ed.), *Imagining Nations* (Manchester, 1998), Chapter 4 in *Transactions of the Royal Historical Society*, 6th series, vol. 11 (2001), Chapter 5 in *Yeats Annual* 12 (1996), Chapter 6 in the *Dublin Review*, no. 2 (Spring 2001), part of Chapter 8 in *Trollopiana*, no. 28 (1995), a small section of Chapter 9 in E. Walshe (ed.), *Elizabeth Bowen Remembered: The Farahy Addresses* (Dublin, 1998), sections of Chapter 10 in the *Irish*

Review, no. 25 (1999/2000) and the *New Republic*, vol. 217, no. 5 (1997) and vol. 221, no. 18 (1999). I should like to thank the electors to the Leland Lyons Lecture at the University of Kent in 1995, the Bindoff Lecture at Queen Mary and Westfield College in 1997, the Trevelyan Lecture at the University of Cambridge in 1998, the Robert Adams Lecture for the Royal College of Surgeons of Ireland in 1999, the Emden Lecture for St Edmund Hall, Oxford, and the Prothero Lecture for the Royal Historical Society, both in 2000, for stimulating some of the ideas which have taken form in these essays, and for providing the audiences that enabled me to try them out.

Poetry, prose and unpublished writings by W. B. Yeats and other members of the Yeats family appear by permission of Anne Yeats and Michael Yeats. The extract from a letter from Ezra Pound to W. B. Yeats on p. 105 is from previously unpublished material and is copyright © 2001 by Mary de Rachewiltz and Omar S. Pound, printed by permission of New Directions Publishing Corp. Extracts on pp. 26 and 96 from *Collected Poems* by C. P. Cavafy, translated by Edmund Keeley and Philip Sherrard, edited by George Savadis, published by Hogarth Press, appear by permission of the Random House Group Ltd and Rogers, Coleridge & White. The extract from Louis MacNeice's 'Autumn Journal' on p. 158 appears by permission of David Higham Associates. The extract from a previously unpublished letter by Isaiah Berlin on pp. 203–4 is copyright © 2001 by the Isaiah Berlin Literary Trust, quoted with the Trust's permission. I am also grateful to the following holders of copyright material: the National Library of Scotland; the Lennox Robinson Collection, Special Collections, Morris Library, Southern Illinois University, Carbondale; the Harry Ransom Humanities Center, University of Texas at Austin; the Henry W. and Albert P. Berg Collection, New York Public Library (Astor, Lenox and Tilden Foundations); and the Robert W. Woodruff Library, Emory University, Atlanta. Every effort has been made to establish contact with the holders of original copyrights; in cases where this has not been possible I hope this general acknowledgement will be taken as sufficient.

Introduction

What stories do people tell each other in Ireland, and why? What stories do they tell themselves? How therapeutic are the uses of invention? The subtitle of this book hints at fabrication, but also at reconciliation; the essays that follow are linked by a preoccupation with the way Irish history, biography and memoir are refracted through narratives of one kind or another, and the way that narrative itself has come to be seen as an agent of making history. This is the specific subject of the first essay, 'The Story of Ireland', and the last, 'Remembering 1798', but it pervades those in between.

Sequential narrative imposes omissions as well as dictating content – every generalizing historian's headache. The heat generated by competing versions of our island story, the dust kicked up when different interpretations collide, obscures some of the most salient questions at issue – such as, whether the country actually is still an 'island' in any meaningful sense. Many of the authors whose stories are assessed in this book have contributed to the process, one way or another: by accounting for themselves and thus helping to make history, or to make it up. The elision of the personal and the national, the way history becomes a kind of scaled-up biography, and biography a microcosmic history, is a particularly Irish phenomenon, but the exclusions thus implied raise wider questions too. P. N. Furbank, in his thought-provoking meditation on identity politics, has put it another way:

however convincingly historians tell the story of the world, one is aware that something is wrong or missing. It is a story not like other stories, of the kind we are familiar with in fables or novels, since from moment to moment the occupants of roles die off and are replaced by a new set. Historical narrative has no way of expressing this all-important fact of birth and reproduction – that is to say, the need for traditions and images of the past and of things as they are to be created over and over again, in the minds of the newly born.[1]

Perhaps this supplies one reason why literary critics using psycho-analytical language have colonized certain aspects of historical interpretation. The need for self-renewing narrative also encourages a swerve into identity politics, a process which at its worst allows the uncritical endorsement by cultural critics of well-worn and jejune 'historical' claims – generally abandoned by historians some time ago. One of the decisive developments in recent Irish cultural debate is the way that a 'globalized' world and the advent of 'comparative' studies have narrowed the terms of interpretation in one direction, while ostensibly extending them in another. Colonial discourse analysis, applying the venerable ideas of Frantz Fanon more or less across the board, has hit Irish studies running. This has produced some invigorating debate, but has also – as Stephen Howe has pointed out in a magisterial and exasperated survey – resuscitated the idea that progressivism and rationalism are innately imperialistic ideas. What some recent critics seem to opt for instead is an anti-developmentalist view, condemning any linear notion of history as whiggish in effect and colonialist by implication.[2]

This too has implications for the way stories get told. As a general rule, the more hermeneutic and convoluted the post-colonial theorizing in the text, the more reductionist, naive and reactionary the political views expressed in the footnotes. Just at the point when Irish historians are blazing new trails in recovering the voices and experiences of the forgotten and marginalized, and thus helping to illuminate structures and mentalities lurking behind the intimate antagonisms of Irish his-tory, post-structuralist literary critics are stridently lecturing them about the role of the state in restructuring and producing ethnic or tribal antagonisms, and resurrecting terms like 'tyranny' to describe the situation of Ireland under the Union at the turn of the twentieth century. When the supposedly 'new' approach to history offered by postmodernized commentators also involves at once condemning 'cosmopolitanism' in modern Ireland, and positing the Irish revolutionary example as the inspiration for worldwide decolonization movements, one cannot but be reminded of the old Isle-of-Saints-and-Scholars view of Ireland's world role peddled a hundred years ago: here we are again, victims and world leaders all at once.

But what lends a novel edge to recent debates, and has spurred several of the combatants into action, is the transformation of Ireland's international position and domestic experience in the last thirty years – the exact period which saw the final abandonment of the introverted, autarchical national view in culture and economics inherited from early Sinn Féin. These processes were, of course, intimately linked to joining the European Union in 1972. There is a popular and attractive argument, pioneered by Declan Kiberd, one of the best of the new historico-literary critics, that Ireland has always been at the cutting edge of 'modernity', and world literary history in this century provides some strong supporting evidence. Historians and economists, however, find aggressive modernization hard to discern before the 1960s. From the 1980s, none the less, the Irish Republic seemed wafted on a tide of wealth, fashionability and the heady excesses of popular culture; twenty years on, the political corruption that accompanied this process is coming under the microscope, but the transformation is still astounding. This is all the more striking since over exactly the same period people in the other part of the island were groping towards some sort of accommodation with each other, and with their own contested pasts. Here, again, the process has sparked off surprisingly unreconstructed opinions among some cultural critics; if the fabric of the Anglo-Irish Agreements from 1985 to 1998 cannot be cut to fit an increasingly sclerotic Leninist view of liberation struggle, it is apparently a sign of 'modernity' to refuse endorsement to the process altogether. But as Ireland enters the twenty-first century, it seems necessary to examine some new ways of interrogating our histories.

Here, at least, the cultural critics and historians can agree: we are all for alternative histories now.[3] 'Cultural history' is certainly one route, and it may be cautiously illuminated by the light of psychological theory – as Richard Haslam has done in a highly suggestive study of the infantilizing imagery inflicted on Ireland, today as in the past.[4] Another possibility – when it can be done – is the kind of microcosmic 'laboratory' afforded by D. H. Akenson's study of the fortunes of the

emigrant Irish in Montserrat, where they emerged as the colonizing
elite, and treated their African slaves as badly as any other colonizers,
anywhere, and worse than many. 'None of this is pleasant to record,'
adds Akenson.

But if the self-replicating cycle of abuser-abused-abuser-abused is to be
broken, the Irish polity, through the historians who are the keepers of its
collective memory, must cease to view the emigrants from Ireland as forever-
passive victims, and therefore as persons who were incapable of hard dealing.
One of the fundamental stories of the Irish diaspora is of Irish emigrants
choosing to do unto others what others had already done to them. In neither
case was that a matter of kind and tender mercies.[5]

This seems a more useful reflection than the musings of at least one
marxisant-decolonist, hailing the 'exhilarating notion' of Irish servants
joining black slaves in joint rebellion throughout the empire as proof
that 'long oppression had led the Irish to oppose oppression wherever
they found it' – but adding mournfully, 'I wish the evidence to support
these beliefs was more widespread than it is.'[6]

   More individual, actualized studies like Akenson's would probably
query the blanket wishful thinking that leads to so many untested
generalizations about the Platonic solidarity between struggling Irish
nationalists and their supposedly analogous fellow victims elsewhere.
The assumptions behind comparative post-colonial studies, and the
undifferentiated (and undefined) meanings of 'colonialism' employed
by those most addicted to the subject, have been comprehensively
examined by Stephen Howe, and this is not the place to paraphrase
his conclusions. There is a case for focusing on the local, the actual,
the lived experience, and trying to reconstruct the terms in which it
was first told (as David Fitzpatrick has shown in his classic studies of
Irish emigrants to Australia). Biography as a 'subject' tends to be
dismissed by theorists, often for good reasons, but the individual's
experience as a kind of national microcosm comes up too insistently
in Irish history and fiction not to be worth examining,[7] and it recurs
in these essays. So does the notion of autobiography as an aspect of
national history. This process can conceal, once again, very large
and untested assumptions; it can also run the danger of collapsing

alternative history into anecdote and psychobabble (or anecdotal psychobabble). As the political moves to the personal, the historian gives way to the pundit and the pop star: spectacularly, and ludicrously, demonstrated in some of the commentaries on the Great Famine during the commemorations of the mid 1990s. The concept of 'recovered memory' was widely used, though hardly relevant to an experience whose occurrence has never been denied. Post-traumatic stress disorder stalked the land, buried 'memories' were indiscriminately exhumed, and 'survivor guilt' was ruthlessly appropriated from Holocaust studies and exhibited in the market place. The process of compensatory identification, in an Ireland rich and well fed as never before, had on one level a certain logic; but, on another, it prompted uncomfortable reflection on Wittgenstein's stricture that 'only a very unhappy man has the right to pity someone else'.[8] The politics, and psychology, of commemorationism are also looked at in this book, but what the subject tells us about Irish history in the 1990s remains an absorbing question. If it finds the right interpreter, it will do at least as much to clarify the modern story of the nation as the acres of print produced since 1995 did to illuminate the history of Famine-struck Ireland in the 1840s.

The dangers of new, deconstructed history, with its stress on the personal and the unmediated, include complacent anti-empiricism and aggressive sentimentalism, often reinforcing each other, and often relying on assumptions that actually contradict recorded experience.[9] In contemporary internationalized Ireland, an enhanced self-image sometimes goes with ahistorical notions of synthetic Celticism peddled by every level of pop culture, from dance spectaculars to feelgood spiritual primers – at a time when 'Celticism' itself is coming in for a certain amount of scholarly scepticism.[10] No matter how successful the achievements of the Irish abroad, however, automatic obeisance is made to victimhood and tyranny: a bestselling and highly talented author, born in the Republic in 1955, can still claim in 2000 that his youthful difficulties with women should be blamed on growing up in 'a small country, trying to find its own identity in the face of British oppression'.[11] Sometimes it is hard to avoid the feeling that the new, modernized, liberated Irish consciousness feels a sneaking nostalgia for the verities of the old victim-culture: which was also, in its way, a culture of superiority. The same approach invades literary criticism: one disgruntled poet has described the process as 'minesweeping Irish literature for markers of weakness and woe: a mutilated tongue, a broken culture – charges that interpret our pain and anger but make a privileged outrage of the history rather than the experience of life in Ireland today'.[12] If there is such a danger, the life and work of (for instance) Hubert Butler, considered in the penultimate essay of this book, provides a counter-example that is at once minatory and inspiring.

Butler, like many of the writers considered in this book, spoke from a vantage which allowed him a particular perspective on nationalism and allied this with a Geiger-counter sensitivity to the exclusivist implications of a certain kind of Irish rhetoric. Tom Nairn, who also occupies a special angle to the Irish landscape, has written arrestingly about the language of European nationalism as it developed from the nineteenth century:

not necessarily democratic in outlook, but invariably populist ... it has to function through highly rhetorical forms, through a sentimental culture sufficiently accessible to the lower strata now being called into battle. This is why a romantic culture quite remote from Enlightenment rationalism always went hand in hand with the spread of nationalism. The new middle-class intelligentsia of nationalism had to invite the masses into history; and the invitation had to be written in a language they understood.[13]

This is recognizable to any student of Irish nationalism in that period. But what is interesting is what happens after the 'invitation into history' has been extended, and accepted; and what this means for 'elites' as well as for 'masses'. David Lloyd has provocatively commented upon the emergence of an 'elite nationalist narrative' of Irish history, an insight which might be taken further.[14] In our age, much of the new cultural criticism, and its populist expressions, concentrates on the 'psychic impact of domination'.[15] At least as arresting – as I tried to show in a previous book of linked essays, *Paddy and Mr Punch* – are the nuanced, mediated and symbiotic cultural relationships which emerged during the Union between Britain and Ireland, and these can be explored in ways which constitute more than simply 'dominant history'. In fact, there may be a case for seeing the Irish middle class of the late nineteenth and early twentieth centuries as subjects marginalized by a new official history. Their occluded narrative deserves some subalternist study of its own and their history epitomizes discontinuities worth exploring in their own right.[16]

Some of the lives, opinions and experiences of people traced in this book might also remind us of the mesh of nuance, complexity and contradiction involved when the stories of nations intersect with those of supposedly emblematic individuals. Anthony Trollope's preoccupation with the superior intelligence of the Irish, for instance, complicates his status as exemplar of anti-Irish 'racism'; and however deeply prejudiced against Irish 'character' he came to be, that prejudice was itself in part a reaction against an early idealization. The version of Leland Lyons that presents him committed to 'the emergence of state institutions as the proper object of history'[17] is queried by the fact that for the last ten years of his life he was preoccupied by analysing the competing cultures which he had defined as marking out the Irish battleground. The privileged aura of Elizabeth Bowen's Edwardian Irish childhood appears, through her highly charged memories, as part and parcel of the alienation and obliqueness which both coloured her relation to Irish life and equipped her to dissect vital portions of its history. Standish O'Grady's influence on the revolutionary generation is well attested, but it is worth examining how his message was preached through books which in fact reversed all the pieties which had come to distinguish Irish nationalism. These relationships between people and their history are uncomfortable, and the boundaries are blurred and complicated; they deserve discussion in terms of what they wrote and the records they left elsewhere, instead of being boiled down into a theoretical reduction. This requires empathy – a word much used in Irish historiographical engagements – of an introspective rather than a possessive kind. P. N. Furbank, again, might be attended to here:

Humanism requires that history be taken seriously – only with a proviso, that the relation of the individual to history is not a straightforward affair and has to accommodate a paradox, that the proper ambition of any human is to be within himself or herself the whole of humankind. But once this is granted, it seems to be the most effective way to study human affairs. To study 'humanity' seems to require two things. It calls for the examination of diverse cultures, and it calls for introspection (i.e. meditating on oneself as an exemplar of the human race): and these are part of the same mental act, a matter of asking, 'What would it be *like* (for oneself) to be so-and-so?'

But the same is true of the attempt to change humanity, for only a human being who regards himself or herself as containing the whole human potential and as able, by introspection, to picture what it might be 'like' (for oneself) to be something quite different from what one happens to be, is in a position to think through false and harmful distinctions of race, class and gender – as a prelude to *un*thinking them.[18]

On one level, this may be taken as an argument that biography *is* a proper subject for historians. It is also a reminder that the prescriptive and dismissive imposition of frameworks taken straight from one theoretician or another, irrespective of context or temporal conditions, can illuminate very little and may obscure a lot. Faced with the complications and confrontations of Irish history, where axes and whetstones lie conveniently to every hand, there is an understandable temptation to simplify the story by adherence to one big idea. Thus the visionary poet and Patrician scholar Aubrey de Vere recalled in 1897 how 'after the lapse of many years the meaning of Irish history flashed upon me. It possessed unity, although not a political one. Religion was Ireland's unity . . . [a] vocation assigned by Providence.'[19] De Vere's path then seemed clear, but at the cost of misunderstanding a great deal about what was actually happening around him.

At almost the same time, under the pseudonym 'Contemplor', an exasperated Irish nationalist 'proud of my Irish blood and descent, and ready to join issue with any foreigner who would defame or belittle my people', wrote a long public letter violently attacking 'sunburstery' and 'Celtic fire' in Irish historical rhetoric, and praising Parnell for 'not everlastingly talking of harps, saints, heroes, martyrs, pikes, green isles, and brutal Saxons'. 'Contemplor' called for a sharply realistic history of Ireland, exposing 'historical half truths', tracing the origin of Irish weaknesses in specifically Irish conditions, and showing how contending cliques obscured the real capacities and potential of a people 'too prone to mistake verbiage for eloquence, fanaticism for piety, and swagger for patriotism'. But, he concluded, 'mine would not be a popular history'.[20] This indicates a belief in attainable truth not very fashionable nowadays, but it strikes a familiar chord. Telling the Irish story from different angles is something of a national pastime; so is the relativity of 'truth' in its competing versions; so is an obsessive and fascinated self-examination, leading to what Joep Leerssen has famously defined in terms of nineteenth-century Irish fiction as 'auto-exoticism', and culminating in the 'over-identity crisis' diagnosed by Cheryl Herr in the 1990s.[21]

At best, the competing cultural critiques of the last generation may have opened the kind of way forward hoped for by 'Contemplor' a century ago; the concept of 'post-nationalism' advanced by writers as different as Richard Kearney, Bruce Stewart and Colm Tóibín offers an indication that this might be so. In the process, the barriers between historical narrative, personal history and national fictions have become mobile – an exciting and intellectually stimulating development, as several of the following essays point out. But what this means for 'memory' (another recurring theme in this volume) gives pause for thought. When a populist pundit can enthusiastically proclaim, in terms of Irish history, 'we must remember what we never knew', we are free to judge the statement either profound emotional truth or self-indulgent idiocy, but historians are more likely to be on one side than the other.[22] Still, there may be several routes towards ascertaining 'what happened'. A warning from Hannah Arendt is relevant here:

Insofar as any 'mastering' of the past is possible it consists in relating what has happened: but such narration too, which shapes history, solves no problems and assuages no suffering; it does not master anything once and for all. Rather, as long as the meaning of the events remains alive . . . 'mastering the past' can take the form of ever-recurrent narration. The poet in a very general sense and the historian in a very special sense have the task of setting this process of narration in motion and of involving us in it.[23]

Arendt was not thinking of the story of Ireland, but her linkage of history and poetry may act as a reminder why so many of the essays in this book invoke or discuss the life, thought and influence of W. B. Yeats, whose role in the Irish story involved mastering the past through visionary narration, and in the process shaping the present and future consciousness of 'the nation' – whoever they were. And constructing a nation, as any historian or poet knows, revolves around the tension created when the affirmation of personal identity intersects with the invention of epic.

I

The Story of Ireland

How may the past, if it be dead
Its light within the living shed?
Or does the Ever-living hold
Earth's memories from the Age of Gold?
And are our dreams, ardours and fires
But ancient unfulfilled desires?
And do they shine within our clay,
And do they urge us on our way?
As Michael read the Gaelic scroll
It seemed the story of the soul;
And those who wrought, lest there
    should fail
From earth the legend of the Gael,
Seemed warriors of Eternal Mind
Still holding in a world gone blind,
From which belief and hope had gone,
The lovely magic of its dawn.

From 'Michael' in AE, *The Interpreters*
(London, 1922)

I

The idea of narrative is back in the air. This pleases me: when I was a
student at Trinity College Dublin in the 1960s, W. E. H. Lecky's great
narrative history was still a set text; when I came to teach at the
University of London in the early 1970s, the idea of deconstructing

narrative was already beginning. Historiography courses were being set up, and the voices of Hayden White and Frederic Jameson were heard in the land. In the intervening years, as old-style ideological certitudes have worn threadbare, the presentation of history itself in narrative form has come back into a certain vogue. But so has the study of the assumptions and exclusions represented by the narrative form itself.[1]

What does this mean for the way Irish history is told? Over the same period, from the 1960s, the questioning of accepted versions of Irish history began to take a firmer and firmer hold, and to advance from academic orthodoxy into public debate. Irish historians, working in many areas, tried to break up the seamless construction of narrative incident which was presented as the story of Ireland, and to analyse the moment, rather than simply follow the flow. But at the same time, the compelling power of the old sequence held its mesmeric force. (I found this myself, when I set out to write a general treatment of Irish history intended to break out of genre, and ended by adhering much more closely than I had realized to the story form.) In that story, personal experience and national history remain woven into an apparently logical and self-referencing construction.[2] And thinking about the shape of Irish history, or arguing about the accuracy and significance of certain generally accepted themes, one is struck again and again by the importance of the narrative mode: the idea that Irish history *is* a 'story', and the implications that this carries about a beginning, a middle and the sense of an ending. Not to mention heroes, villains, donors, helpers, guests, plots, revelations, and all the other elements of the story form. And the formal modes of *Bildungsroman*, ghost story, deliverance tale, family romance, all of which have lent motifs to the ways Irish history has been told.[3]

However, Irish history has inspired such a broad and compelling range of narratives, reiterated in every generation, that scope must be restricted. The title of this essay, and book, is not new. To trawl any library catalogue with variants on *The Story of Ireland* nets a rich haul of authors taking in novelists like Emily Lawless, politicians like A. M. Sullivan and Justin McCarthy, prophets like Standish O'Grady – right down to twentieth-century commentators like Sean O'Faolain and Brian Inglis; the title has most recently been employed by William Magan's family history published in 2000.[4] This is a thought-provoking sample. The compelling notion of a Story of Ireland, with plot, narrative logic and desired outcome, reached its apogee in the later nineteenth century. The historiography thus created is intimately connected with the discovery of folk tale, myth and saga as indices of the national experience; the development of Irish nationalism is strongly influenced by the transference of these forms into a narrative of nationality;[5] and many of the *fin-de-siècle* literary generation who were mediators and brokers in this process lived to query the validity of the powerful determinist vision – at once a consolation, a consecration and a call to arms – which they had given to 'the nation'.

II

In Lady Morgan's influential novel *The Wild Irish Girl* (1806) the innocent hero inherits a house in the west of Ireland and discovers a locked library containing books of history – about which he is ignorant. For the rest of the novel, he pursues the supposed facts of Irish history. The closed book is opened; something potent enough to keep under lock and key is released. It is a recurring motif in nineteenth-century historical novels, and closely related to the Irish approach to narrative. This is not simple. 'We Irish' (Bishop Berkeley's phrase) have an idiosyncratic approach to telling stories. A powerful oral culture, a half-lost language, the necessary stratagems of irony, collusion and misdirection which accompany a colonized culture, maybe even the long wet winter nights – all these give a distinctive twist to the way the Irish account for themselves. A recurring theme is the deliberate gap in the narrative: the momentous elision, the leap in the story. Maria Edgeworth's *Castle Rackrent* was originally to be about a family called the 'Stopgaps'. Given that they carry Irish history, so to speak, on their backs, it is an important conceit. The other characteristic Irish mode is the story within the story – a key to Sterne, Maturin, Le Fanu, Flann O'Brien and, most of all, Joyce. And the assertion that Irish literary culture is deficient in great novels may simply indicate that Irish writers had neither the time nor the inclination for novels that were formal in conception and linear in structure, as in the great age of English or French fiction.

This carries its own importance for the construction of a national history. We may not have in Ireland the kind of *Bildungsroman* that, in Walter Benjamin's formula, 'integrates the social process with the development of a person',[6] or treats the novel as 'the private history of nations' *à la* Balzac. But we do have other characteristic literary modes. And the thesis that asserts a close connection between the emergence of the novel and the growth of a sense of national identity needs to be interrogated sharply for the Irish case. A popular collection of writings on the subject of nation and narration notably glides over the Irish question;[7] those connections which are made by literary critics are not always convincing. Might this be because in Ireland history – or historiography – is our true novel?[8] Certainly at the point in the eighteenth century when the English novel was allegedly emerging as a contributing factor to the sense of nation, discourse in Ireland was obsessed by history-writing – a competitive genre of national story-telling, preoccupied by who owned the narrative.[9] Historiography was also invested with the moral authority conferred by a story with a known or expected ending – that secret known to all Marxists.

Romanticism in early-nineteenth-century Ireland, as elsewhere, sustained the idea of national history as transfiguring wonder tale; it is a period when fiction is preoccupied by historical subjects, but also when history-writing is obsessed with constructing a compelling fiction.[10] This fertile era provided the seedbed for the work of two inspirational storytellers of Ireland, whose names will recur. One is Samuel Ferguson, producing from the 1830s stories, poems and reconstituted bardic epics that interrogate the disputed question of an Irish identity which could be both Protestant and nationally minded.[11] The other is the Young Ireland revolutionary John Mitchel, equally a product of those un-Irish figures Carlyle and Herder, but arguing the nationalist morality tale with all the zeal of a Presbyterian convert. Today remembered for his *Jail Journal*, Mitchel's other narratives of Irish history compel attention. His history both responded to and forged the Irish emigrant consciousness of a national story from which England, wicked stepmother, had written them out.[12]

By the time of Mitchel's death in 1875, the Story of Ireland had emerged from myriad retellings in its accepted narrative form. The phrase 'wicked stepmother' has almost inadvertently emerged, as well as the earlier 'wonder tale'. The Russian structuralist Vladimir Propp, in *The Morphology of the Folk Tale* (1928), argued (indeed, wrestled) his way through to certain basic conclusions about the function of fairy tales:

1. Functions of character serve as stable, constant elements in a tale, independent of how and by whom they are fulfilled.
2. The number of functions known is limited.
3. The sequence of functions is always identical.
4. All fairy tales are of one type in regard to their structure.

Certain literary critics have applied Propp's ideas to classic fictions.[13] Moreover, by the later nineteenth century, the Story of Ireland (already a favourite title) seems to have adhered obediently to Propp's law. The received version uncannily conformed to the classic structure of the fairy tale. One can, for instance, review Propp's 'functions' themselves and relate them to canonical episodes in the story, such as the Norman invasion or Hugh O'Neill's resistance to the Elizabethan state. Here is the latter mapped against Propp's first nine functions:

1. *One of the members of a family absents himself from home.* O'Neill is sent from Ulster to be brought up among the English aristocracy.
2. *An interdiction is addressed to the hero.* He is made to swear fealty to the queen.
3. *The interdiction is violated.* O'Neill makes a bid for overlordship in Ulster.
4. *The villain makes an attempt at reconnaissance.* Sir Henry Bagenal is repulsed at the battle of the Yellow Ford.
5. *The villain receives information about his victim.* Bagenal suborns local chieftains.
6. *The villain attempts to deceive his victim in order to take possession of him or of his belongings.* The news of the queen's death is withheld from O'Neill.
7. *The victim submits to deception and thereby unwittingly helps his enemy.* O'Neill signs the Treaty of Mellifont.
8. *The villain causes harm or injury to a member of the family.* Red Hugh O'Donnell is poisoned by English agents.

9. Misfortune or lack is made known; the hero is allowed to go or he is dispatched; the hero leaves home. The Flight of the Earls.

One could go on, as this kind of thing is addictive; Propp's narrative modes and functions lend themselves uncannily to the *ur*-stories of Irish national history. In the fairy-tale form, of course, the hero reaches Function 15 ('led to the whereabouts of an object or search') or even Function 19 ('The hero returns'); whereas in the Stories of Ireland these last happy stages did not happen to O'Neill, or O'Connell, or Parnell, or Hibernia herself. Still less did they ever attain Function 31, 'The hero is married and ascends the throne.' (Parnell's Home Rule Story, alas, was the only one that ended with a wedding, at Steyning Register Office, and that was shortly followed by a funeral.) The point of the Story of Ireland as retailed in classic form was, in fact, that though all the elements were there (villains, heroes, helpers, donors) it had not yet reached its ending. But through omission of elements that did not suit the fairy tale, and adherence to established narrative forms, the right ending could be inferred.[14] This might be illustrated by looking at the most famous book written under the title *The Story of Ireland*, first published by A. M. Sullivan in 1867.

The edition I work from is, in fact, the twenty-fifth, published in 1888 but substantially the same text. Sullivan, a journalist and politician from Cork, helped create the popular Irish concept of nationalism through his newspaper the *Nation* and his oft reprinted *Speeches from the Dock*. In *The Story of Ireland*, written (he said) 'hand to mouth . . . with printers like wolves at my heels for copy',[15] he produced one of the great bestsellers of all (Irish) time, rapidly shifting 50,000 copies and going into dozens of editions. It is worth dwelling on this hugely influential text, because it best encapsulates the formalities, motifs, elisions, parallelisms and – of course – gaps that characterize the story. Sullivan defended his decision to present a narrative based on 'chief events' that were 'easily comprehended and remembered'; minor incidents or qualifications which might 'confuse and bewilder' were dropped.[16] He addressed himself to the young, the 'Irish Nation of the Future', telling them Ireland's story 'after the manner of simple storytellers'. But the sequence and emphasis were really aimed at a far wider audience. The theme was established from the beginning: Ireland as the Isle of Destiny, invaded from Spain by the Milesians (and thus implicitly linked from its origins to Catholic Europe). Archaeology was used to buttress claims of rule by accomplished sovereigns from about 1500 BC, 'liberal patrons of art, science and commerce' instituting orders of chivalry and 'regularly convened parliaments'.[17] The themes are legitimate independence, equal status with other European nations, the capacity for self-government: Home Rule 3,000 years *avant la lettre*. This mercilessly present-minded preoccupation drives on through Christianity, accomplished peacefully in Ireland alone: St Patrick's prayers and litanies 'express such doctrines as are taught in our own day in the unchanged and unchanging Catholic Church'. Columba, the wandering saint, is presented as the first involuntary emigrant (condemned to leave Ireland, he also, incidentally, conforms to Propp's First Function);[18] in fact, he goes off to Scotland and brings about 'the independence of the young Caledonian nation' – Home Rule all round.

On the story rolls, through centuries of bondage; native kings like Brian Boru are beset by false friends, magical donors, renegade relations; 'national unity' is forever dangled as the object of the quest and, just as often, cruelly removed; justice, of a sort, is searched for in every narrative twist. Despite 'the innate virtue and morality of the Irish national character',[19] the Irish kings *deserve* the Norman invasion because of their factitiousness; however, virtue triumphs. 'It is a singular fact – one which no historian can avoid noting – that every one of the principal actors on the English side in the eventful episode of the first Anglo-Norman Invasion ended life violently, or under most painful circumstances.'[20] Nevertheless, the English win dominion because, for all their faults, they are nationally minded – even Cromwell, 'a despot, a bigot and a canting hypocrite, was a thorough nationalist as an Englishman'. And where an Irish hero nearly wins – as with our old friend Hugh O'Neill – it is as reward for demonstrating his patriotism and commitment to 'national independence and freedom'. This distinctly nineteenth-century language is constantly used for all periods of what is seen as an ideologically consistent struggle; thus in the seventeenth century Irish exiles organize revolutionary cells 'in the design of returning and liberating their native land' (Propp's Function 20). And the evidence adduced is also garnered from the early-nineteenth-century treasurehouse of Irish Romanticism: Tom Moore's historical ballads, Samuel Ferguson's bardic fantasies and the writings of John Mitchel.

There are high points. In 1641 the Irish unite at last in a bloodless rising against the oppressor, and the Ulster Protestant plantation vanishes 'like the baseless fabric of a vision' (perhaps the most fantastical element of all in this fairy tale). However, with the advent of James II the Irish fall foul of Propp's 24th Function: 'A false hero presents unfounded claims.' Loyalty to the Stuarts condemns them to suffer throughout the eighteenth century 'an agony the most awful, the most prolonged, of any recorded on the blotted page of human suffering'.[21] Grattan's Parliament, another false dawn, precedes the betrayal of the Union and the selling into bondage. 'In cruelties of oppression endured, Ireland is like no other country in the world.'[22]

There is, however, an end in sight, and it uses the language of another story: nation becomes religion. 'It could be no human faith that, after such a crucifixion and burial, could thus arise glorious and immortal! This triumph, the greatest, has been Ireland's; and God, in His own good time, will assuredly give her the token of victory!' The Story ends for the moment in the year of publication, 1867, with the failed Fenian Rising; a hopeless skirmish in a snowy wood.[23] Sacrifice, we are explicitly told a half century before Patrick Pearse, will redeem the nation's soul.[24] But if the message is the right to revolt, Sullivan's own politics were those of a moderate Home Ruler; Ireland would thus, in the end, export virtue back to England, where family life, Sullivan airily remarked, was 'one black catalogue of murdering, wife-beating and infant-choking'. Most importantly, the Story of Ireland must not be absorbed into England's corrupt narrative, substituting 'her history of falsehood, rapine and cruelty for ours of faithfulness, noble endurance and morality – giving us the bloodstained memoirs of her land and sea robbers in place of the glorious biographies of our patriots and our saints'.[25]

III

Sullivan's book constructed (often by careful exclusion) the accepted Irish national memory; and it was the kind of memory which, in Michel de Certeau's phrase, 'is linked to the expectation that something alien to the present will or must occur'.[26] In so doing it supplied the canon for Irish history as taught for generations by the Christian Brothers; and it was followed by a rash of volumes under variations of the title *The Story of Ireland*, which must have been thought to guarantee financial success. Emily Lawless's and Justin McCarthy's *Stories*, as well as countless others under less barefacedly imitative titles, used Sullivan's structure, though often fitting the tale into a series of 'stories of the nations' which carried a distinctly imperial message. Overall, however, the story conformed: it began with Mediterranean origin myths and proceeded to the advent of Home Rule via Christianity and suffering, asserting moral authority over debased England. Determinism was explicit.[27] The formula brilliantly popularized by Sullivan from 1867 created the terms learned by the succeeding generation. And this generation not only lived through the rise of Home Rule, and the assertion of a popular nationalist culture in Catholic Ireland; it also saw the foundations laid for an Irish cultural revival using the sources of ancient Irish history and literature, which carried their own highly charged narrative forms.

These had entered public circulation at the time Sullivan was writing – the 1860s – through publications like the *Revue Celtique*, the *Transactions of the Ossianic Society* and O'Curry's *Manners and Customs of the Ancient Irish*; the preoccupation went back to the end of the eighteenth century.[28] But what matters is when they were popularized. It is worth noting a book which appeared in 1868, the year after Sullivan's *Story of Ireland*. This was *The Story of the Irish before the Conquest* by Lady Mary Ferguson, whose husband, Sir Samuel, was well known for his bardic sequences and Irish translations. Her volume owed much to such effusions, and was profusely illustrated with poems by Aubrey de Vere, Thomas D'Arcy McGee and Ferguson himself, lending it a distinctly present-minded tone. Also, like her husband's work, Mary Ferguson's moral was in the end distinctly unionist.[29] But the important thing was that her accessible, effective treatment made popular both the stories of mythic heroes and heroines like Cuchulain and Deirdre, and the division of early Irish history into 'The Mythic Period', 'The Heroic Period' and other categories which (taken with Sullivan) constructed a powerful sense of national destiny and nationalist *amour propre*. (At this point of self-education, if not at many others, Irish nationalism fits easily into the 'Ruritanian' model proposed by Ernst Gellner.[30]) And for the poets and writers of the next generation, the clean lines and simple colours of Sullivan's *Story of Ireland* were overlaid with the subtle shades and cloudy vapours of mythic retellings and folklore rediscoveries. It is at this intersection that we encounter the Dublin art students and apprentice littérateurs of the mid 1880s, George Russell (who would rechristen himself with the Gnostic symbol AE) and his friend William Butler Yeats. They would inculcate a school of reinvented national literature, drawing heavily on the myths and beliefs of ancient Ireland, in the 1890s. But when they looked back at their youth and recalled their inspiration, they did not remember the popularizers A. M. Sullivan and Mary Ferguson; a much more towering presence was the bardic historian and outsized eccentric, Standish James O'Grady.

O'Grady's work was not popular: when he produced his *History of Ireland: The Heroic Period* in 1878, he had to subsidize its publication himself. But it was, in trade terms, a 'sleeper'; subsequent volumes of early history, and stories based on them, were popular with many, and holy books for a few. AE wrote later of O'Grady as a man out walking who passed a grass-grown rath, or dun, sensed the ancient warriors sleeping within and released them to ride rampantly through the modern Irish consciousness. This was written after the 1916 Rising, in which Cuchulain was a sort of invisible brigade commander, and thus with knowledge of its associated rhetoric. But O'Grady himself tells a more literal tale about his own awakening, which still has a metaphorical resonance. An ignorant Trinity student, son of a rector, he was staying in a country house. One day, kept inside by the rain, he took down at random a book and discovered the lost world of heroic Irish pre-history, with its myths, sagas and heroes larger than life.[31] This is, in essence, the image used by Lady Morgan long before: the secret narrative, suddenly released. The book makes history.

And in fact O'Grady – unionist, Carlyean, anti-democratic, at once scourge and champion of the landlord classes – was obsessed by what he called (a hundred years before Homi K. Bhaba) 'the national narrative'. In his bardic histories of early Ireland, published in 1878 and 1880, he put it into the most arresting and imaginative shape he could: actually confronting the question of narrative modes and national consciousness, discussing the different strategies (annalistic, anecdotal, all-inclusive) and rejecting them for his own poetic version. In his first volume, *The Heroic Period*, he attempted to re-create a bardic history from the material reassembled by scholars earlier in the century, and by using archaeological insights and poetic vision. The point was to re-create the heroic age, recognizing that 'all the great permanent relations of life are the same'. This hit the mark with the Yeats generation, perhaps partly because all O'Grady's poetic epigraphs are from Keats, Shelley, Milton and the canon of Palgrave's *Golden Treasury* (the most Irish name I can find is Edgar Allan Poe). And the influence of that unrecognized founding-father of Irish national rhetoric, Carlyle, is stamped upon this epiphanic history as on Mitchel's, twenty years before.[32]

Moreover, O'Grady was determined to substitute his own poetic insight for the straightforward acceptance of the narrative dictated by the 'Annals' put together by medieval Irish monks about which he was mercilessly funny.[33] Early Irish history, he maintained, was bardic invention and should be appreciated as the imaginative and psychological record of a nation, its wished-for history made magically coherent. As for himself, he wanted to summon up the atmosphere of legendary Ireland, retailing sagas, freely interpreting poetic tradition, revolving around symbolic points of focus like the royal hill of Tara,[34] the Lia Fáil (or crowning-stone of destiny), gods like Lugh Lámhfhada, and the whole panoply of the Red Branch saga (Deirdre, Cuchulain, the cattle raid of Cooley). A brutal Irish friend remarked that O'Grady 'did very well considering that all the materials in his history were lost in the Flood'.[35] But the salvaged elements were familiar from the *Transactions of the Ossianic Society*, or even Lady Ferguson, though their composition dates were assumed to be much earlier than is now thought to be the case.[36] O'Grady assembled them into a range of atmospheric references plundered by Yeats and made sacred by Maud

Gonne, Ella Young and a host of other forgotten national revivalists. He did this by telling the story in a series of visionary epiphanies, Pre-Raphaelite in clarity and precision, depicting 'life' through exact, tiny details about buildings, decorations, dress (he seems to have been mildly fetishistic about 'thonging'). And as usual there was a present-minded note as well: pre-Christian Ulster (Ulla) is described as 'the black country . . . a people altogether given up to the making of weapons and armour, where the sound of the hammer and the husky voice of the bellows were forever heard',[37] which must owe more to the Harland & Wolff shipyard than the *Táin* saga.

It is easy to mock, and he was at first mocked. His second volume begins with a ninety-page introduction which implicitly apologizes for the imaginative excesses of the first. But he reiterated the subjective nature of the Irish narrative, 'floating loosely in a world of imagination'.[38] He would create his audience, and retrieve the true bardic sense of sequence, regulated and determined by their chronology rather than that of later monks. (O'Grady, as we shall see, had considerable trouble with monks.)

Like a true romantic, O'Grady believed the essence of history was revealed in epic poetry; the development of the critical spirit, demanding formal perfection and consistency, had smoothed away the reality of history. He would restore the colour and the vehemence.[39] John O'Daly's translation of the *Táin* for the Royal Irish Academy remained a basic text, but O'Grady emphasized the sacred places of Ireland (Newgrange as temple, not tomb), and this would greatly influence the Yeats generation. Some surreal anachronisms remained (Cuchulain visits Dublin, looks in shop windows and rails against the cash nexus);[40] but essentially O'Grady tried to restore to the Irish their mythological pedigree.[41] By the mid eighties he had found his audience: young revivalists were buying his books, the reviewing circle around the young Yeats was plugging them at every opportunity. The heroes were released into the general imagination.

IV

We should pause here and, like Cuchulain looking in the shop windows, think in contemporary terms. The audience O'Grady really wanted to reach were the leadership classes of Irish life, who had lost their spirit and whom he attacked in savage polemic at this very time. The enemy was Gladstonian democracy and its allies, the Catholic Church triumphant and the Home Rule Party. He had a cult of Lord Randolph Churchill and Tory democracy; he wanted to head off modern nationalism and revive feudal values (including fealty to a king of England). But these were not the priorities of the literary generation who (like AE) explored Ireland's holy places with O'Grady's volumes as their vade-mecum, who put themselves (as Maud Gonne did) under the occult protection of gods like Lugh, or who assembled at Tara to prevent the local farmer from allowing the British Israelites to excavate it in search of the Ark of the Covenant.[42] From the mid eighties (not, as Yeats would later have it, after the fall of Parnell in 1891) literary societies were meeting in Dublin and invoking O'Grady, but they were distinctly advanced-nationalist in their politics. In Yeats's memoirs, written as a heroic frieze, O'Grady is immobilized as a spiritual father-figure,[43] calling the Irish to their past and releasing those buried warriors. The aspect of his teaching that warned (in 1882) that Irish nationalist politics would end in 'anarchy and civil war . . . [and] a shabby sordid Irish republic, ruled by corrupt politicians and the ignoble rich' was left aside. His followers used material from O'Grady's Story, but filtered it through the ideology of A. M. Sullivan's.

As his disciples flirted with Fenianism, O'Grady travelled further and further towards his own wilder shores of unionism. There is no time here to deal with how he tried to bring his message to the gentry of Kilkenny in 1898 by taking over a local newspaper, and was run out of town in a storm of libel writs,[44] or to discuss his subsequent newspaper the *All-Ireland Review*, largely constructed of heroic serials and savage skirmishes between O'Grady and outraged letter-writers. (To one innocent correspondent the editor simply replied: 'Were you momentarily mad, or in London, when you wrote?'[45]) It is odd to realize that O'Grady lived on until 1928, exiled in England; as with Henry Grattan, the received story of Ireland writes him out as soon as his allotted part is played, and he remains preserved as heroic prophet of nationalism.[46] Any other life is incompatible.

But we have to look at one more facet of this extraordinary man. His heroic bardic histories were published in 1878 and 1880; his political polemic became more and more frantic through the 1880s as Home Rule appeared to reach its apotheosis; and in 1893, the year the second Home Rule Bill passed the Commons (but was thrown out by the Lords), O'Grady produced a book called . . . *The Story of Ireland*.[47] His *History of Ireland: The Heroic Period* is often referred to but rarely read. *The Story of Ireland* is neither referred to nor read, and the reasons are clear.

The familiar title is not accidental. Like Sullivan's, it was addressed to youth; like Sullivan's, it was a work of passion and colour. But it was written directly against Sullivan and the whole school of nationalism apparently coming into its own. It begins, traditionally, with the Milesian invasions, and ends more idiosyncratically with O'Grady's memories of the recently deceased Parnell. The narrative structure follows little linked mythic stories, rather predictive of Italo Calvino: gods, heroes and saints succeed each other in the early chapters. But there is a subversive undertow. O'Grady always had reservations about the early Christians, and here he comes out into the open. They represent, he tells his young audience, 'a lack of straightforward, bold and honest dealing, which afterwards became a national vice, so that many of our great saints were also great liars, and fell under the just scorn and contempt of those who had no religion at all but simply preserved the old instinctive Pagan abhorrence of falsehood and doubledealing'. Monasteries 'perverted the understanding of those who lived there'; the *Book of Kells* was 'an appalling monument of misdirected labour and too ingenious toil'.[48] As one reads on and devious saints overthrow good pagan kings, 'pagan' clearly stands for Protestant and 'saint' for priest, while the bards obviously prefigure O'Grady himself: poking fun at abbots and exposing the vices of crooked monasteries.[49]

His scheme could hardly be plainer, and we need not be too surprised when we read on and discover that the Irish deserved all they got in the

Viking invasions. Indeed, 'Ireland, as distinguished from the monks, rather welcomed than withstood the Norsemen' – reliable, fair-minded (and fair-haired), honest and sincere.[50] Contrary to monkish propaganda, Brian Boru was not killed at prayer but in battle. The Norman Conquest 'ought to have been a great blessing [to the Irish] as it had been to the Saxons'.[51] King John *was* a good king. Norman barons and Irish chieftains were brothers under the skin, affectionately sharing beds with each other after signing peace treaties. 'Ireland' liked the Tudors. And Cromwell – merry, animated, decisive, charismatic, like the best kind of pagan – was 'a most sagacious ruler and a most valiant fighter', disciplining his soldiers, preventing looting, trying to discuss religion with the Dublin Catholics who 'for one reason or another, probably bad reasons, frequented his rude and simple court'. 'Bold as the prophecy may be, I predict the coming of a day when his memory will be dearer to Ireland than that of the greatest Irish worthy that we can furnish down to date. He was, to go no further, the first fighting man who waged war in Ireland with any approximation to civilized methods.'[52]

It is hard to exaggerate the offensiveness of this revisionist view, but O'Grady happily ploughed on with his narrative *tour de force* – providing *inter alia* a wonder-tale description of James II's flight across Ireland,[53] and a brilliant image of *nouveau* landowners in the eighteenth century occasionally entering a tenant's cabin and 'seeing a ghost': the supplanted former owner, or his heir, being deferentially entertained. The picture of the nineteenth century is largely predictable: the Anglo-Irish 'dropping out of our historical saga', displaced by the 'fraudulent and theatrical' O'Connell. But O'Grady's story takes some unexpected twists: the revolutionary James Fintan Lalor is a hero, possibly because he began his career by exhorting landlords to their duty, much as O'Grady himself did. And the O'Grady view of Parnell anticipates that of Paul Bew: 'I think he had planned out ways and means of preserving the Irish gentry, not at the cost of the Irish peasant but at the cost of the imperial Treasury, also that he intended to manoeuvre so as to have Ulster on his side not at his flank.'[54] In this as in much else O'Grady's *Story of Ireland* not only reflected the conditions of the early 1890s – the second Home Rule Bill and the era of constructive unionism; it also completed his own expiation for the unintended encouragement which his early work had given to national-ism.[55] And it changed the characters in the story in order to suggest a different moral and even a different ending.

V

What did this mean to the generation of brokers of nationalist culture who had put themselves under O'Grady (as Maud Gonne had put herself under the god Lugh)? Notably, what did it mean to their central figure, Yeats? He gave O'Grady's *Story of Ireland* to his sister Lily for Christmas, and he certainly read it closely: interestingly, it contains phrases which recur in his later work (including 'a terrible beauty'[56]); he quoted from it, without attribution, in letters to the papers. But though he reviewed other work of O'Grady's at this time,[57] he avoided mentioning *The Story of Ireland*, which had rapidly and unsurprisingly become the target of violent abuse in the nationalist press. Finally Yeats excused its controversial content on the grounds of 'impressionism'.[58] In 1895 his list of 'the Best Thirty Irish Books' included no fewer than six of O'Grady's, including the controversial *Story*;[59] in unguarded moments he could praise O'Grady for his sub-versiveness,[60] puncturing 'the mystery play of devils and angels which we call our national history'. But he nervously took issue with his mentor over assertions such as the lack of national consciousness among the Irish rebels against Elizabethan rule;[61] and as Yeats's opinions became more openly Fenian in the later 1890s, guru and disciple moved on to different sides. For his part, O'Grady let Yeats away with very little – complaining (perceptively) at the way that the poet juggled advanced-nationalist ideas in Ireland with an eye fixed firmly on the London literary market, and objecting to the uses made of his own writings. 'Among the other interesting barbarians whom you are exhibiting to the Philistines I, too, am being trotted out to show my paces.'[62] Their relationship became increasingly awkward: as with John O'Leary, Lionel Johnson and other friends of Yeats's youth, their actual relationship went into decline long before their deaths, and was subsequently resurrected for Yeats's autobiographical purposes. Only an echo comes through from O'Grady's side, through one of his inimitable home-truth letters. 'Frankly, and quite between ourselves, I don't like at all the way you have been going on now for a good many years. You can't help it, I suppose, having got down into the crowd.'[63]

Despite this uneasy personal history, and the spectacular political incorrectness of O'Grady's real opinions, the influence of his impressionist and prophetic history lies behind the ideas of Yeats, AE, Maud Gonne and others as they rediscovered their national 'story' in the 1890s. Moreover, his apocalyptic vision and his rediscovery of heroic myth interacted potently with the currents of occultism and mysticism which also characterized their circle (and the age). As the millennium approached, Yeats and his friends became preoccupied by the implication which I have already mentioned: if Irish history were a 'story', and its beginning and middle were, as they thought, well established, then what was its end? By the late 1890s they had become convinced that a millennial 'ending' was just round the corner. Horoscopes, the French illuminati tradition, Theosophy, the Golden Dawn and the Celtic propaganda of Fiona MacLeod had much to do with this; but so, in the Irish context, had the notion of history as a story.

The people thus affected were an identifiable group, who had usually graduated from Protestant bourgeois backgrounds via the avant-garde art-school underworld to claiming Celtic identity through occult affinities. They required a visionary answer to the confusion left by Parnell's collapsed enterprise. Particularly in AE's personal religion, figures from the Irish past created by O'Grady were built into a structure of promised revelations – and a promised liberation. In his writings and painting, AE peopled the Irish landscape with prophetic avatars carrying Gaelic names and shimmering in violet light. (He saw the most mundane matters in apocalyptic terms; writing to excuse himself for a missed deadline, he could not resist announcing 'the devil has appeared to me in the form of a wife and children'.) With Gonne, Yeats and Fiona MacLeod, he frantically worked on organizing an Order of Celtic Mysteries, to midwife the new age; its symbols, names and inspiration owe much to cabbalistic traffickings but even more to O'Grady.

In this millennial surge towards the end of history, two further inputs need to be noted. One was the highly selective approach to Irish folk tales and their deconstruction,[64] pioneered by Yeats; through his eyes, many of these tales could be read as narratives of Irish history, rather than as variants of international models. The other input was the millennial influence of advanced Irish nationalism in the 1890s, epitomized by the Irish Republican Brotherhood (IRB), or Fenian movement.

For in the late 1890s the IRB, and its offshoot the Irish National Alliance, to which Yeats and Gonne were affiliated, also had expectations of the millennium, centred on their commemoration of the 1798 Rising and their hopes of international unrest in South Africa. The cleansing war which Yeats divined in Irish folk prophecy and his poetic visions of the stars being blown about the sky were reinforced by the discussions with Irish nationalist cabals in rooms off Chancery Lane. They were also, it must be added, reinforced by experiments with mescaline and hashish, but more relevant for our purposes is the way that the arguments were underpinned by that belief held – in their different ways – by A. M. Sullivan and Standish O'Grady and reiterated in their Stories: Ireland's special idealism would show the rest of the world the way. They also interacted with AE's own expectation that the story was reaching its end, and his letters of the time are peppered with highly specific injunctions: the gods are returning to Ireland; the old beliefs are reviving; 'a new avatar is about to appear and in all spheres the forerunners go before him to prepare'. The latter was tracked, in a highly specific vision, to a Donegal cottage with a fallen tree in front of it, he told Yeats. 'Don't spread this about.'[65]

As it happened, when the new age dawned in 1900, the apocalypse stayed away. The 1798 celebrations, apart from one tremendous street party, were a damp squib; Fenian politicking ended with squabbles about funding and the exclusion of Maud Gonne from public platforms. AE's own visionary future failed to deliver, and he became disillusioned with Fiona MacLeod ('every time she bobs her head out of the Astral Light I will whack it, at least so long as it bobs up in connection with Irish things'[66]). And Yeats's personal horoscope turned out to have cruelly scrambled its message.[67]

All this is from another story, though Yeats's biography might also be construed as a Story of Ireland. The narrative laid down by both Sullivan and O'Grady, and the uniquely influential generation of literary power-brokers reared by them, presumed an ending round about 1900; but the anticipated year came and went without writing the final page. Even the Boer War, important in many other ways for Irish history, failed to provide the expected final severance. O'Grady buried himself in his idiosyncratic new paper. And Yeats took to the theatre, as a continuation of hieratic secret-society organization by other means.

Initially he was aided and abetted by the scandalous novelist George Moore; and Moore wrote an account of these years (*Hail and Farewell*) that provides another version of the Story of Ireland. This is written to reverse the St Patrick story: the hero is sent back to Ireland to *rescue* it from Christianity. Yeats too was becoming bent on subversion. The subject matter of his theatre pointedly involved all the characters reinvented by Lady Mary Ferguson, Standish O'Grady and company – Cuchulain, Deirdre, Senchán, King Guaire, and Diarmuid and Gráinne – interpreted in a manner that infuriated Standish O'Grady beyond reason. But the stories of Ireland which Yeats's theatre told were more and more at odds with the received version; as time went by he used the theatre to wage war on nationalist pieties, leading to a lasting ideological break with Gonne and a personal break with AE. As for AE, he had by then devoted himself to the agrarian cooperative movement, remarking gloomily: 'O'Grady writes no titanesque romances but edits a local newspaper. I am not of the mighty but I knelt at the inner shrine and now I explain to a hungry looking audience how advantageously they might spend a pound or so in buying pigs.'[68]

The end of the story was not what had been expected. After 1900 it seemed that the old Home Rule version, back on the agenda, was going to provide a diminuendo closure.[69] In fact, *that* future evaporated too; in the next decade new storytellers appeared, like James Connolly, a Marxist who wanted to turn the clock back to pre-capitalism, believing (*à la* O'Grady) that ancient Ireland had pioneered communism. And, much more influentially, Patrick Pearse would bring A. M. Sullivan's story of the Christ among nations to its own preordained ending. After the rising of 1916, this national narrative would predominate, and many of the alternatives be forgotten – especially those alternatives dreamt up by a subversive intelligentsia of *déclassé* Protestants. As it turned out, the story was not ended by the cultural revivalists' New Age; nor by the Home Rulers' old one; nor even by the Sinn Féin Republic.

It remains no less important to recapture what the future looked like up to about 1912: though, if Anthony Smith is right in seeing nationalism as a strategy for solving the crisis of an intelligentsia, it signally failed to solve the various crises of the *fin-de-siècle* generation. Rather like generals always fighting the previous battle, cultural revolutionaries rarely get the revolution they expect. If a metaphorical hero finished the story by coming home in the end, it was not the epic hero Cuchulain but the threatening old man of the West with his 'redrimmed horny eyes' conjured up by James Joyce's Stephen Dedalus in a parody of Yeats, AE and solipsistic national culture.[70] And it would be Joyce who would, in the end, subvert the idea of the novel as the story of nations. As for the accepted story, in a partly independent Ireland, determinism ruled: the wonder tale shadowed out by Sullivan, where a virtuous Ireland finally reached the desired destination, fulfilling the final function delineated by Vladimir Propp.

This involved forgetting a lot; and it is that rigid morality tale which Irish historians have tried to query in recent years – though in some quarters it has just been replaced by a simplistic application of Frantz Fanon's One Big Idea to an Irish situation sweepingly redefined as 'post-colonial'.[71] The old form of the narrative continues to exert a compelling attraction for lost souls from the larger island, beached by receding tides of intellectual fashion (structuralist as well as Marxist). This can sometimes appear to the exhausted Irish as a new kind of colonial exploitation: at other junctures, one is reminded of nineteenth-century English travellers being told by sophisticated Irish locals what they know will make the visitors happy. From unexpected quarters, we sometimes hear the old insistence on the seamlessness of the web of national narrative: political correctness demands chronological elision.[72] This often posits a highly questionable version of the order in which things happened,[73] and requires a strangely limited notion of state, nation, allegiance and identity. It is sometimes asserted that modern cultural limitations have made us forget our history; with Irish history, the problem may be that we remember too limited a version. Ernest Renan pointed out long ago that creating a nation involves getting one's history wrong;[74] but those who have subsequently tried to rearrange the narrative are – interestingly – attacked in terms that are sometimes both religious and racial.[75]

However, political events at the close of the last millennium have shown that Irish people can reinterpret their experience away from supposedly preordained patterns and endings; and subversive history-writing has played its part in this. Irish historical interpretation has too often been cramped into a strict literary mode; the narrative drive has ruthlessly eroded awkward elisions. There *are* ascertainable facts and progressions, often unexpected; and there *is* a history beyond received narrative conditioning (though postmodernists may not admit it). There are other models, tales within tales, which might allow more room for alternative truths and uncomfortable speculations.[76] Perhaps Standish O'Grady's determination to re-create atmosphere was not so off-beam after all. There is a need for a historical strategy that recaptures uncertainties and thereby unlocks contemporary mentalities; for instance, group biography, or local history, can re-create realities that are not forced into episodes in the preordained national narrative. One might do it, indeed, by looking at the conditioning and expectations of those nineteenth-century writers and readers of the Story of Ireland – and the way they had to change their minds.

And one might in the end look back to AE, who, like many of that generation, was thrown out of kilter by the events of the unexpected future. His instincts – like several of his forgotten contemporaries – reached out to pluralist, pacific, cooperative endeavour; but the apparently compelling narrative logic of 1916, both foretold and enacted by Patrick Pearse, would hijack the story.[77] AE still worried away at the national narrative, determined to change perspectives and conscious that the story needed retelling. In 1914, just as the plot took a new twist, he dined with the writer of fairy tales Lord Dunsany. That evening, like Lady Morgan's fictional hero or the real Standish O'Grady, he fantasized about discovering a book of Irish history written from a new vantage. 'In his beautiful voice,' recorded Lady Dunsany,

he sketched . . . how the small holdings of the nineteenth and twentieth centuries gradually come into the hands of large owners, in the eighteenth century progress has been made and the first glimmerings of self-government appear, religious troubles and wars follow until the *last* Englishman, Strongbow, leaves the country, culture begins, religious intolerance ceases with the *disappearance* of Patrick, about AD 400, and we approach the great age of the heroes and gods. It is finally discovered that the publisher has bound the book backwards by mistake.[78]

2

Theme-parks and Histories

In his erratic but from time to time impressive youth, Ezra Pound spent three wet winters sharing a cottage in the Ashdown Forest with W. B. Yeats and acting as the great man's secretary. Perhaps driven beyond endurance, he wrote towards the end of this experiment an obscure and splenetic essay called 'The Non-Existence of Ireland'.[1] In this Pound attacked, among much else, the 'myths' retailed about the achievements of the ancient Irish, 'making ironclads and developing stage-plays in the fifth century of our era', claimed that Irish peasants were 'as rare and fictional as fairies' and asserted that 'there is no state, no recently promoted territory in the Union, which has not more claim to being a nation in itself than has this John Bull's Other Island, this stronghold of ignorance and obstruction'. I do not know if Yeats ever noticed the piece; or if it was read by any of those who proved Pound wrong the very next year, 1916, by beginning the Irish revolution which ended in an appreciable degree of independence. Of course, Pound had a way of being astonishingly wrong about things: it is a delectable irony that by 1924 he was trying to get Yeats to procure for him one of the Irish passports proudly issued by the new Irish Free State. This document was not forthcoming: a fact which Pound may have regretted in 1945, when, interned for Fascist collaboration in an army prison near Pisa, he wrote those deeply atmospheric *Cantos* which recalled his winters in Stone Cottage with his Irish mentor. The 'non-existence of Ireland' must by then have rung rather hollowly in his mind, but it served him right.

One of the themes of this book is Irish self-validation: the Existence of Ireland. But also its creation: and, particularly, the re-creation of 'Ireland' by communal acts of remembering and celebration. This brings us at once to self-presentation, particularly abroad. But the Irish self-image also relies upon a domesticated popularization of history: 'making history' in a second sense, which has more to do with packaging and marketing. It is canonically defined in a document issued by the Irish Tourist Board a few years ago called 'Heritage Attractions Development: A Strategy to Interpret Ireland's History and Culture for Tourism':

Irish history, due to the influence of many peoples, cultures and conflicts, is not easily understood by visitors . . . Visitors' time is also limited . . . so it is important to help increase visitors' understanding by creating interpretative 'gateways' into our heritage. This will heighten their experience, increase satisfaction levels, and help in awareness and appreciation of individual sites. The end result will be more repeat business, better word of mouth publicity, and the creation of a strong brand image of Ireland as quality heritage destination, with unique heritage attractions.[2]

So the plan is to emphasize a fixed number of 'storylines' in Irish history, linked to tourist sites and presentations: easily tapped into, easily understood. If only. This suggests that, if America was allegedly the only country to pass from barbarism to decadence without experiencing civilization, Ireland seems to have moved from archaism to postmodernism without really allowing the time to become modern. But it also suggests that 'history' can be arranged and packaged into presentations, or pantheons, or waxwork shows, or interpretation centres (where the interpreting is, of course, done for you in advance). And it is impossible not to wonder who this is for. Historians are often exhorted to write for 'the general reader', and some try to – though for most practising academics, the 'general reader' is a bit like the stray neighbourhood cat: you feel vaguely sympathetic towards it, you know it's someone's responsibility to look after it, but you're damned if you're going to do it yourself. However, over the last few years Irish historians have been increasingly presenting their wares for a popular audience: tourists on one level; and those attending commemoration ceremonies on another. This is responding to a felt need, but it is also dictated by hard-nosed motivations in the (supposedly) real world of politics as well as that of marketing.

Of course, it was ever thus. Versions of Irish history have been a contested area since the territory of Ireland itself was contested, with the coming of the Normans. There is a tradition of Irish history written to present an agenda, from one side or the other, which becomes especially notable in the seventeenth century and is an accepted strategy of intellectual debate by the eighteenth – a sort of parlour game for scholarly clerics of opposing faiths. With the Act of Union in 1800 the process moves into popularizing mode. On one side, a version of Irish history is promulgated by the Victorian state which is designed to demonstrate that Britain and Ireland really are one country: history is presented as a process that denies Ireland's separate development and illustrates the benefits of British rule and imperial membership. Naturally enough, those who did not agree set themselves to marketing a historical account which reversed these messages: through discussion groups, journalism, public demonstrations and history textbooks. We have already seen how A. M. Sullivan's *The Story of Ireland* presented Irish history as a self-enclosed liberation narrative, in the style of European Romantic nationalism, a story whose ending was pre-ordained, with separation from Britain as both a moral imperative and a historical inevitability.

The important thing is that both versions of this particular island story presupposed heroes and villains, both deliberately elided the complexities and paradoxes of Irish history. And by the time of the great revival of cultural nationalism around the turn of the century, movements like the Gaelic League, which preached a gospel of national liberation, had taken this fully on board. 'God wished us to be by ourselves out in the ocean, with our own particular language, music, religion, customs and other things. In addition he made the ancient Romans afraid to come near us, so that we are not like any other nation in Europe.'[3] Among the unwanted foreign complications thus airbrushed out were the overlapping waves of settlement, the interplay between religion and cultural identity, the unique balance of social, religious and political forces in the north-east, the parallels and connections with Europe, the development of distinctive Irish class and economic structures from the eighteenth century, the relationship of the Irish economy to industrialization, the takeover of many areas of privilege by a Catholic *haute bourgeoisie* by the turn of the twentieth century, and several other factors which lie behind the diversity and complications of our history. Much of this also shadows the way that partial independence came about in 1916–21 (though you would not guess it from the movies). And when independence did come in the 1920s, to the surprise of false prophets like Ezra Pound, with it came the need to rewrite history for the new state.

The expectant atmosphere of Ireland after the Anglo-Irish Treaty of 1921 might invoke Cavafy's poem 'Waiting for the Barbarians', in which people in a frontier city towards the end of the Roman Empire, living on rumour and obsessed with the threat of the barbarians coming, learn that the threat no longer exists. There are, in fact, no barbarians any more. The city-dwellers are suddenly nonplussed. 'Now what's going to happen to us without barbarians? / Those people were a kind of solution.'[4] The same was true regarding our own particular barbarians, the British government as represented in Dublin Castle: when it did not exist any more, on certain levels of intellectual life a *raison d'être* was removed. So from independence a version of Irish history had to be constructed by the state which stressed the 'Story of Ireland' in relation to the removal of the British: developments within the island, especially post-1921, tended to receive rather short shrift. 'Outstanding personages' and 'striking incidents' were to be emphasized, according to a contemporary Department of Education guideline.[5] In fact, theme-park history was being constructed *avant la lettre*. Certain strains in the national story – or stories – were painted up, others written out. (The First World War is just one obvious example, now being energetically reinserted.[6]) The process of censorship worked on more subtle levels than merely erasing love scenes from films or ferreting out books describing birth control (or 'Race Suicide', as the *Catholic Bulletin* crisply referred to it in the 1920s). The historical record was itself subject to a policy of enforced silence.

But, being Ireland, there was a counter-movement too. From the late 1930s a new generation of historians emerged, who set themselves to producing a more inclusive and sometimes dissenting version of Irish history, following new historical methods and approaches developed in the United States and Britain. They were based in universities throughout the island – Dublin, Cork, Galway and Belfast. The historians who pioneered this collaboration, Theodore Moody and

Robin Dudley Edwards, are sometimes presented nowadays as dry-as-dust pedants, convincing themselves that they were achieving impartiality by being even-handedly anaemic: to anyone who was taught by those spectacular personalities, this is laughable. They were empathetic and passionate scholars, but they did try to advance reinterpretation on various key issues, to edit a historical journal to the highest standards, and to produce a massively conceived *New History of Ireland*, written by divers hands. A revolution was set in hand which would affect the school textbooks of the next generation, and introduce a new attitude to the learning and teaching of Irish history, as a more complex and plural development than the old Story of Ireland – without throwing out the heroic or catastrophic elements in the story along with the bathwater. The next essay in this book looks at the process in some detail.

By the 1960s this approach was firmly fixed in the universities; by 1970 it had aroused its own reaction, and attracted a new description: revisionism. Philip Larkin's lugubrious verse claims that sexual intercourse began 'In nineteen sixty-three / (which was rather late for me) / Between the end of the *Chatterley* ban / And the Beatles' first LP.' For my Irish generation, revisionism 'began', or was identified, about the same time – somewhere between the death of the Pope and Thin Lizzy's first LP, if local references are desired. We were the generation of Irish historians formed by that intellectual development, and also excited by the advances in historical analysis in France and America, especially during that decade. We wanted to apply them to Ireland. Could approaches to Irish history be illuminated by Eugene Genovese's reconstruction of American slave culture, or Theodore Zeldin's *petite histoire*, or Eric Hobsbawm's political reading of Sicilian banditti, or Eugene Weber's analysis of how peasants turned into Frenchmen? But more immediately, and overtaking – tragically – that internationalizing moment, we were also influenced by the explosion in Northern Ireland that broke out during our studenthood, and enforced a rigorous examination of the political uses to which history is put. Historians like Conor Cruise O'Brien and F. S. L. Lyons made this specific connection, in books like *States of Ireland* and *Culture and Anarchy in Ireland*. And one regrettable result was that an opposing movement developed, claiming – I think wrongly – that so-called 'revisionists' were themselves censoring history, in the interests of present-day politics: understating the 'extreme nationalist' elements in the Irish past for fear of encouraging the IRA in the present.

Interestingly, it was some of the post-1960s generation, as well as more old-style commentators, who in turn gave revisionism a pejorative meaning, though they tend to be journalists or polemicists rather than professional historians. The concept nowadays tends rather to exercise newspaper columnists, professional polemicists, fringe conference-groupies with a grudge, underemployed politicians and refugees from post-post-structuralist university departments of English or sociology. There has been a fair amount of slanging, with the revisionist generation accused of 'corrosive cynicism' and endemic scepticism. There have been some good jokes: the most famous – indeed, by now canonical – defines an Irish revisionist as someone who thinks that the Famine was caused by a mass outbreak of anorexia nervosa, and is, significantly, attributed to P. J. Mara, spin doctor to the late disgraced Taoiseach, Charles Haughey. At best, the controversy has meant a healthy revival of why and how we teach history – and a stimulating dialogue around important issues of interpretation. At its worst, it has provided a bogus mantle of radicalism for the refurbishment of traditional preoccupations. The process has also led to some well-qualified scholars endorsing (intentionally or not) an odd view of the historians' task: redefined as a duty to reinforce the self-understanding of a 'people', no matter how it relates to the historical record (or the self-understanding of other people).

And that leads me to a consideration of how we make history by remembering things – because one of the sites where some very interesting historical 'marketing' has been going on is the industry of commemoration. Here, as in the seminar discussions of the 1960s, the fashion is set by France, where the notion of the present validating itself through remembering and citing the past is a long intellectual tradition. Lewis Namier, in one of those lapidary essays for which he should be remembered at least as much as for the *History of Parliament* project, pointed out that in 1940 it was very difficult for the Free French to convince their fellow countrymen that a base for resistance could be established outside the country, simply because it had no historical precedent. Such an idea, the newspaper *France-Libre* said, 'remains an abstraction since no memory, no tradition sustains it'.[7] It is this habit of mind which the historian Pierre Nora and his colleagues have investigated in a five-volume study translated (with a slightly Scott Moncrieff flavour) as 'Realms of Memory'.[8] Nora's word is 'lieu': a place or site where national memory settles and coheres and colonizes, through remembrance of an event, or a symbol, or an actual location. Most relevant, perhaps, for the Irish parallel is his idea of how memory operates in our day and age. As Sunil Khilnani has put it,

the collapse of a single national narrative and the dismantling of a regulated collective memory have encouraged the emergence of little narratives, attached to shared collective sites and speaking diverse and sometimes contradictory meanings. National history has ceded to national memory, which establishes more intimate but also more capricious relations between individuals and symbols of collective memory.[9]

In Ireland, under similar circumstances, the idea of self-validation through received memory has grown apace. This used to be a relatively low-level affair. For instance, the centenary of the Famine in the mid 1940s was commemorated by a government-funded programme of folklore-retrieval and a heavyweight volume of essays on the event, as well as several local observances. By contrast, the 150th anniversary was big business.[10] The government decreed exactly the period it was to cover (it had to be over by 1998, to make way for the next commemoration: so, by a government decision, the span of the actual, historical Famine was interestingly reinterpreted). It was linked to exploiting tourist sites and attracting interest from the Irish diaspora. The Cashel Heritage Society produced a luridly jolly brochure promising 'a colourful Pageant of Music, Song, Dance and Drama' to commemorate the 150th 'Anniversary of this dark period of our past', with five days a week of fancy-dress events over the summers of 1995, 1996 and 1997. A 200-acre Famine Theme Park was opened on Knockfierna Hill in west Limerick; 'it will be possible', promised the hand-out from the Great Famine Commemoration Committee, 'to experience first hand in this remote area how 1,000 people struggled for survival at the height of the Famine'. Coffin ships were energetically reconstructed in New Ross and Tralee, and Atlantic crossings planned. A life-sized bronze group of starving figures was erected on Custom House Quay in Dublin, and members of the diaspora were encouraged to have their family names 'cast in bronze' and set in the cobblestones around the sculpture (£750 payable to the Irish Famine Commemoration Fund, Payment Plan Option available for those who wished to spread the cost). Ministers were put in charge of the commemorative enterprise and given scripts to read. And all this, of course, took place against a background of controversy already existing, as regards the terrible event. Traditionally, the Famine was seen as at worst a deliberate English policy of genocide, at best wilful neglect on the part of the British government – an interpretation boosted in the 1960s by a great work of popular history by Cecil Woodham-Smith. Subsequent academic research tried to concentrate upon the contemporary context of similar disasters and the current beliefs about government intervention, and to understand how such a horror could have happened, rather than simply apportioning blame. But the effect of the commemoration year (or years) was to highlight the issues of guilt and pain, driven by the idea that some sort of empathy could be achieved, and a therapeutic catharsis brought about. The language of popular psychotherapy replaced that of historical analysis. This was popularized by a strange alliance of populist journalists, local political wheeler-dealers, erratic rock stars and those born-again newly Irish Eng. Lit. academics again. Performance artists staged presentations where they wept for hours in public to demonstrate what they felt about the Famine. Journalists and even historians wrote that we had 'suppressed the memory' of the Famine through 'survivor guilt' and had to get back in touch with ourselves, 'reappropriating that buried experience . . . reclaiming our Famine ghosts from their enforced silence', 'liberating ourselves into a fuller and more honest sense of who we are', or we would be 'culturally lonely' for ever. Thus the language of individual psychology was unthinkingly scaled up to communal identification. More hard-headedly, historians who had written judicious theses on the Famine turned their findings into books for the popular market, often turning up the volume of blame to a markedly strident level. Famine museums were opened, and 'Famine diaries' rediscovered and republished. The one that sold most turned out to have been a fake created by a novelist half a century after the Famine, as was painstakingly demonstrated in a long journal article, but the bookshops went on selling it under 'history' regardless.[11]

Meanwhile in the USA, a movement began among politicians in search of the ethnic vote; the Famine was defined as genocide in certain states and put on the curriculum of 'Holocaust Studies'. A fringe republican group circulated a map showing the location in Britain today of army barracks housing regiments which had been located in Ireland during the Famine years, exhorting the right-thinking Irish public to go and do their historic duty – you can guess how.[12] Finally the British prime minister Tony Blair made a public apology for the deeds and policies of his predecessor Lord John Russell in the 1840s. This – following the principle of party inheritance – should surely have been left to Paddy Ashdown, if anyone, but it followed the same logic of historical time-travelling as the British queen apologizing to the Maoris, the Pope apologizing about the treatment of Galileo and 400 latter-day Crusaders arriving in Jerusalem in July 1999 to apologize for the sacking of the city by their predecessors 900 years before. Pedigrees of inherited responsibility were asserted which raised, at very least, interesting questions about historical analysis.

Back in Ireland, all this activity (sourly referred to in some quarters as 'Faminism', an appellation which the more humourless practitioners quickly appropriated for themselves) produced a historical pay-off. This took the form of some first-rate and important local research, a number of extremely worthwhile conferences, and a shift among historians towards a consensus of concentration upon the role of the British government, specifically the economic assumptions of the then Liberal prime minister, Lord John Russell, and his ministers and civil servants. But the overall effect, while it boosts popular interest in a kind of Irish history, may not really lead to much illumination. The same has to be said about the next great commemorative binge: the failed rising of 1798, which from late 1997 ruthlessly shoved the Famine celebrants into the wings. Again, government ministers were detailed; again, the decks were cleared for public events; again, a political and marketing agenda was easily discerned, and in fact articulated. The 1798 Commemoration Committee stressed that remembering this event 'will benefit the country tourist-wise', and so the rebellion was commodified and packaged with a 'heritage trail', tea-towels, videos, reconstructions. The question has to be confronted, however, whether reconstruction in the 1990s has much to do with what can painfully be re-established about whatever the contemporary reality may have been: a subject returned to in the last essay of this book.

When history is commodified in this way, and put to such clear political uses – even when the objective is as valuable as the peace process or European Community membership – it is hard to suppress a faint shiver. We are so sensitized to our history in Ireland, and know, or think we know, it so intimately that this kind of exploitation is inevitable. Hugh Leonard wrote a satirical play thirty years ago called *The Patrick Pearse Motel*. It is a mordant farce set in a modern Irish hotel where all the rooms were named after events in Irish history. The illicit lovers were apprehended in the Parnell Suite, while the restaurant was called the Famine Room. How we laughed, in 1971. But the spectacle of the Famine Museum right beside the restaurant at Strokestown House, County Roscommon, or the old Wicklow gaol in its new tourist-friendly incarnation, full of resting actors in period costume, suggests that at least one great Irishman, Oscar Wilde, would appreciate the way that reality slavishly imitates art.

At the same time, it is worth noting the anniversaries that do not get commemorated. The 150th anniversary of Daniel O'Connell's death went unnoticed, though if we must have heroes he is surely one of the greatest figures in the pantheon – if unpopular, perhaps, in certain quarters today. We barely noticed the centenary of the foundation of the Irish Cooperative Movement in 1998. The 150th anniversary of Thomas Davis's death also went more or less uncommemorated, and indeed shares in the Young Ireland movement remain at a fairly sluggish level of performance altogether, though it had a more pluralist and forward-looking agenda than many movements in Irish history. Nor are investors in historical memory taking up many options in the eighteenth-century Catholic Committee – less glamorous than the United Irishmen but arguably more representative and more influential. And Charles Stewart Parnell's birth and death dates do not seem to arouse huge effort or industry. There are other subjects we seem to avoid as well. Ireland is, after all, a familial country; Irish history, and

Irish inter-communal relations, often seem to take on the character of a family quarrel. And we all know how families get through their days of festival and holiday: by not talking about certain subjects. In some ways, this kind of avoidance must be what the more psychotherapeutically inclined commemorationists mean when they talk about the trauma of suppression. But a certain amount of suppression might be desirable. It is hard to feel comfortable with the idea of historical memory as a feelgood happy-clappy therapeutic refuge; or as a fantastical theme-park like the short-lived Celtworld Mythology Centre in Tramore, County Waterford, which opened in 1992 and collapsed three years later, having received IR£1.8m in EU grants;[13] or as a sort of time-travelling computer menu which you can scroll down and pick your event to reconstruct. But the question that occurs is: why do we now see a boom in pop history, with a distinctly make-believe feel to it, and the revival of simplistic and fusty versions of the Story of Ireland, just at the point when it seemed that the analysis of Irish history had reached a new level of professionalism, impartiality and nuance?

Perhaps a number of causes have intersected. First, there is, of course, a worldwide fashion for theme-park reconstructions and soundbite-sized, digestible history-as-entertainment: it is impossible to expect that Ireland would have missed out, especially as history has always been of such absorbing interest to the general public here. (Indeed, that is one of the great delights of being an Irish historian.) Lewis Namier, again, described how we predicate our expectations about what will happen on what we think we know about what has happened: 'One would expect people to remember the past and imagine the future. But in fact, when discoursing or writing about history, they imagine it in terms of their own experience, and when trying to gauge the future they cite supposed analogies from the past: till, by a double process of repetition, they imagine the past and remember the future.'[14] For any historian, this carries the ring of a recognized truth. Then there is the question of generations and Oedipal reactions, which happens at a wider level than just within the family. The generation of so-called 'revisionists' who were Young Turks once are now middle-aged professors: the generation beneath them will make their own reputations by querying the interpretations of their elders. This is a kind of 'revisionism' in its own way, and will go on for as long as people need jobs.

There is also another, more controversial question of changing historical context. While the Northern nightmare was at its bloodiest, there was an imperative to turn a searchlight upon various disputed versions of our national past, and to investigate the supposed verities in the name of which both sides were conducting war. This produced, for instance, a self-conscious but wholly admirable and productive attempt among intellectuals in the Republic to try to understand the roots of the unionist view (not always reciprocated from the North). It is easy to have fun at the expense of the language used by politicians, but in many ways the public rhetoric of the state has altered astonishingly over the last ten or fifteen years; and this is the outcome of reconsiderations enforced in the first place by new approaches to our history. However, since 1994 the Northern nightmare has receded; for all the cliffhanging and postponements in the negotiations, ceasefires have held; hopes are raised again and again; we are no longer looking over the brink. This relaxation has, perhaps, made people less conscious of the dangers inherent in historical interpretations that tend to self-congratulation, tub-thumping or professional victimhood, all of which unwelcome characteristics have surfaced in aspects of recent commemoration fever. And, perhaps, in the unguarded language that sometimes slips out amid the welcome Newspeak of Irish politicians, North and South.

This is a personal diagnosis, but I am not going to offer a prognosis as well: historians prefer to leave that to commemorationists. My own belief is that the most illuminating history is often written to show how people acted in the expectation of a future that never happened ('remembering the future and imagining the past', once again). But one might recur to W. B. Yeats, with whom I began. Quoting Yeats sometimes seems like the last refuge of a scoundrel, but there is a case for citing Yeats as a more realistic prophet than his friend Ezra Pound. Yeats is often seen as a figure wrapped in cloudy and archaic preoccupations, but he was very conscious of the need for Ireland to be modern in a fulfilling, independent sense. And in several essays and speeches from about 1910, he attacked the idea of sanitized and idealized history, and the creation of pious and backward-looking stereotypes of Irishness which created 'images for the affections'. Time and again he spoke of the perils of nostalgia, and the need to bring Ireland to the cutting edge of the European and international experience. He also preached that a realization of our cultural independence was a necessary precondition of true independence, and that what must be emphasized was 'Ireland's inner subtle intellectual life' rather than the 'public, passionate life of the struggle for self-aggrandizement'. He also spoke out against what he called 'attacks on opinion pretending to be defences of morals' and the dangers of intolerance.[15] At the time of the Home Rule debates of 1912–14, he stressed that the national claim – to which he was deeply committed – should not be based upon 'national vanity'; and, in a public lecture after independence, he said that if that national freedom meant anything, it was the ability to cease being vain and to become proud instead.

When a nation is immature it is exceedingly vain and does not believe in itself, and so long as it does not believe in itself it wants other people to think well of it in order that it might get a little reflected confidence. With success comes pride, and with pride comes indifference as to whether people are shown in a good or bad light on the stage. As a nation comes to intellectual maturity, it realizes that the only thing that does it any credit is its intellect.[16]

By 'intellect' he means, I imagine, culture and achievement.

If the Irish are to remember or commemorate anything, it is worth recalling the great upward curve of Irish cultural achievement from about 1890 to 1914, and the fact that this went with an opening out of attitudes, a modernization of nationalism, an exploration of cultural diversity, a questioning of too-readily-received forms of authority in public and indeed private life. That was the period when, in a sense, modern Irish history was 'made'. And there are obvious parallels to the recent historic period through which the country has passed. We can make history by rereading it, and by realizing and accepting the fractured, divergent realities, and the complications and nuances behind the various Stories. The ambiguities of Irish history are, in many ways, the most distinctive thing about it. 'Making it up' for commemorative reconstructions will not get us any closer to those very aspects. Should we go so far as to follow the suggestion[17] that the next commemoration might take the form of raising a monument to Amnesia, and forgetting where we put it? Not entirely: as a historian, I have to be rather shocked by the idea. But as an Irishman I am rather attracted to it.

3

'Colliding Cultures': Leland Lyons and the Reinterpretation of Irish History

The Irish have become used to history meaning something more than war and the conduct of public affairs. The histories of the unwritten are crowding in: the subaltern voices of emigrants, of women, of subcultures like that of the Palatines in County Limerick or millenarian prophets in the 1790s, the forgotten voices of nineteenth-century schoolmasters trying to record a vanishing culture.[1] Historical geography and folklore studies are prospected for new ways into the Irish historical experience. Most of all, though, the study of Irish history has been opened up by analysis of Irish culture, or cultures. This has been true of the historical profession elsewhere too, where such an approach was often pioneered by scholars who had spent much of their professional lives defining themselves against conventional academe: E. P. Thompson or Eric Hobsbawm in Britain, Eugene Genovese or Natalie Zemon Davis in the USA. In Ireland, however, the idea of bringing the history of culture into the historiographical arena was pioneered by someone known up to then as a supreme practitioner of conventional political history.

Francis Stewart Leland Lyons published *Culture and Anarchy in Ireland* in 1979. He was the most distinguished product of Theodore Moody's history school at Trinity College Dublin, though he developed his new approach when he was living and working outside Ireland, holding a chair at what was then the new University of Kent. It was at Kent, while drafting courses like 'Education and the Idea of Culture', that he came to conceive of a new key to understanding Irish history. This would not be through the conventional study of political crises and the careers of politicians, to which he himself contributed so notably in books like *The Irish Parliamentary Party*, *The Fall of Parnell* and *John Dillon*; nor through magisterial overviews with a social and economic bias, like *Ireland since the Famine*; but rather through the analysis of cultures, where 'culture' stands for a system of beliefs, attitudes and ways of thought, in a sense mediated and refined through an understanding of history. In so doing, he put down markers for an interpretation of Irish history deeply influential in the next generation – so influential, indeed, that it seems almost imperative to reassess it for the coming millennium.

In Ireland, Leland Lyons came to think, there were several distinct 'cultures' in this sense: sometimes overlapping, more often sealed into separate, self-justifying compartments. It was not simply a 'Protestant' versus 'Catholic' tradition: varieties of identification certainly took religious labels, but as often as not the religious identification was simply a flag for a whole range of attitudes and values. And within Protestantism, for instance, there were the utterly distinct cultures of Ulster Presbyterianism and Southern Ascendancy identity. The resources of the country (psychological, geographical, political) could not accommodate the implicit friction, which broke out again and again. Nor could one really hope for a 'solvent', so to speak, which would meld or blend them into a less confrontational whole. In his last and most challenging book, *Culture and Anarchy*, he remarked that Irish diversity was

a diversity of ways of life which are deeply embedded in the past and of which the much advertised political differences are but the outward and visible sign. This was the true anarchy that beset the country [in the early twentieth century]. During the period from the fall of Parnell to the death of Yeats [1890–1939], it was not primarily an anarchy of violence in the streets, of contempt for law and order such as to make the island, or any part of it, permanently ungovernable. It was rather an anarchy in the mind and in the heart, an anarchy which forbade not just unity of territories but also 'unity of being', an anarchy that sprang from the collision within a small and intimate island of seemingly irreconcilable cultures, unable to live together or to live apart, caught inextricably in the web of their tragic history.

> Out of Ireland have we come.
> Great hatred, little room,
> Maimed us at the start.[2]

This involves the sombre concept of 'colliding cultures', rather like colliding planets, in a universe where interpenetration, fusion or commingling is simply not a physical possibility. The idea preoccupied Leland Lyons in what would turn out, with tragic unexpectedness, to be his last years; the phrase recurs in his Rankin Memorial Lecture two years later, when he remarked – speaking in Belfast – that 'the fact that historians are inarticulate about the different cultures which collide with each other in this island is merely a symptom of a more profound ignorance which runs right through our society and is exhibited *in excelsis* on the other side of the Irish Sea'.[3]

How far does this idea still apply to Irish history, past and present? What is the evidence for predetermined 'collision' between the culture of an Irish Ireland and that of an English England? And how do these ideas relate to Leland Lyons's work, and the tradition of history-writing which he did so much to influence?

In a sense, the pessimistic and slightly sardonic tone of that passage, and of that whole book, was a new development in his work. Lyons's intelligence was notably subtle, reflective and interrogative, and the Lyons oeuvre is distinguished by its refusal to go for easy answers, or to adopt simple and self-justifying stances: in this it was markedly different from the popular and populist versions of Irish history which he did much to displace. He was once asked by an interviewer where he would place Parnell 'in the pantheon' and crisply replied, 'I hate the whole idea of pantheons, quite honestly.'[4] This was an unfashionable attitude at the time. At the same time, he had made his early name by writing political studies which implicitly subscribed to the generally accepted notion that Irish national independence, achieved constitutionally but with the implicit threat of insurrection, was an inevitable if not always productive process in Irish history; that the nationalist tradition was the predominant and, in a sense, predetermined one; and that the achievement of the independent Free State and, later, Republic was a successful and by and large admirable enterprise. Much of this is of course true. But from the time of *Ireland since the Famine*, published in 1971, a certain saturnine doubt creeps in. In a book review of 1976, he permitted himself a sharp reflection:

I do not find it easy to recognize any Ireland that I know of in [the author's] assessment of the country at the beginning of the century. 'Today many Irishmen view the patriotism of this period in their country's history as an embarrassing memory, associated in the mind with the green beer and shamrocks of St Patrick's Day observances. What they forget, perhaps, is that a sense of patriotism and nationalism existed in Ireland at the turn of the century which, sentimental as it may have been, united men of a variety of political creeds, from unionists and Orangemen to militant republicans, in a genuine love of Ireland.' This seems to me to be wrong on two counts. I suspect what we feel now for those bygone days is nostalgia rather than embarrassment, and if we feel nostalgia it is, ironically, because perhaps we still do not sufficiently realize the depths and intensity of the feelings by which, already at that date, men were divided rather than united.[5]

The emphasis of his thought was already falling on division rather than unity. One simple but insufficient explanation might be that he had moved back to Ireland. A memorable exchange was reported by the great Irish botanist David Webb, a key figure in Trinity College Dublin, where he was known (and in some quarters much appreciated) for his fearsome brusqueness and – in intellectual encounters – for taking no hostages. He read *Ireland since the Famine* and immediately taxed Lyons with subscribing to 'sentimental nationalism' (an accusation no one could have levelled at Webb himself). Lyons's reply was worthy of his antagonist as well as of himself: 'Yes,' he admitted, 'but you must remember I was living in England then.'[6]

It is, of course, easier to sustain an old-fashioned and unquestioning belief in Irish history as an apostolic succession of national liberators if you do not live in the country itself. (This might be drawn to the attention of some English and American fellow-travellers.) But it is not a sufficient reason to explain Lyons's increasingly quizzical view of Irish history. The process is clearly prefigured in some aspects of *Ireland since the Famine*. By then events in Northern Ireland were well set on what would turn into a quarter-century of bloodshed, spilling over into Britain and the Republic; and the use made of 'sentimental nationalism' in that struggle would give many analysts of Irish history pause for thought. Through the seventies and early eighties Lyons lived in Ireland, and saw this at close quarters; he had differences with colleagues – usually not historians – who went in another direction on the issue. He himself had roots in the North (an Ulster Presbyterian father), as well as a strong identification with the South, and an English education. Conflicts of cultures were not new to him. But the 1970s in Ireland, when he was beginning to study the life of W. B. Yeats and to work on the lectures that would be published as *Culture and Anarchy*, should also be seen in a longer perspective. And this requires some consideration of the historiographical tradition of which Lyons was a part.

The generation of Irish historians before Lyons centred round Robin Dudley Edwards, David Quinn, J. C. Beckett and most of all the man Lyons described in that Rankin lecture as his own 'beloved teacher', Theodore Moody. These were notable people. Trained in the 1930s, they were much influenced by the work being done by scholars at the Institute of Historical Research in London, and in the great American universities: where, in both areas, a new analytical spirit was abroad, using geography and economics to re-examine long-accepted ideas about the patterns of national history. In American or British terms, this might entail querying sacrosanct notions about 'manifest destiny', the Founding Fathers or the nature of parliamentary development. In Irish terms, it could mean something even more subversive.

It has already been pointed out that Irish history since independence in 1921 had been very specifically oriented, and that the function of studying and teaching it was seen as highly specific and indeed highly instrumental. The object was to stress the continuity of the separatist tradition, and the determinist development of the movement or independence; as well as implicitly (or indeed explicitly) to stress the fact that British rule in Ireland was always an undesirable and undesired imposition, taking the form of oppression and exploitation of a people struggling rightly to be free. (The periods of Irish history where this was not very obvious were, therefore, treated as regrettable interludes when the 'national spirit' was temporarily dominated by collaborators, or simply *reculant pour mieux sauter*.[7]) Elements in the national history, and indeed the national population, whose history did not subscribe to this apostolic pattern were seen as at best deluded or, more generally, 'un-national'.

This may sound like a caricature, though readers of the *Catholic*

Bulletin or the pronouncements of Thomas Derrig (minister for education in the 1930s) will be unsurprised. And it should be stressed that from the late 1920s, and especially through the 1930s and 1940s, a small but vocal group of Irish intellectuals challenged this teleology. Some, like Frank O'Connor, did so because they had become disillusioned by the purist Irish Republicanism which they had embraced in their youth; the key text here is O'Connor's short story 'Guests of the Nation', and indeed the whole collection under that name, published in 1931. Others, like Sean O'Faolain, did so because they had discovered a wider world of cosmopolitan literary culture, which included the kind of England not so easily demonized; still others, like Hubert Butler or, later, Owen Sheehy-Skeffington, did so because they saw themselves as Irish nationalists but were reared outside the Catholic tradition and, in Butler's case, had close connections to the Protestant community of the North. And there were still others, like Louis Mac-Neice, who might not have described themselves as Irish nationalists but who felt their Irishness was denied by the purist stream.

Not enough work has been done on these dissentients, though it is the sort of theme that would have appealed to Leland Lyons.[8] But perhaps it is worth linking the work of such intellectuals, principally grouped around that great periodical *The Bell* in the 1940s, to the contemporary movement in Irish historiography. For just when O'Faolain and his friends were planning their literary magazine, the first number of a new Irish scholarly journal had appeared – in 1938. This was the brainchild of Moody and Edwards, and in turn followed the establishment of two scholarly societies: in the North *and* in the South, but closely connected. They were the Ulster Society for Irish Historical Studies, based in Belfast and focused on Queen's University, and the Irish Historical Society, based in Dublin and equally focused on UCD and Trinity. From these two societies emerged a single journal, *Irish Historical Studies*, created by Moody and Edwards. Announcing it, they specifically declared an intention to set up in Ireland a journal which would be the scholarly equal of the *English Historical Review* or the *Historical Journal*, and they bemoaned the lack in Ireland of any clearing-house for historical research on the model of the Institute of Historical Research attached to the University of London.

Fair enough, you might say; but it is worth remembering the temper of the times. In the late 1930s it was very much the fashion to stress Ireland's cultural *superiority* to England; de Valera's political enterprise was in many important ways based on just such an assertion. Material and industrial disadvantage was, in fact, directly linked to moral and cultural superiority. It was an axiom of the *Catholic Bulletin* that in ancient Gaelic society, the poorest rural families sat around the fire discussing scholastic philosophy.[9] This was not subscribed to by the distinguished schools of medieval Irish history developing in UCD, Trinity and, indeed, Maynooth, but it struck the popular imagination. To state, however urbanely, that Irish historical scholarship could benefit by following English example automatically raised hackles. So, in some quarters, did any enterprise which was closely linked to the Northern state. In some important if implicit ways, the efforts made by Moody and Edwards to encourage a modern-minded and unpoliticized historical profession were bound to arouse suspicion. There are those who will say that an unpoliticized historical profession is itself an impossible and even undesirable aim, and in some circumstances one would have to agree. But the objectives of historical study in the Ireland of the late 1930s could certainly have benefited in terms of scholarship (and imagination) by becoming a great deal less politicized. And even if an 'impartial' mind may be impossible for the historian to achieve, impartiality, like virtue, is there for us to aim at, if never to reach. Nor does it exclude passion and commitment, as a glance at Moody's own biography of Michael Davitt's early years will show us.[10]

The preface to the first issue of *Irish Historical Studies*, then, gave a number of hostages to fortune, beneath its apparently unexceptional statement of intent:

We aim at doing, to the measure of our ability, what in England is distributed among several journals. We hope to be of service to the specialist, the teacher, and the general reader who has an intelligent interest in the subject. We have set before us two main tasks, the one constructive, the other instrumental. Under the first head are to be included articles embodying the results of original research, and articles on reinterpretation and revaluation, in the light of new facts, of accepted views on particular topics. The latter type of article, under the title 'Historical Revisions', has been standardized in *History*, the journal of the Historical Association, to whose example we gratefully acknowledge our indebtedness. We hope that this feature will prove of special value to teachers, and will help to reduce the time-lag between historical research and the teaching of history. Under the second head are to be included articles on the scope and the teaching of Irish history; articles on research methods and problems; select documents, with editorial comment; select and critical bibliographies and guides to sources, manuscript and printed; annual lists of writings on Irish history including articles in periodicals, annual lists of theses on Irish history completed and in progress in the universities of Ireland, reviews of books and periodicals dealing with, or having a bearing on, Irish history . . . We aim at coordination and co-relation of historical work . . . This journal is produced in the belief that it will attract sufficient public interest to set it on a secure and permanent foundation.[11]

It did, and it was. Could anything sound more acceptable and worthy and, indeed, patriotic? It was even dedicated, in the manner of ancient Irish historians, 'dochum glóire Dé agus onóra na hÉireann'. And the foundation of *IHS* was also the foundation of research schools, German-type seminars in Irish universities, the *New History of Ireland*, many monographs and a number of general synthesis works, written by university teachers rather than polemicists, which tried to present Irish history as more complex and less Manichaean than the old handbooks of the revolutionary generation.

It was against this background that Leland Lyons became first a student and then a teacher of Irish history, and his own work took a foremost place in the kind of scholarly study which placed Irish historiography on a new and firmer footing. At the same time, however, this process helped to destabilize some older assurances. The word used innocently by Moody and Edwards in 1938, 'revisionism', would be adopted nearly fifty years later as a hostile term for a kind of history which did not subscribe to the traditional pieties; and, in turn, to indicate a kind of history which, it was supposed, either intentionally or unintentionally made excuses for England.

The idea of 'revisionist historiography' as a conspiracy against nationalist probity has gathered pace after Lyons's death; it certainly gathered volume from the late 1980s. Those historians who subscribed to the demonic notion of revisionism were very rarely specialists in the modern period, though their arguments were often marshalled on this ground (Father Brendan Bradshaw, for instance, the doyen of the faith-and-fatherland school, is a historian of the early sixteenth century, but prosecuted a particular mission against those who reinterpret the late nineteenth and early twentieth centuries[12]). Perhaps because of this, no anti-revisionist historian produced a general synthesis of Irish history, reasserting the view of A. M. Sullivan, though that would have been the logical outcome of their position: the one exception roundly proves the rule.[13] And a certain inhibition might perhaps have been induced by the fact that revisionist historians were rapidly incorporated into the demonology inveighed against by Sinn Féin speakers at their annual Ard-Fheiseanna in the 1980s and early 1990s.

The *Kulturkampf* in Irish historiographical debate is discussed elsewhere in this volume and may be left there. But it is worth considering how Leland Lyons's work fits in to this debate. The arguments about revisionism only really gathered pace after his untimely death in 1983; accepting the Wolfson Prize (for *Culture and Anarchy*) in 1980, he grimly remarked that the real historical revisionists were the gunmen. But when the polemicists call out the roll of those supposed to have subverted Irish historiography from is rightful role of expressing the 'pain' of Irish history, his name is always there. Lyons was not around to respond to Bradshaw's declaration – in, ironically, *Irish Historical Studies* – that the traditional faith-and-fatherland view of Irish history was salutary and should be sustained, '*its wrongness notwithstanding*'. But his response can be guessed. And if one work of Lyons's takes a prominent place in what is conceived of as a revised view of the revolutionary period in Irish history, it must be *Culture and Anarchy*.

One reason why this was so was because here, unusually, Lyons confronted directly the question of contemporary politics in a historical study. He had become increasingly conscious of the potential for abuse of history by the polemicists. When the British government seemed to be inclined towards reintroducing the death penalty, after the assassination of Airey Neave, he was asked to sign a public letter from historians of Ireland, which made the case that such a step would only create a martyr-culture of the kind which had sabotaged Anglo-Irish relations in 1867 (the Manchester Martyrs) and 1916 (the Easter Rising), and would give a great propaganda victory to the IRA. In a letter of characteristic laconic courtesy he refused, presenting the exact opposite argument: he felt that such a letter would, as he put it, 'give comfort to the Provisionals', and that he could not associate himself with a statement which might carry such a risk. Whether he was right in this case or not (and the effect of the subsequent hunger-strike campaign argues against him), he was very closely attuned to the possible political implications of historical arguments. In *Culture and Anarchy* his chosen period ended in 1939, but on the first page he made a deliberate link to the carnage of the present, repeating yet again the image of cultural collision:

Political solutions are indeed urgently needed, but they will continue to be as unavailing in the future as in the past if they go on ignoring the essence of the Irish situation, which is the collision of a variety of cultures within an island whose very smallness makes their juxtaposition potentially, and often actually, lethal. Recent events in Northern Ireland have certainly shown us that two very different communities are at death-grips with each other, but the fact that this conflict is so often described in religious terms has still further confounded confusion, leaving many observers convinced that a people so inveterately addicted to its ancient, obscure quarrels is best left to its own murderous devices.[14]

This was the tone which struck the ear, and the pessimism of the book is perhaps one reason why it made such an impact. Its success surprised Lyons himself, who characteristically criticized it far more stringently than any of the reviewers, and privately remarked that more weight was being put on it than it could really bear. (He also noted, with astringent humour, its unpopularity in some quarters in Ireland.) In a sense, the pessimism of *Culture and Anarchy* was also the sign of a break with his mentors. In 1980 he described Moody's values as those of 'the liberal historian of the old school who still cherishes a lingering belief, if not in the perfectibility of man, at least in his improvability, and who has not entirely discarded the idea of progress from his mental equipment'.[15] But a bleaker and less optimistic note was already sounding in his own work. It had been a characteristic of historians from his tradition, working in independent Ireland, to conflate differences of culture; to play down the more irreconcilable and sectarian manifestations of Irish political life; to downgrade the confessional identification present at every level of Irish society, at least until quite recently. In the quotation from his Rankin lecture, Lyons put this avoidance down to ignorance or myopia, but it may have been more strategic than that. It is relevant to remember Moody's great admiration for the integrity and commitment of the nineteenth-century Fenian movement, which he constantly emphasized, at the expense, perhaps, of the openly sectarian Ancient Order of Hibernians, who, it could be argued, were far more influential in shaping Irish politics in the early twentieth century. The point here was that, speaking from the tradition (and the institution) which Moody represented, his (completely genuine) admiration for the moral sense of the early Fenians was a valuable counter to the suspicions and prejudices of those from the 'other side', with whom he was determined to work in the cause of historical research. Joe Devlin might be tactfully left for later. But in *Culture and Anarchy* Lyons confronted the cutting edge of Irish differences, and traced the expression of antipathies which often seem as much tribal as sectarian. Scholars like Vincent Comerford, Paul Bew and David Fitzpatrick have carried this further in their generation; but in 1979 it struck a new and resonant note.

It may have been encouraged by the fact, as mentioned earlier, that Lyons was living in Ireland then (he had returned to Trinity as Provost in 1974). But it probably also reflected his work on the biography of W. B. Yeats. What stage had his thinking on Yeats reached, at the time he was writing the Ford Lectures which became the book *Culture and Anarchy*? I suspect that he had noted how early, and with what vehemence, Yeats was assailed by literary and political enemies who were prepared to impeach him on the grounds of Protestant Ascendancy background, as well as moral and political unsoundness. This reaction is usually associated with his speeches in the Senate during the 1920s, notably his great polemic against building Catholic moral teaching into the fabric of Irish law regarding divorce. But through Yeats's protean life, two developments are constant. One is his own conviction, and determination, that he would be famous: possibly developing from about the age of fourteen. The other is his distancing from the conventional nationalist pieties of the day, and his belief that these political beliefs were too closely interwoven with the Catholic establishment to accommodate either artistic or political freedom.

Yeats was sharply conscious of this at the turn of the century, even before the separations and traumas of the following decade. It would, as discussed later in this book, dominate his creative imagination in the late 1920s, and set the tone for how he was remembered after his death.

Thus the analysis of *Culture and Anarchy* was inspired by Lyons's tracing of Yeats's personal political odyssey; and it was, so to speak, framed by Yeats's own political disillusionment with the prospect of a pluralist Irish national culture by the very early 1990s. Yeats was a fighter, and went on preaching this cause, as well as creating a national theatre which often challenged the pieties of the day head-on. The climax of this was the first week of *The Playboy of the Western World*, opening at the Abbey Theatre in January 1907, when the outraged audience rioted against the version of Ireland created by Synge. 'I stood there watching,' Yeats recalled, 'knowing well that I saw the dissolution of a school of patriotism that held sway over my youth.'[16] But in fact it had dissolved for him several years before. (And his youth had passed too.)

One of the reasons why *Culture and Anarchy* is a wonderful book is because it is founded on a similarly passionate moment of insight and self-interrogation. It also stems from an odd and little-noted Irish subculture: Trinity College nationalism. The conflation of nationalism and Trinity may seem surprising: the initial reaction may be as sceptical as the TCD classical scholar A. A. Luce's withering remark when Conor Cruise O'Brien said he was writing a book about the Congo. ('Is there a book in that, do you think?'[17]) The culture of what the *Catholic Bulletin* used to merrily describe as 'the Elizabethan rat-pit' seems by nature inimical to Irish nationalism. The university was used as a barracks and prison in the Jacobite wars, was defended against the rebels in 1916 (by a younger A. A. Luce among others) and insisted on playing 'God Save the King' at college functions up to the 1950s. There is, of course, a well-rehearsed roll-call of nationalists who were connected with Trinity (Tone, Emmet, Davis, Luby, Butt, Galbraith, Hyde), but they are no more representative than the equally well-worn roll-call of Protestant patriots (Fitzgerald, Parnell, Childers) who were not. None the less the Trinity mind could be nationally minded in a manner which, if not nationalist, was not unionist either. Like much else, this was grounded in an eighteenth-century cast of mind, when the idea of 'nation' signified not a claim to territory but an ethos of government and culture. It was well expressed by a Trinity-educated bishop: 'If we understand [by "nation"] a compass of wall, or an extent of land: our notions are too narrow, and material. We must understand by it that system of law and polity by which we are kept together in peace and order, and preserved in security from our enemies and ourselves. And this is the civil sense of the word.'[18]

The Irish Protestant intellectual tradition, grounded in this belief, is not automatically assimilated to a 'British' view; this can be established not only by instancing Thomas Davis, but others of his 1830s Trinity generation, whether they followed him politically or not: John Mitchel, Isaac Butt, Sheridan Le Fanu, Samuel Ferguson, James McNevin, James McCullagh, John Blake Dillon. (Davis's tutor, Thomas Clarke Waller, called himself 'Professor of Things in General and Patriotism in Particular'.) The ethos of the College was, and remained, firm against public disorder but hospitable to hybrids. The founder of Irish Home Rule, Isaac Butt, for instance, was far more than simply a John the Baptist to Parnell's Messiah; Joseph Spence has brilliantly demonstrated that he was an original and 'national' thinker, preaching a nationalism based on 'Irish facts' (especially economic facts), rather than 'English Theories' – a very Trinity distinction.[19] And Ferguson's 'Dialogue between the Head and Heart of an Irish Protestant' is a text that has retained its canonical importance from the 1830s to today.

Trinity's national-mindedness need not necessarily be seen as a variety of liberalism. Although the College treated Catholics and Dissenters in the nineteenth century far better than either Oxford or Cambridge, its first Catholic fellow was in fact a maniacal unionist, later implicated in peddling forgeries to *The Times* in an effort to discredit Parnell. And while early Home Rule had a certain College following, it dropped off as the cause radicalized. By the turn of the century Trinity's ethos seemed summed up by a lethally laconic and dismissive Toryism. But there was none the less a strain of cultural nationalism which could invoke C. H. Oldham, Douglas Hyde, T. W. Rolleston: mentors and allies of the young W. B. Yeats, and figures very important to Lyons in *Culture and Anarchy*. Yeats's own relations to Trinity were troubled and ambivalent, especially in his Fenian youth

– though even then, the College was neither as upper class nor as West Briton as claimed.[20] And even if A. A. Luce manned a rifle in 1916, and the Trinity history don W. Alison Phillips wrote the most stinging study of 'The Revolution in Ireland', the doomed 'Convention of Ireland' trying to bring together nationalists and unionists before the deluge met in Trinity's Regent House. The new Free State regime was not friendly towards the College (as is clearly evidenced in the handbook edited by Bulmer Hobson), but its revenues were guaranteed. De Valera built a close relationship with several provosts, and an evident regard for the institution itself (possibly in reaction to the symbiotic links between his opponents in Fine Gael and University College, Dublin). Certainly by the 1960s Trinity (like the *Irish Times*) was settling itself into new-look nationalism. And Lyons himself sustained this tradition during his memorable tenure as provost, taking a leading part in Dublin life and, for instance, entertaining the winners of the all-Ireland Gaelic football final in the Provost's House. The version of Trinity's relation to Ireland entertainingly conjured up by Denis Donoghue in 1982, when he delineated an institution presenting a 'surly' rebuttal of the world outside its gates and refusing to allow 'papists' to occupy the Provost's House, was by then wildly out of date.[21]

In fact, the questioning scepticism of Lyons's mind owed much to his Trinity conditioning. Reactionary as Trinity has sometimes been, the inclination of the College has never been towards the pious belief that everything in Irish history was fine until some outsider came along and spoiled everything. Trinity historians do not, as a rule, believe in Golden Ages; they are more inclined (like Arthur Balfour) to argue that, since there was once an Ice Age, so there must one day be another. It is an approach antipathetic to romanticism, but also to sentimentality. Theodore Moody once remarked that he found Gerry Adams's politics perfectly comprehensible: what was unforgivable was his 'sanctimoniousness'. This is not only a typically Trinity distinction, but a characteristically Trinity reaction to the verities of old-style nationalism.

It is against this background that Lyons's later interpretation of Irish history – when he returned in triumph to Trinity in 1974 – might be seen. In these years, he was studying the political and intellectual world of Ireland at the *fin-de-siècle*. The effect of saturation in the polemic and journalism and political point-scoring and literary skirmishes of Ireland a century ago can induce scepticism and weariness; but other perspectives are possible too. One is inevitably struck by the vehemence, immobility and barely suppressed hysteria of the extreme views on both sides: Orange and Green, unionist and nationalist, Protestant and Catholic. But equally notable is the fluidity and openness of the middle ground: the little magazines, the discussion groups, the cultural initiatives that tried not to be politicized in a reductionist and jejune way. There was, along with the public confrontations, a deliberate attempt to circumvent the 'zero-sum' version of Irish antagonisms in cultural politics or religious issues, as well as in the attempts made to settle the land question and the devolution issue, by people who had been vituperating against each other for a generation.

Most of all a picture emerges of the political mentality during the first decade of this century in Ireland as characterized by an expected future: the future of Home Rule, achieved constitutionally. This is an aspect increasingly stressed by historians of Edwardian Ireland such as Paul Bew, Patrick Maume and Senia Paseta. And many of the cultural agendas, and the fringe societies, and the discussion groups were concentrating on the shape that life would take under this expected new dimension. The apocalyptic and revolutionary rhetoric which presaged 1916, and which – with all its inspirationalism – also implied the institutionalizing of irreconcilable divisions between the various Irish cultures, came into focus only from the political crisis of 1910–12. Lyons's view was that the argument for 'cultural fusion', when it recurs, appeals only and always to a small group of the already converted. Writing in 1979, this seemed all too true. But at the turn of the twenty-first century it is not sentimental or Golden-Ageist to discern cultural debate opening up in Ireland and the growth of a dialogue – along with notions of imaginatively reinterpreting the questions of sovereignty and allegiance, which have so often been restricted to 'zero-sum' options.

In 1989 the Cultural Traditions Group was launched in Northern Ireland, and discussions revolved around these issues – optimistic though it seemed at the time. Need nationalism always imply the politics of old-fashioned separatist republicanism, given the alteration of the Republic of Ireland into a kind of state which bore less and less resemblance to the picture traditionally nurtured by both sides in the North? Did cultural self-confidence have to be yoked to a determinist and ideologically redundant notion of unilaterally declared nation-statehood? Might we be coming to a juncture, in the history of both Irish states, where the credentials for being Irish were being redefined, as in early-twentieth-century Ireland? Might 'modernized' nationalism mean not only accepting cultural diversity, but moving towards a secular ethic as a reasonable aspiration in both parts of the island? Finally, it was thought,

there may be grounds for hope that the discovery of an outward-looking and inclusive cultural nationalism, not predicated upon political and religious differences, will be the salient business of . . . intellectuals and educators in this current crisis of both Irish states. If such a process, teamed with economic optimism, achieved its own momentum, hopes of vague 'political movement' might be left for later. More importantly, the message that cultural diversity need not imply political confrontation might get through to the rockface of attitudes in the housing estates of Belfast and Derry.[22]

In 1989 this may have seemed utopian. But the subsequent decade has seen a cultural and political upheaval in the Republic; the astonishing ascendancy of President Mary Robinson, with her long and public commitment to secularism, feminism and recognition of diverse cultural traditions; an equally seismic change in the public perception of the Catholic Church and its political influence; and the establishment of a coalition government including ministers from a party once seen as revolutionary socialists of the deepest dye. In the North, republican and loyalist paramilitaries went out on a limb by suspending hostilities without receiving any of the long-outdated and discredited shibboleths which had always been demanded as necessary guarantees. The communal breath was held as we saw something like a semblance of normality return to life, in the very arena of those colliding cultures of which Lyons had written so brilliantly twenty years ago.

In the process, we were roughly divided into Sceptics and Romantics; and there is little doubt about which side Lyons would have occupied. Many others, trained in the same school, would usually be inclined towards scepticism. And during all the euphoria about the 'peace process' some chilling notes were struck, notably from people within the opposing monoliths, now prepared to say the unsayable in public. Prominent among them was the testimony of Sean O'Callaghan, an IRA volunteer, shortly to leave the prison where he was serving life for murder, after fifteen years in the organization.[23] He now recounted how he had changed his mind. Interestingly, O'Callaghan did not come from the 'rockface' of a Belfast or Derry housing estate; he had grown up in County Kerry, surrounded by the comfortable verities of old-style rural nationalism. And he had set off, as he saw it, to 'free the North', migrating to the killing fields of east Tyrone in the 1970s and what he now calls 'a world so paranoid and fanatical that it is almost beyond the understanding of soft Southern nationalists'. He argued, therefore, that those who had helped to bring about the ceasefire, and spoke in terms of a brave new world beyond it, had no comprehension of the forces they were dealing with, and were being strung along by implacable bigots.

However, this grim analysis can be taken in a different way. True, the perceptions of what nationalism means in South and North have by now diverged irreconcilably. But one does not need to be Pollyanna to believe that the new style of politics in the North reflects at last a recognition among republican politicians that the fundamentalist and myopic 'nationalism' of the IRA in Northern Ireland is a different culture than 'nationalism' as redefined in a dramatically altered South; and that it is the worldview of the Northern republicans that must change – including a change in their recognition of the unionist community, who themselves know there is no going back to the old conditions of their supremacist statelet.

English commentators have a tendency to talk about 'violence in Ireland' or 'war in Ireland', in a way that denies the manifest, fractured reality: the fact of how widely society, expectations and consciousness have diverged in the Republic and in the North over the past quarter-century. And the limitations of the old manifest-destiny notion of Irish nationalism have been exposed as mercilessly as the bankruptcy of old-Marxist historical theories about 'logical positions' and 'inevitable contradictions'. Here the revisionist historians have played their part, if only in trying to indicate that Ireland is a complicated place, characterized by diversity as much as by uniformity; and, more broadly, that history is not about manifest destinies, but about unexpected and unforeseen futures.

And it should also be written to illuminate ambiguities: especially when dealing with the history of a country which over seventy years has developed a stable, mature and increasingly confident polity while manipulating multiple forms of ambiguity in terms of national identity and political ethos (opposite parties standing for the same things, a 'first national language' spoken by next to nobody as their first national language, a claim on territory that few politicians really wanted, and a booming economy dependent on international hand-outs). In his palmy days Charles Haughey received much flak for coining the phrase 'Irish solutions for Irish problems': I rather liked it, and believe that it may indicate sophistication as well as sleight-of-hand. It may, indeed, apply to the future of nationalism in Ireland, and the collision of cultures. It is time to reiterate that people can reconcile more than one cultural identity within themselves; abandonment of the old, prescribed positions may be a liberation for both sides; the border may be crossed by so many channels of media communication, leisure activities, economic cooperation, joint initiatives in energy and tourism that the variety of EU passport carried by those on either side becomes less and less relevant.[24]

This is not to forget that as recently as the 1980s someone could leave the easygoing certitudes of life in Tralee in order to follow the dictates of Irish history as he had learnt it, and adhere to Wolfe Tone's eighteenth-century ambition: 'to unite the whole people of Ireland, to abolish the memory of all past dissensions, and to substitute the common name of Irishman in the place of the denominations of Protestant, Catholic and Dissenter'. Who would not want to do as much? But the path he took, he now tells us, led him to become enmeshed in implacable tribal hatreds, and a policy of ethnic cleansing which led him to kill two Protestants before he was twenty. Is this the ultimate logic of colliding cultures? Certainly, the logic of exclusivist Irish nationalism can too easily point that way. And it must be a worry that, in the current rapprochements, elements in Southern politics will feel it necessary to adopt Northern nationalism's discredited rhetoric of political correctness, instead of Northern nationalism following some of the redefinitions pioneered by the South.

At the same time, Southern Irish political culture has been characterized since about 1921 by the tradition of giving up something in order to gain a lot; this could be seen as the reappearance of that reconciling element discernible in the early 1900s, before the whirlwind. We have already seen that the rewards of realism may mean civil security and political cooperation in a redefined Northern Ireland. And Irish public opinion may be following the lesson taught by historians over the last two generations: that Irish nationalism and Irish identity should not be interpreted as an immutable graven image, but as a protean and fabulous beast.

The work of Leland Lyons did much to teach that very lesson, not least because of his developing commitment to cultural rather than simply political history. Less than a year before his death he wrote privately: 'The literary-historical genre is infinitely beguiling and I can't ever imagine going back to straight political history again, especially Irish political history, which is (in fact) anything but straight.'[25] None the less, the politics entered the literary-historical genre, as he well knew. Elsewhere he wrote that he wished research students would invade the history of culture and colonize it more intensively than they seemed prepared to; and here too he was prescient. I have referred to him as a Sceptic, but in his Rankin lecture he allowed himself a more optimistic reflection than any in *Culture and Anarchy*:

Whether one looks at the nineteenth-century arguments about Home Rule, or at the twentieth-century arguments about devolution or about republicanism, the crucial questions have tended to be posed primarily in political terms. Will there be self-government for the whole of Ireland? Once partitioned, will Ireland be reunited, and if so, how and when? What should be the relations of Dublin and Belfast with each other and of both with London? So the questions go on and on, and the political solutions, which are in fact no solutions, go round and round in a vacuum that seems increasingly unreal. Why is the unreal vacuum there? Why do the questions and the answers seem in the end so inane? Very large, in my view, because over the last hundred years few people have tried to relate political solutions to cultural realities. Here in Northern Ireland, under the pressure of horrendous events, you have begun to come to terms with this problem. Indeed, a longer perspective than any we can envisage now may yet reveal that out of all the suffering of the past decade has come a far more sympathetic response to the sensitivities of the different cultures than was evident before the Troubles began, or has been evident in the South at any time.[26]

Events may now have shifted into that longer perspective: where Irish cultures are understood as parallel and, in the end, coexistent and even complementary, rather than colliding for eternity. If this is so, the process owes something to the kind of history advocated by Lyons, because to study 'cultural history' is to interrogate concepts of 'state' and 'nation' – which bristle with complications in the Irish case.

Lyons's own view of history looked hard at such complications and distrusted pantheons and personality cults. In this he may have been influenced, not only by his work on Yeats, but also by his interest in that other giant of twentieth-century Irish cultural achievement, James Joyce. The way that Joyce has recently and ingeniously been claimed for nationalism is considered elsewhere in this book, but it is worth remembering what he wrote. As early as 1905 – the era of *Culture and Anarchy* – he told his brother, 'I am sure that the whole structure of heroism is, and always was, a damned lie.'[27] He subsequently produced *Ulysses*, a novel constructed against the accepted structure of heroism, and against conventional, exclusivist pieties. Leopold Bloom is a Jewish advertising-man but no less an Irish hero for that. In the great pub scene which presents Irish national rhetoric, retailed in saloon-bar anecdote form, a discussion develops about nation and culture, in which aggressive questions alternate with hackneyed apostrophes celebrating the heroic version of Irish history. In the middle of it all Bloom makes tormented stabs at definitions of culture and nation. What is a nation? 'A nation is the same people living in the same place.' Ridiculed, he adds, 'Or also living in different places.'

– What is your nation if I may ask, says the citizen.
– Ireland, says Bloom. I was born here. Ireland.

This provokes a great parody of the chauvinist catalogue of Irish historical icons, which makes Bloom think of his own race's history and persecution.

– But it's no use, says he. Force, hatred, history, all that. That's not life for men and women, insult and hatred. And everybody knows that it's the very opposite of that that is really life.[28]

To stringently study the kind of history that illuminates 'life', in a welcome or unwelcome way, seems the intellectual legacy left by Lyons's work and tradition. Had he lived something nearer his allotted span, would his pessimism – well founded in the 1970s – have been moderated? Probably. He knew well that Irish history, past and present, is marked by sudden and devastating changes of mind as well as by tragically immobile attitudes. Some of these convulsions, like Gladstone's conversion in 1885 or de Valera's in 1926, decisively altered the terms of political history on the ground. But it might be more apposite, given Lyons's own restrained scepticism and his own interest in cultural and intellectual history, to end with A. M. Sullivan, whose classically nationalist *Story of Ireland* provides the *leitmotif* of this book. Late in life he was elected an MP for the Irish Nationalist Party and came to the satanic empire, home of wife-murderers and infant-chokers, which he had spent his life denouncing. He found he rather liked Westminster; surprised his colleagues by expatiating on the virtues of the British character; and finally admitted that he 'looked back with intense regret upon the unreasoning hatred in which I have grown up'.[29] So he became – though the word was not yet coined – a 'revisionist'. He wrote another book called *New Ireland* which preached the national story in conciliationist terms, calling for 'free and friendly communication' between Britain and Ireland, 'leagued together for purposes of mutual protection and prosperity'. But it was too late; nobody read it.

4

Yeats at War: Poetic Strategies and Political Reconstruction

'Memory' is a subject which has achieved a historiography all its own, starting – as with so many high historiographical fashions – in the *ateliers* of Paris.[1] But it is not a novel preoccupation in Ireland, where the importance of structured memory has been recognized by the widespread practice of its obverse: therapeutic voluntary amnesia. Until recently, this was conspicuously the case regarding the First World War. For many years the 'Great' War was seen as a topic of some embarrassment: the political correctnesses of the new state established in 1922 demanded that the participation of hundreds of thousands of Irish people in the war to end all wars, fighting for the British Empire, be forgotten or at best politely ignored. This was, of course, because the war was in part a prelude to Ireland leaving the Union: but in other ways, Irish commitment to the war raised awkward questions about commitment to the Union as well.

So 'Not talking about the war' was elevated to a fine art in public rhetoric – and this affected historiography too. Over the last twenty years or so, this has been reversed: the war has been seen as centrally important in modern Irish history; the experiences of combatants, the treatment of ex-soldiers, the centrality of the war to the planning of the Easter Rising, have all been topics treated at length in excellent books, and the way that the war interacted with the fortunes of John Redmond's brand of constitutional nationalism has also been closely inspected.[2] Moreover, the war has become an acceptable part of official memory too: symbolized by the restoration of Lutyens's memorial garden at Islandbridge, Dublin, and by the president of Ireland joining Queen Elizabeth in ceremonies remembering the war dead.

This is all emphatically to the good; it represents a facing up to the many-faceted nature of modern Irish history, and a recognition that there may have been alternative futures to the one that actually happened. At the same time, it should be remembered that during the years 1914–18, the war and what it represented were already, for many nationalists, a subject of some ambiguity and embarrassment. Nor did they have to be revolutionaries. Clearly, some constitutional nationalists were prepared – like the Nationalist MPs Tom Kettle or Willie Redmond – to fight for Britain; equally clearly, others felt more doubt. W. B. Yeats was not a Nationalist MP, though he was once suspected of having such ambitions.[3] By 1914 he was also very far from being a revolutionary. But the day after the war broke out, he wrote doubtfully to an Abbey Theatre colleague: 'I wonder how the war will affect the minds of what audience it leaves to us. Neitsze [sic] was fond of foretelling wars for the possession of the earth that were to restore the tragic mind, & banish the mass mind which he hated . . . In Ireland we want both war & peace, a war to unite us all.'[4]

Redmond thought that this was exactly what the war effort against Germany would do – specifically, that it would bring a recalcitrant Ulster into line with their comrades to the south. This did not happen; and after the 1916 Rising and its aftermath, the Anglo-Irish War, or war of independence, proved to be the 'war that united us all' – if 'we' were to be conceived as the nationalists of twenty-six counties. Other disunities remained painfully evident. Through it all, Yeats remained preoccupied by the intellectual effect of the war. And the way his own intelligence, creative and political, responded to both wars – the Great War and the small Irish war that followed it – is central to the story of his life. In the process he adapted his public persona in order to emerge as a founding father of the new nation in 1922. In this, as in so many ways, his biography is the history of his country.

From August 1914 Yeats's attitude towards the war effort epitomizes the ambiguities and sensitivities inseparable from the subject in Ireland. He was a convinced Home Ruler, who had given many speeches for the cause (and went so far as to make the Abbey Theatre put on a terrible play by Redmond's daughter for nakedly political reasons). However, the arguments he sometimes produced for Home Rule were quintessentially Yeatsian (including the impartially offensive argument that it would 'educate Catholics mentally and

Protestants emotionally').[5] By 1914 he was emphatically an 'establishment' nationalist; he lived part of the year in London, where he was on dining terms with Asquith and Balfour; he would shortly refuse a knighthood; he was far estranged from extreme nationalism. But he also had an early record of Fenian activity, and of criticizing the monarchy. From the start of the war, he refused to align himself with public statements on behalf of 'men of letters' condemning Germany, and was careful not to identify the Abbey Theatre with official war-effort benefit performances.[6] As news came through from the front, he was critical of the apparent incompetence and 'useless heroism' of the British officer class: 'England is paying the price for having despized intellect.'[7]

At the same time, to be anti-war in Dublin was effectively to identify yourself as an advanced nationalist, and he elaborately refused to do this – notably when he had to share a platform with the ostentatiously 'advanced' Patrick Pearse at a public meeting, for which Trinity College refused to act as host on the grounds of Pearse's anti-recruiting activities. Yeats trod a very careful line at this meeting, disassociating himself from Pearse's politics while defending free speech: but he noted astutely that when Captain Tom Kettle turned up at the debate in military uniform, fresh from the Western Front where he would subsequently meet his death, he was booed. While Yeats kept apart from the 'bloody frivolity' of the war, it raised issues which could not be evaded, and which penetrated unexpected areas of life.[8] Attempting to organize a pension for James Joyce from the Royal Literary Fund, for instance, he came up against Edmund Gosse at his most cavilling and blimpish:

Neither his own letters nor yours expressed any frank sympathy with the cause of the Allies. I would not have let him have one penny if I had believed he was in sympathy with the Austrian enemy. But I felt that you had taken the responsibility in the matter.

Yeats's reply was masterly:

It never occurred to me that it was necessary to express sympathy 'frank' or otherwise with the 'cause of the allies'. I should have thought myself wasting the time of the committee. I certainly wish them victory, & as I have never known Joyce to agree with his neighbours I feel that his residence in Austria has probably made his sympathy as frank as you could wish.[9]

Thus literary politics were, like every other facet of life, affected by the war. Nor was Yeats as absolutely detached as he liked to pretend. He did give his strategy of detachment poetic form, when Edith Wharton asked him to donate a poem for a war-effort compilation called *The Book of the Homeless.* Close friends and collaborators of his like Edmund Dulac turned out a great deal of work for such enterprises, but Yeats kept himself aloof: he told Henry James (Wharton's inevitable intermediary) that this was the only thing he would write about the war, and the poem conveys a certain impatience at the whole exercise, as well as a contrived staginess. (Great ladies brought out some of the best in Yeats, but also a lot of the worst.)

> I think it better that at times like these
> We poets keep our mouths shut, for in truth
> We have no gift to set a statesman right;
> He's had enough of meddling who can please
> A young girl in the indolence of his youth,
> Or an old man upon a winter's night.[10]

Actually, he did take part in a reading for the Belgian Relief Fund a year later; and though he kept his head down, wartime conditions impinged on his life in various ways. A boy shouted 'Kitchener wants you!' at him when he was going into his club. The London blackout altered his urban landscape in a way he approved: no more illuminated advertisements for Bovril, he remarked. While living in Ashdown Forest, his erratic secretary and amanuensis, Ezra Pound, was taken briefly into police custody for being an 'alien in a prohibited area'.[11] Most bizarrely of all, wartime paranoia interrupted Yeats's experiments in St Leonards-on-Sea with David Wilson, a mildly deranged chemist who had invented a machine which received and amplified messages from the spirit world. Yeats's excitement about this was immense, and he tried to raise money for developing it commercially. But Wilson recklessly published a message received in German, and the police impounded the machine as an illegal wireless: Yeats had to intercede with Gerald Balfour (fortunately interested in psychical research) and highly placed contacts at the Home Office. But he could not stop Wilson being conscripted, and the experiments came to an end. It could have been, Yeats thought, 'the greatest discovery of the modern world'.[12]

This bizarre episode happened in 1917. In that same year, Yeats was in correspondence with the Foreign Office about giving a series of lectures under their auspices in France. But, significantly, one of the reasons why this idea was dropped was that he wanted to talk about 'modern Ireland'. And since the events in Dublin of a year before, this was a dangerous subject. Those same events had initiated a process of political adaptation in Yeats's own life which would dominate his publication strategies as well as affect the content of his poetry over the next five years – until three-quarters of Ireland emerged into quasi-independence in 1922, and Yeats emerged alongside as the poet of the revolution.

Yeats, like nearly everyone else, was astonished by the Easter Rising of 1916, when Patrick Pearse and his companions defied the majority of their IRB comrades as well as the British Empire by launching a hopeless insurrection. Several of his friends noted that his surprise was coloured by his deep dislike of Pearse, whom he had, according to Pound, been denouncing for years as 'half-cracked and wanting to be hanged – has Emmet delusions same as other lunatics think they are Napoleon or God'. Pound also pointed out, regarding the proclamation of the republic, 'Yeats dont like Republics – likes queens, preferably dead ones.'[13] Several of the revolutionaries and their sympathizers had been known to him; some, like Arthur Griffith, founder of Sinn Féin, had become serious enemies through disagreements about the relationship of artistic freedom to nationalism and – more elementally – jealousy over Maud Gonne. At just this time Griffith attacked Yeats as an 'imperialist' who had gone over to the enemy: 'a poseur in patriotism precisely as Chesterton is a poseur in Catholicism'.[14] Others, like Constance Markievicz, had been friends in his youth and were now estranged. Living in England, Yeats was reliant on letters from friends to find out what had happened: and these provide a fascinating barometer of changing opinions. His sister Lily sent a bracing sketch of some of the principal revolutionaries, which gives a rather different portrait than the one her brother would later construct canonically in his poem 'Easter 1916':

What a pity Madame Markievicz's madness changed its form when she inherited it. In her father it meant looking for the North Pole in an open boat, very cooling for him and safe for others. Her followers are said to have been either small boys or drunken dock workers. I don't think any others could have followed her. I would not have followed her across a road. I often heard the elder Pearse speak at his school prize days and such things. I thought he was a dreamer and a sentimentalist. MacDonagh was clever and hard and full of self-conceit. He was I think a spoilt priest.

As for the alcoholic John MacBride, she added, 'it must have been some humorist who got him the post of water bailiff to the corporation'.[15]

Thus we have exactly the 'mocking gibes' that Yeats would later write into his poem of apparent atonement about the rebels. The letters from his closest friend Augusta Gregory at Coole Park similarly begin with references to 'corner-boys' and 'rabble'; but they change, particularly with the executions. Her opinions, in fact, run well ahead of Yeats's. 'It seems as if the leaders were what is wanted in Ireland & will be even more wanted in the future – a fearless & imaginative opposition to the conventional and opportunist parliamentarians.' Yeats sends her articles from the *Westminster Review* stressing the rising as a German plot; and she retaliates with quotations from Shelley on the execution of people who deliberately risk the death penalty from motives of political idealism: 'persons of energetic character, in whom as in men who suffer for political crimes, there is a large mixture of enterprise & fortitude & disinterestedness, and the elements, though misguided and disarranged, by which the strength and happiness of a nation might have been cemented, die in such a manner as to make death not evil but good'.[16] These are the very ideas explored in the poem Yeats would write about the rising: 'Easter 1916'. The seedbed of that complex poem contains not only Maud Gonne's remark to Yeats that 'tragic dignity had returned to Ireland', but also Gregory's reflections on Shelley, and the Dublin mockery retailed by Lily – all to be changed utterly.

Yeats wrote 'Easter 1916' over the summer, staying with Maud

Gonne in Normandy, with echoes of the European war in the wings; but Ireland had come to the forefront. Just as influential is the fact that he finished the poem at Coole Park, under Gregory's influence again. Appropriately, it is in some ways a classically ambiguous text – as Gonne smartly spotted when she told him it didn't come up to the mark ('My dear Willie, No I don't like your poem, it isn't worthy of you & above all it isn't worthy of the subject.'[17]). The life of that poem is itself a complex subject. Its arrival at Gonne's seaside house, sent from Coole, galvanized arguments between Maud and her daughter over the nature of sacrifice; it was then circulated as a samizdat among trusted friends; in early December Yeats read it at Lindsey House, Cheyne Walk, to a reception so electric that Gregory had to defuse things by declaiming some Hilaire Belloc;[18] it made a ghostly appearance on a draft contents list for his 1919 collection, *The Wild Swans at Coole*, but subsequently disappeared. Eventually it was published in the *New Statesman* in 1920, and absorbed into the canon of inspirational revolutionary literature, creating phrases recycled into countless chapter and book titles: 'All is changed, changed utterly: / A terrible beauty is born.'

Despite this endorsement, and its future life on posters and tea-towels, 'Easter 1916' is in fact a very ambivalent reaction to the rising, emphasizing the 'bewildered' and delusional state of the rebels as much as their heroism, and moving to a plea for the 'flashing, changing joy of life', as Maud Gonne put it, rather than the hard stone of fanatical opinion, fixed in the fluvial stream of existence.

> Hearts with one purpose alone
> Through summer and winter seem
> Enchanted to a stone
> To trouble the living stream.
> The horse that comes from the road,
> The rider, the birds that range
> From cloud to tumbling cloud,
> Minute by minute they change;
> A shadow of cloud on the stream
> Changes minute by minute;
> A horse-hoof slides on the brim,

And a horse plashes within it;
The long-legged moor-hens dive,
And hens to moor-cocks call;
Minute by minute they live:
The stone's in the midst of all.

Too long a sacrifice
Can make a stone of the heart.
O when may it suffice?
That is Heaven's part, our part
To murmur name upon name,
As a mother names her child
When sleep at last has come
On limbs that had run wild.
What is it but nightfall?
No, no, not night but death;
Was it needless death after all?
For England may keep faith
For all that is done and said.
We know their dream; enough
To know they dreamed and are dead;
And what if excess of love
Bewildered them till they died?
I write it out in a verse –
MacDonagh and MacBride
And Connolly and Pearse
Now and in time to be,
Wherever green is worn,
Are changed, changed utterly:
A terrible beauty is born.

A textual analysis of the poem reveals this ambiguity, and also the inheritance of phrases and reflections which Yeats had been entrusting to notebooks and essays since long before the First World War.[19] But in the mood of 1916, it would be read as republicanism pure and simple. This was still far from being Yeats's position, though he was being accused of pro-Germanism: there were rumours his own Literary

Fund pension would be withdrawn, and he had to visit Asquith to quell these very assertions. And there is another way in which one of the unexpected contingencies of the Great War restrained his actions. He was much involved in the endless campaign to repossess the great collection of paintings which the art connoisseur Sir Hugh Lane (Gregory's nephew) had left to the Dublin National Gallery when he drowned in the *Lusitania* disaster in 1915. The bequest was in an unwitnessed codicil, revoking his previous bequest to the National Gallery in London; the London gallery, and powerful friends in the government, stood on the letter of the law and claimed the paintings belonged to them. (Curzon was seen as a particularly obsessive enemy on this score, though his biographer believes it meant rather less to him than Yeats thought.[20]) Yeats and Gregory spent a phenomenal amount of time, energy and ink fighting this cause. In 1916 they were pursuing it through the corridors of power, by means of Yeats's friendship with Asquith, Birrell and others. But they were also particularly cultivating both Carson and Craig, now influential in government – but also, of course, the leaders of implacable Ulster Unionism. Yeats's chances of keeping them on side, once he had emerged as an apologist for the Dublin rebellion, may easily be imagined. His sense of political possibilities was always finely developed; indeed, he told John Quinn that he could include 'Easter 1916' in his next collection only if the war came to an end before then, well aware that in many people's eyes pro-rebel equalled pro-German.[21]

What the years from 1916 to 1920 are remarkable for, therefore, is a good deal of writing that was withheld from publication. There were unambiguously nationalist poems like 'The Rose Tree', Fenian ballads of a kind which Yeats had experimented with in his youth but, apparently, resolutely turned away from in the intervening years. There was a Fenian Noh play, *The Dreaming of the Bones*, dealing with the iniquities of the fatal lovers whose scandal supposedly led to the Normans being invited into Ireland in the twelfth century – whose eternal existence as wandering ghosts is strangely bound in with that of a 1916 rebel, on the run in County Clare. It is a play which departs from Noh conventions in coming down on the side of revolutionary confrontation rather than reconciliation – with an invocation of that classical symbol, the red cock of revolution. Yeats was well aware that it packed a strong revolutionary punch: too strong, at that moment, for it to be performed.[22] And from the summer of 1916 he returned to writing his memoirs.

Like most people's memoirs, these cast more reliable light on the author at the time he was writing them than on the actual events they purport to describe: in fact, he takes sweeping liberties with chronology and personnel in order to build his pattern. This particular draft was unpublished as such until 1972, but he quarried it for the marvellous volume called *The Trembling of the Veil* that appeared in 1922. In 1916 Yeats set himself to writing about the 1890s, but with the sharp consciousness that Irish history post-Parnell's death in 1891 was going to produce a revolution twenty-five years later. The theme he returns to again and again is the conflict between nationalist propagandist politics and the imperatives of the creative artist: stressing that the artist's influence, while remaining independent, will play its own political part, by radicalizing the new Ireland. This was the thesis that he would reiterate again and again, finally and most memorably delivering it as part of his speech in receiving the Nobel Prize in 1923, the year after Ireland achieved some kind of independence: an event Yeats would cannily relate to the honour bestowed upon himself.[23]

That is to look ahead. For the moment, he watched as Irish opinion settled in a new direction over 1917–1918. This was a period of personal *Sturm und Drang* for Yeats, from which he emerged with a new wife, a rejuvenated interest in occult and psychical research, and a new home – the Norman tower which he bought in 1916 and had begun to renovate. In Irish politics, helped greatly by a series of government blunders, political support was swinging to Sinn Féin, the party of Yeats's old enemy, Arthur Griffith. Again, the opportunities were provided by wartime conditions: the government's paranoia about the involvement of radical nationalists in a trumped-up 'German plot', for instance, and the great crisis in 1918 over the decision to impose conscription on Ireland if need be. In this year of transition, Yeats's movements repay close attention.

First of all, he finally wrote a war poem – though not in the way that, perhaps, Edith Wharton would have expected. In January 1918 his friend Augusta Gregory's only son, Robert, was killed flying his plane over Italy: a shattering blow for the Gregory circle. She wanted a memorial of him and Yeats obliged, writing an obituary and several elegies. It is notable how carefully he avoided the actual circumstances of Gregory's death for king and country. The first attempt, 'Shepherd and Goatherd', is an awkward and archaic piece of pastoral (only achieving interest in a stanza describing Yeats's own evolving theory of the journey of the soul). The most substantial effort, 'In Memory of Major Robert Gregory', is also self-centred – a sombre celebration of the poet's own new state of life (wife, tower, remembrance of dead friends) – written under the firm tutelage of Lady Gregory, to Yeats's irritation. He affected to long for Urbino-style patronage, but disliked being ordered to produce a stanza 'to commend Robert's courage on the hunting field'; he provided it, but confided to his wife, 'I have firmly resisted all suggested eloquence about aeroplanes and the "blue Italian sky".'[24] Augusta Gregory was allowed to play Isabella d'Este only so far. But this was not only an aesthetic reluctance. To praise the manner of Robert Gregory's death in an Ireland where, in 1918, even moderate nationalist opinion had turned against the war effort, and farmers' sons were determined to stay home and bring in the harvest rather than be conscripted for slaughter in Europe – this would have upset the political balance he was so carefully and discreetly keeping in his public life. So the one poem for Robert in which he faces up to the manner of his death, takes good care to reverse the message of king and country:

An Irish Airman Foresees His Death

I know that I shall meet my fate
Somewhere among the clouds above;
Those that I fight I do not hate,
Those that I guard I do not love;
My country is Kiltartan Cross,
My countrymen Kiltartan's poor,
No likely end could bring them loss
Or leave them happier than before.
Nor law, nor duty bade me fight,
Nor public men, nor cheering crowds,

A lonely impulse of delight
Drove to this tumult in the clouds;
I balanced all, brought all to mind,
The years to come seemed waste of
    breath,
A waste of breath the years behind
In balance with this life, this death.

This was Yeats's 'war poem' at last, written in June 1918 and published after the Great War was over, in 1919. But it placed the warrior-airman as an exponent of Nietzschean tragic joy; and attributed to him a lack of sympathy for the imperialist cause which was the exact opposite of what Gregory apparently actually felt. There would be one more Gregory elegy, which was not published in Yeats's lifetime, though that was Lady Gregory's decision, not his. And it would stem from the circumstances of the subsequent war – in Ireland.

For the moment, in 1918, Yeats held back his nationalist writings, and very carefully monitored the plays to be put on at the Abbey, rejecting several as too political for present circumstances; he also refused to be a signatory to the Irish Convention hastily arranged by his old friend George Russell (AE), to bring together nationalists and unionists and attempt a compromise Home Rule settlement. 'I dont want to take a political part, however slight, in haste.'[25] Since AE was calling for a pluralist solution to the current impasse, and the greatest possible diversity of thought, this is rather odd: Yeats had spent many years arguing for exactly the same thing. But in late 1918 he was restraining himself. He cancelled a projected lecture on 'the poetry of the Irish rebellion', privately remarking 'times are too dangerous for me to encourage men to risks I am not prepared to share or approve'.[26] At the same time, there are signs that he had decided the way the cat was going to jump. As early as January 1918 he had suggested to Gregory getting de Valera and Sinn Féin on board the Lane pictures campaign – a full ten months before the general election that proclaimed them the coming power.[27] And when the conscription crisis broke that summer, he took a firm line. The man who had insisted that poets had no gift to set a statesman right decided to do just that, approaching Asquith (though warned by Horace Plunkett that 'Squiffy isn't Gladstone') and initiating a correspondence with Lord Haldane which deserves quotation.

I write to you because you are a man of letters, and we, therefore, may speak the same language. I have no part in politics and no liking for politics, but there are moments when one cannot keep out of them. I have met nobody in close contact with the people who believes that conscription can be imposed without the killing of men, and perhaps of women. Lady Gregory, who knows the country as few know it, and has taken down, for instance, hundreds of thousands of words in collecting folk-lore from cottage to cottage, and has still many ways of learning what is thought about it – is convinced that the women and children will stand in front of the men and receive the bullets. I do not say that this will happen, but I do say that there is in this country an extravagance of emotion which few Englishmen, accustomed to more objective habits of thought, can understand. There is something oriental in the people, and it is impossible to say how great a tragedy may lie before us. The British government, it seems to me, is rushing into this business in a strangely trivial frame of mind. I hear of all manner of opinions being taken except the opinion of those who have some knowledge of the popular psychology. I hear even of weight being given to the opinions of clergymen of the Church of Ireland, who, as a class, are more isolated from their neighbours than any class known anywhere to me. I find in people here in Dublin a sense of strain and expectancy which makes even strangers speak something of their mind. I was ordering some coal yesterday, and I said: 'I shall be in such and such a house for the next four months.' The man at the counter, a stranger to me, muttered: 'Who, in Ireland, can say where he will be in four months?' Another man, almost a stranger, used nearly those very words speaking to me some two weeks ago. There is a danger of a popular hysteria that may go to any height or any whither. There is a return to that sense of crisis which followed the Rising. Some two months after the Rising I called on a well-known Dublin doctor, and as I entered his room, an old cabinet-maker went out. The doctor said to me: 'That man has just said a very strange thing. He says there will be more trouble yet, for "the young men are mad jealous of their leaders for being shot".' That jealousy is still in the country. It is not a question as to whether it is justified or not justified, for these men believe – an incredible thought, perhaps, to Englishmen – that the Childers Committee reported truthfully as to the overtaxation of Ireland, that the population of Ireland has gone down one-half through English misgovernment, that the union of Ireland, in our time, was made impossible because England armed the minority of people with rifles and machine-guns. When they think to themselves: 'Now England expects us to die for her,' is it wonderful that they say to themselves afterwards: 'We shall bring our deaths to a different market.' I read in the newspapers yesterday that over three hundred thousand Americans have landed in France in a month, and it seems to me a strangely wanton thing that England, for the sake of fifty thousand Irish soldiers, is prepared to hollow another trench between the countries and fill it with blood. If that is done England will only suffer in reputation, but Ireland will suffer in her character, and all the work of my life-time and that of my fellow-workers, all our effort to clarify and sweeten the popular mind, will be destroyed and Ireland, for another hundred years, will live in the sterility of her bitterness.[28]

The preoccupation with hereditary bitterness infecting the accumulated efforts to 'sweeten the public mind' anticipates the two great poem sequences which the Irish revolution inspired him to produce: 'Nineteen Hundred and Nineteen' and 'Meditations in Time of Civil War'. But for the moment, as Ireland descended into guerrilla war from 1919, Yeats kept his counsel; to judge from references in his friends' correspondence, he was considered to have lost touch with public affairs, immured in his tower with his wife and new baby. It is true that from time to time he thought of withdrawing altogether, to Italy or even Japan. He was putting together the beginnings of his bizarre study of the philosophy of history, A Vision, and preoccupied with the belief that the Christian era was ending, in an apocalyptic downward spiral of world revolution: his attention to events in Russia was closer than is often realized, reflected both in his poem 'The Second Coming', written at this time (a world-historical poem about world revolution), and in the strangely prophetic essay 'If I was Four and Twenty', which ends with an odd anticipation of totalitarian rule in Europe.[29]

In early 1920 Ireland lurched deeper into guerrilla war, and Lloyd George's government responded by sending over the mercenary forces known as the Black and Tans and the Auxiliaries. The actions of these troops, with their unofficial policy of 'reprisals' against the civilian population, drove once unlikely people to join Sinn Féin. Before they came, Lily Yeats had joked that to be a true Sinn Féiner you had to believe the RIC were obligingly shooting each other to make propaganda for the British government; after some experience of the Tans, she would write in December 1920: 'As you know I was no Sinn Feiner a year ago, just a mild nationalist, but now –'[30]

From early 1920 her brother was on a lecture tour in the USA. Here, as so often before, his responses to journalists are worth decoding. He was, in a sense, unmuzzled, but also had to keep a wary eye to Irish-American Fenianism, especially as de Valera was touring the States at the same time. (A meeting was actually arranged, which Yeats described to Gregory. 'I was rather disappointed – a living man, all propaganda, no human life, but not bitter or hysterical or unjust. I judged him persistent, being both patient and energetic, but that he will fail through not having enough human life to judge the human life of others. He will ask too much of everyone & ask it without charm. He will be pushed aside by others.'[31]) In the event, Yeats's public statements were distinctly un-republican. He attacked the 'oppression' of the military, criticized censorship, but also stressed the advisability of granting dominion status and said that Ulster should not be coerced. The British had created Sinn Féin's success by bungling: now they might 'be criminal enough to grant to violence what they refused to reason' (a very conservative reflection indeed).[32] Political fanaticism, he said, was 'a bitter acid that destroyed the soul'; he reprised this in reading his poem about Constance Markievicz feeding a seagull on her window-ledge in prison, a strange mixture of sympathy and contempt:

> Did she in touching that lone wing
> Recall the years before her mind
> Became a bitter, an abstract thing,
> Her thought some popular enmity:
> Blind and leader of the blind
> Drinking the foul ditch where they lie?

And he did not read 'The Rose Tree' or 'Easter 1916'. Sinn Féin sympathies had their limits. Griffith and he, Yeats told a journalist, had not been on speaking terms for some years.[33]

Strangely, at this time, in an instruction from prison, Griffith told his Sinn Féin comrades: 'Mobilize the poets . . . Perhaps Yeats will use his muse for his country now.'[34] However, he did not. He stayed away from Galway, irritating Gregory with his inquiries about the safety of building materials at his tower; in Oxford, he worked on his philosophical system. But in the autumn and winter of 1920 he also wrote the section of his autobiography called 'Four Years', recalling his London apprenticeship from 1887 to 1891. This looks like an escape from current horrors: but reading between the lines offers a different interpretation. The text is preoccupied by how a 'nation or an individual' might achieve, through emotional intensity . . . a symbological, a mythological coherence'; and in a passage written at this time, but incorporated into a later volume, he recalled his own early efforts at creating a culturally revolutionary organization, relating the gestation of his own youthful opinions to what he actually calls 'the future birth of my country'. The artist's integrated life provides the platonic parallel for the creation of a national myth. The ringing conclusion of 'Four Years' should be read not only as emotion recollected in an Oxford study, but as a product of observing Ireland in the process of revolution and remaking.

I used to tell the few friends to whom I could speak these secret thoughts that I would make the attempt in Ireland but fail, for our civilization, its elements multiplying by division like certain low forms of life, was all-powerful; but in reality I had the wildest hopes. Today I add to that first conviction, to that first desire for unity, this other conviction, long a mere opinion vaguely or intermittently apprehended: Nations, races, and individual men are unified by an image, or bundle of related images, symbolical or evocative of the state of mind which is, of all states of mind not impossible, the most difficult to that man, race, or nation; because only the greatest obstacle that can be contemplated without despair rouses the will to full intensity.

A powerful class by terror, rhetoric, and organized sentimentality may drive their people to war, but the day draws near when they cannot keep them there; and how shall they face the pure nations of the East when the day comes to do it with but equal arms? I had seen Ireland in my own time turn from the bragging rhetoric and gregarious humour of O'Connell's generation and school, and offer herself to the solitary and proud Parnell as to her anti-self, buskin followed hard on sock, and I had begun to hope, or to half hope, that we might be the first in Europe to seek unity as deliberately as it had been sought by theologian, poet, sculptor, architect, from the eleventh to the thirteenth century. Doubtless we must seek it differently, no longer considering it convenient to epitomize all human knowledge, but find it we well might could we first find philosophy and a little passion.[35]

And he knew what he was doing. At this time, he wrote to Gregory describing his memoirs: 'they are mainly history of my kind of national ideas & how it formed in my head – the rags I picked off various bushes. I think it will influence young Irishmen in the future, if for no other reason than that it shows how seriously one lived & thought. I know from my own memory of my youth in Dublin how important biography can be in Ireland.'[36]

Moreover, by the late autumn a series of climactic events was pushing him to, at last, come out on the side of revolution. Near his local Galway town of Gort, the Black and Tans committed two horrific atrocities, when a young mother sitting at her cottage door was shot dead from the back of a lorry, and when two local boys were murdered for 'impudence' and their bodies dragged behind a lorry for miles; meanwhile the Sinn Féin mayor of Cork, Terence MacSwiney, died on hunger strike in prison. Three days before MacSwiney's death (by then inevitable), Yeats published 'Easter 1916' at last – in the *New Statesman*, which had been campaigning for clemency towards him. Simultaneously he accepted a play of MacSwiney's for the Abbey, and redrafted his own play about hunger-strike, *The King's Threshold*. (He carefully published the revised ending in *Seven Poems and a Fragment* in October 1922.) MacSwiney's impending death, Yeats remarked hard-headedly to Gregory, 'may make it tragically appropriate'. MacSwiney's own play, while a bad piece of work, 'would greatly move the audience who will see the mayor in the play's hero'.[37] Suddenly the Abbey stage was to be a forum for politics after all. (And the audiences for MacSwiney's play, *The Revolutionist*, reached record levels, reversing a period of declining profits.)

And at this point too Yeats wrote his last Robert Gregory poem: 'Reprisals', a distinctly agit-prop piece about the Black and Tan atrocities at Gort, addressed to Gregory's shade and implicitly contrasting his war-effort and heroic death with the reality of the grubby Empire in whose name mercenary soldiers now were murdering his tenants. But Lady Gregory, who thought it an insincere poem and disliked the use of her son's name, asked him to withdraw it from the *Nation*, which he did – with some annoyance. (It remained unpublished until 1948.) 'I had long hesitated before I wrote,' he told her, 'as I have hesitated about other things in this tragic situation.'[38] This was certainly true.

But by the spring of 1921 the time for hesitation was past, and he came out on 17 February with a famous denunciation of the government's policy in Ireland – at the Oxford Union, attacking the establishment from, so to speak, inside. An Irish undergraduate, Joseph O'Reilly, has left a description:

He denounced and defied the English . . . In twelve minutes of bitter and blazing attack on the English in Ireland he ended pointing at the busts of the Union's Prime Ministers. 'Gladstone! Salisbury! Asquith! They were Victorians. I am a Victorian. They knew the meaning of the words 'truth' and 'honour' and 'justice'. But you do not know the meaning of them. You do not know the language I speak so I will sit down.'

There was no acting or posing, added O'Reilly. 'No one who heard that speech could question his sincerity as an Irish nationalist.'[39]

No one who read his collection *Michael Robartes and the Dancer*, published the same month, could doubt it either: here were, in deliberate sequence, 'Easter 1916', 'Sixteen Dead Men' and 'The Rose Tree'. Griffith's challenge to use his muse for Ireland seemed answered.

Moreover, the rewriting of his political position would continue, in many ways. Notably, it affected the publishing life of the sequence he began just after the publication of *Michael Robartes and the Dancer*, entitled 'Thoughts on the Present State of the World'. This was, in its way, a war poem: at least, it began as a poem about the apocalyptic world events of the past few years, posited against the belief held by a deluded bourgeoisie before 1914 that life would go on for ever. 'Many ingenious lovely things are gone / That seemed sheer miracle to the multitude'. Comments in letters, and recurrent phrases and images, establish that he is thinking of the world before the Great War, as well as of Ancient Greece and (I believe) the Irish Georgian Ascendancy. But the poem deliberately shifts to the current Irish war and the Gort atrocities:

> Now days are dragon-ridden, the nightmare
> Rides upon sleep: a drunken soldiery
> Can leave the mother, murdered at her door,
> To crawl in her own blood, and go scot-free;
> The night can sweat with terror as before
> We pieced our thoughts into philosophy,
> And planned to bring the world under a rule,
> Who are but weasels fighting in a hole.

Thus he introduces 'Reprisals' by another route: but it is linked to preoccupations with historical cycles and world chaos. The interesting thing is that, as time went by, he evidently decided to stress the *Irish* war as the poem's theme, rather than the more cosmic conflict which really lies behind it. Hence his retitling it a few years later by the name we know: 'Nineteen Hundred and Nineteen'. This has always been something of a conundrum, at least to simple-minded historians, for the poem was written in 1921 and deals with events from 1920. But by choosing that name some time after the poem was written, he shifts the chronology of the poem away from the Great War and into the Irish war. When he wrote, in 1921,

> We, who seven years ago
> Talked of honour and of truth,
> Shriek with pleasure if we show
> The weasel's twist, the weasel's tooth.

he was obviously thinking of 1914: that recurring memory of being assured by a friend watching a military display in the park that this was all part of the past, and modern civilization had done away with war. But when we read 'seven years ago' in a poem titled 'Nineteen Hundred and Nineteen', we obviously think of 1912 – and the introduction of the Home Rule Bill, with all its brave hopes. And by the time this title was attached to the poem, readers would also know that

1919 was the date when the Anglo-Irish War began. Thus Yeats turned his poem about the dislocations of the world after the Great War into a poem about the Irish war instead. This perfectly parallels the general repositioning of his stance which he pursued since the aftermath of the Easter Rising: which both parallels and expresses a national shifting of stance, and a certain elision of memory.

From late 1921 the British government entered upon negotiations with Sinn Féin. Yeats continued to write his memoirs, now dealing with the 1890s and recurring to the idea that extreme-nationalist abstractions were like the fixed ideas of hysterical people, turning the mind to stone: while unionist prejudices are their mirror image. Simultaneously he separates out events, misrepresents the political alignments of the time, draws out the role of himself and his collaborators as the midwives of what was evidently, as he wrote, a revolution drawing to its close. The last words of the volume published as *The Trembling of the Veil*, covering the late eighties and the nineties, announce that 'the coming generation, to whom recent events are often more obscure than those long past, should learn what debts they owe, and to what creditor'. Superficially referring to Gregory, he has her here stand for Synge and himself too: the makers of drama and language through which revelation had come, with the fabulous moment of the trembling of the veil of the temple.

And as he finished these memoirs, the new dispensation was being born, with the Anglo-Irish Treaty of December 1921. Yeats's private letters show his heavy forebodings, but with remarkable speed he decided to return to Ireland. He had written himself back into Irish history. 'We have to be "that old man eloquent" to the new governing generation,' he told Gregory. 'If we write our best, the spiritual part of free Ireland will be in the books & the Free State's struggle with the impossibilists may make even some of our unpopular struggle shine with patriotic fire.'[40] He must have been annoyed when an old sparring-partner reviewed his memoirs and decided that they showed Yeats's generation had been consigned to history by the Anglo-Irish War. John Eglinton wrote, 'Each new phase of Ireland's political and social history seems to require new personalities to express it: and just as Griffith and Collins have blotted out Redmond and Devlin, so the literary influence of Patrick Pearse and his band has seemed, at all events for the moment, to cast into the shade the movement in which Mr Yeats was so recently the protagonist.'[41]

This of course was exactly what Yeats had so strenuously devoted himself to disproving. And in 1922 he seemed right, and Eglinton wrong. It was all working out very well – even if the president of the new Free State was his old enemy Arthur Griffith. On the same day as he wrote that letter about making their unpopular deeds shine with patriotic fire, Yeats sent an equally frank letter to AE:

I am by constitution a pessimist & never thought they would get so much out of Lloyd George & so am pleased nor am I distressed to see Madame Markiewicz and other emotional ladies among the non-jurors. I expect to see Griffith, now that he is the universal target, grow almost mellow and become the fanatic of broad-mindedness and accuracy of statement. Hitherto he has fired at the coconuts but now that he is a coconut himself he may become milky.[42]

Thus the poet who had no gift to set a statesman right, and who assured Haldane that he had neither interest in nor aptitude for politics, and whose dislike of Pearse and enmity to Griffith had been so well attested in 1914. He even held high hopes that Griffith would make him minister for fine arts in the new government, and began to plan how he would apply art to industry, as in Germany: a prospect he found very tempting. Griffith had more sense than to make Yeats a minister, but he was appointed a senator, carried out a number of discreet government missions (notably during the Civil War that followed), cultivated key ministers like Desmond FitzGerald, Ernest Blythe and Kevin O'Higgins, and immediately took his place at the head of prestige cultural events such as the Irish Race Convention and the Tailteann Games: the cultural commissar of the new order.

Yeats had won his war. His poetry and prose continued to cast an eye (sometimes cold, sometimes not) back over the events of the Anglo-Irish War. But in common with so many other Irish people, he practised a deliberate amnesia about the 1914–18 war which had done so much to create the conditions for the Irish revolution. In 1928 he famously turned down Sean O'Casey's play about the World War, *The Silver Tassie*, because it seemed to him a subject irrelevant to O'Casey's genius (he told O'Casey that while he had written about the

Irish war out of passionate involvement, 'you are not really interested in the Great War', a pronouncement O'Casey ventured, not unreasonably, to contradict[43]). And in the 1930s Yeats excluded most of the First World War poets from his Oxford anthology of modern verse on the grounds that 'passive suffering is not a subject for poetry'. But the path he had followed through those years of European chaos was both a complicated and a self-conscious one, realizing throughout the necessity to lay claim to the events which were building to revolution all around him and emerging in a position which would have seemed – to say the least – unlikely, considering the political and ideological position he had occupied in 1914.

The same was true of many of his compatriots, not least Arthur Griffith, the newly milky coconut who was suddenly president of Dáil Éireann. But Yeats stands as a powerfully absorbing exemplar of the Irish propensity to therapeutic forgetting: the ability to change footing and gloss over the past. Contemporaries recognized it too. In the heady days of the new state the writer James Stephens recorded a conversation with Griffith. He wanted – reading between the lines – to find out what kind of politician the new president was, and what qualities had enabled him to survive the revolution and emerge at its head. Stephens approached the issue by addressing a hypothetical question.

'If by touching a button you could kill a person in China and get all his goods without fear of detection or punishment either here or in hell, would you touch the button?'

Mr Griffith laughed, but focused the problem.

'I would not touch the button,' he averred.

'Would Connolly?' I urged. 'Or Montgomery? Or Gogarty?'

'Yeats would,' said Mr Griffith.[44]

5

'When the Newspapers Have Forgotten Me': Yeats, Obituarists and Irishness

On 28 January 1939 the poet W. B. Yeats died at his long-established home on Cap Martin. He had previously lived 'several years' in New York, where 'socialists flocked to him as an intellectual leader and standard bearer'; then, 'with his greatest work *The Wind Among the Reeds* behind him, he retired to the seclusion of the South of France'. Previously he pursued 'a brilliant academic career' at Cambridge where his students included John Masefield. 'He had one son, who died.'

This splendidly counterfactual version of Yeats's life retailed by the *Cleveland Press*[1] comes as something of a diversion after the blanket coverage in the world's newspapers throughout early February 1939. Literary evaluations and special numbers of journals piled up; reminiscences accumulated; one is left with the impression of a continuous memorial service, in default of a public burial in Ireland. Certainly, the absence of such an occasion was sharply felt. Even the Taoiseach's telegram of sympathy had ended pointedly: 'We hope that his body will be laid to rest in his native soil',[2] while the Abbey Theatre directorate had been even more peremptory: 'Ireland insists that Yeats be buried here Dean of St Patrick's offers grave in Cathedral'.[3] But there had never been any question of that, as George Yeats made clear to close friends. 'He returns, by sea, to Sligo in September,' she told Thomas MacGreevy. 'That is earlier than he had asked. His actual words were "If I die here bury me up there and then in a year's time *when the newspapers have forgotten me*, dig me up and plant me in Sligo." He did not want the sort of funeral AE had.'[4] A family conference amplified this, as his sister Lollie confirmed. 'We all agreed there must be no public funeral. Also he said "I want to be buried as a poet, not as a public man." '[5] There was, in fact, a service in St Patrick's,

Dublin, on 7 February, where Lollie sharply noted that her brother's Catholic friends were constrained not to enter the church ('they should work now to get that obsolete law of the Church done away with. Now that they are "on top" & also in the majority it seems to me so foolish'[6]); and later on, a London memorial service at St Martin-in-the-Fields on 16 March, arranged by John Masefield.[7] But in one respect at least, the dying poet's expectations were not fulfilled; for the newspapers showed little sign of forgetting him.

For their different audiences, journalists produced different versions. American papers were heavily swayed by Macmillan's recent publication of a one-volume edition of the *Autobiographies*, which had come out in September 1938; some articles combined the function of review and obituary, and most stressed the early life and family background as presented in those disingenuous masterpieces. (This, as will be seen below, exercised a decided influence on discussion of Yeats's family tradition and influences in Ireland.) The *New York Times* honoured him with a first leader, as 'the first Irish and perhaps the first English man of letters of his time'[8] – followed by a lengthy appreciation from Padraic Colum in the *Book Review* a fortnight later.[9] This dealt knowledgeably with Yeats's career in its many phases, making several points which would not be missed by cognoscenti: the Fays and others who had been squeezed out of the theatre movement after quarrels with Yeats were given their full due, though Colum admitted that the establishment of the Abbey remained 'an event in the history of the Irish mind'. In the end, he judged, Yeats was himself 'a Byzantine, one, like El Greco, strayed into the western world, and expressing in our time that unaccountable affinity that the Ireland of the ninth and tenth centuries had for Byzantine civilization'. As a subtle evasion of the thorny question which would dominate many of the post-mortem evaluations – how Irish was Yeats? – this was worthy of the magus himself.

Others had similarly special interests to advance. The *New York Evening Post* was lapidary:

He ranked at his death as the First Poet of English. He was known more widely than any living Irishman except George Bernard Shaw. He was a writer of shining prose, poetic Irish plays, elegant essays, and constructive criticism of Irish art and letters. He was a Nationalist patriot when that took courage; he was a Senator of the Free State from 1922 to 1928; in 1923 he won the Nobel Prize.

Beyond that, he was a little daft.[10]

The *Providence Journal and Rhode Island Bulletin* recalled the poet's early contributions to the *Providence Sunday Journal*, and inferred proudly from these that 'he held a warm spot in his affections for Providence and its people';[11] its obituarist owed much to Horace Reynolds, who had edited those early contributions, and ignored all Yeats's work since the 1890s except *Purgatory*, apparently included only because one of the paper's journalists had attended the Abbey first night. John Devoy's *Gaelic American* similarly followed its own agenda: the 'Irish renaissance of the 1920s' was emphasized, and Yeats's greatness was located in his influence on others (with a particular and rather surprising emphasis on Eugene O'Neill). His 'inability to be natural even when in the company of friends and associates brought him much sorrow and discomfort, in the later years of his life . . . his visible eccentricity of conduct and manner of dress seemed to annoy political and literary associates'.[12] Otherwise, most of the *Gaelic American*'s space was devoted to a reprint of Yeats's speech on the centenary of Robert Emmet, delivered at the New York Academy of Music on 28 February 1904 – from the paper's viewpoint, the high point of Yeats's creative career. (This is rather reminiscent of recent biographies of Maria Callas, which imply that her chief achievement was to lose a lot of weight.) Above all, however, he was a patriot – English contacts notwithstanding. 'He was ever active in the cause of freedom.'

On the other side of the Atlantic, the emphasis tended to be on his towering personality. There was some demurral about his arbitrary symbolism and wilful commitment to strange gods; *Cathleen ni Houlihan* was judged his greatest play, and the early work generally preferred (or at least emphasized) above the bewildering profusion of his last poems. (A rare exception was David Garnett in the *New Statesman*, who hailed the poems recently published in the *London Mercury* as his best work.[13]) *The Times* produced a lengthy, straightforward and comprehensive piece, choosing to stress Yeats's quarrels with conventional Irish nationalism from the time of *Responsibilities*; finally, though, 'Yeats's differences with his own countrymen seem insignificant when we take into view not merely what he gave Ireland but what Ireland, through him, has given to the world.'[14] A magisterial evaluation came, predictably, from Desmond MacCarthy in the *Sunday Times*, who still managed to strike the personal note. 'He was the only poet I ever talked with whose talk and attitude (pose if you like to call it) never allowed you to forget that he was a poet';[15] characteristic phrases were recalled or adapted ('I ought to spend ten years in a library and Lionel Johnson – ten years in a wilderness without a book') and the 'enigmatic impressiveness of his romantic appearance'.

Thomas Bodkin in the *Birmingham Post* again stressed the appearance, the personality and the deliberate elaboration which 'sometimes irritated those who might have wished to be familiar with him'; there may be an autobiographical resonance here, which would explain the otherwise incomprehensible statement that Yeats was 'not a man who enjoyed friendships'.[16] (Yeats had done his best to block Bodkin's appointment as director of the National Gallery of Ireland fifteen years before.) Oliver St John Gogarty, writing in the *Evening Standard*, offered a fulsome contradiction, claiming full possession of Yeats's friendship with all his characteristic self-importance.[17] But generally, those who knew him took the opportunity to make clear why they had not been allowed to know him better.

The Irish note was different, and allowed the expression of some intimate enmities. In the *Observer* Stephen Gwynn concentrated on Yeats as 'a great personality' and recalled his impact from early meetings at Edward Dowden's house. Beneath the artistic pose he was capable of shrewdness 'even to cynicism'; but his artistic sincerity was uncompromising.

First and last he was smashing idols in the market-place; at first, the cheap rhetoric of drum-beating ballads, false models in poetry; later, justifying work which his artistic sense approved as vital, while the crowd denounced it as 'an insult to Ireland'. First and last, he was a champion of freedom – but, above all, against the tyrannies of democracy. And in the end, the democracy which he never spared to resist and rebuke, marches, to its credit, behind his coffin.[18]

St John Ervine also wrote from a personal angle, emphasizing Yeats's affectation and lofty approach to life. 'He had no common qualities, no small talk, no familiarities'; in conversation he preferred mono- logue, either holding the floor or leaving it; he was completely unable 'to be familiar with his friends'.[19] This provoked Robert Smyllie of the *Irish Times*, writing as 'Nichevo', not only to deny that Yeats's Christian name was out of bounds (AE always called him 'Willie') but also to give a memorable description of attempts to teach Yeats golf at Carrickmines in the mid 1920s. ('Occasionally, having played a shot, he would allow his club to fall to the ground and stalk away after the ball, leaving me or [Alan] Duncan to retrieve it. He would roar with laughter when Cruise [O'Brien] foozled a shot; and in the clubhouse afterwards, when he insisted on buying drinks for the three of us, although he took none himself, he would regale us with vastly entertaining stories of his younger days.'[20]) P. S. O'Hegarty wrote a piece for the *Dublin Magazine* that appropriated Yeats in a different way, relating him to 'Revolutionary Ireland of His Time', stressing his commitment to the 1798 Centenary commemorations (where O'Hegarty had first encountered him), and discussing *Cathleen ni Houlihan* as 'a play of the captivity', whose impact was impossible to recapture in the independent Ireland of 1939.[21] And the *Irish Press* (currently serializing Maud Gonne's autobiography *A Servant of the Queen*) produced a leader which traced the canonical connection between Yeats, the literary revival and Easter 1916.[22]

Overall, except for MacCarthy and a few other professional critics, obituarists showed a distinct reluctance to evaluate the work, except in a way that fitted the general interpretation of a man of masks (Bodkin remarked that 'his prose writings are often tainted by a slight affectation of a learning he did not really possess'). This task was left to special issues like the commemoration number of *The Arrow*, and a series of articles in *The Bell* the following year. Here, a judicious review of the work and its development was counterpointed with memories of the extraordinary personality behind it, who would – it was generally accepted – dominate Irish literature for the foreseeable future. A deliberate effort was made to reclaim Yeats from the 'English' identification stressed by MacCarthy, Garnett and others. Even the

Irish Times had mischievously remarked that 'when, in 1930, the English Poet laureateship became vacant, he was made a candidate by leading literary authorities in England'; and Lord Dunsany, asked for a reaction to the poet's death, likened his loss to that of Kipling, Barrie and Housman.[23] (Dunsany, it should be remembered, had nurtured resentments against Yeats too.[24]) This Anglocentric approach was pointedly countered by O'Hegarty, speaking for his generation, when he remarked 'we felt that Yeats and Russell were Ireland's in an intimate sense in which Shaw and Moore were not'. Lennox Robinson also stressed that 'besides his gifts as poet, thinker and philosopher, he was passionately Irish – Irish, from his first meeting with John O'Leary thirty-five years ago; Irish in his work as Senator of the Irish Free State; Irish to the last day of his life'.[25] (The implication that Yeats achieved Irishness only by political commitment was probably unintentional.) F. R. Higgins asserted that Yeats's artistic inspiration was authentically native-born, drawing as heavily and uncritically on the *Autobiographies* as nearly everybody else. The late poetry 'became more Gaelic in feeling', influenced by translations of Irish verse and songs (mediated, naturally, by Higgins himself). 'When we were together he sang in his own uncertain, shy, way some of these poems . . . In writing his own songs we worked together welding his occasionally meandering words to Gaelic tunes. That exercise was latterly his constant delight.'[26] Austin Clarke, in his very different way, also chose to stress Yeats's Irishness: 'no poet could be less representative of English genius than this Anglo-Irish poet'. Clarke went on to emphasize Yeats's openness to influence, a 'susceptibility to eddies and currents . . . increased by an astute awareness of literary fashions', but related his English dimension to Irish influence:

In England the sheer art of [his] poetry has proved a useful influence and has schooled even the best known of the younger modernists. In Ireland, where the artistic tradition of the literary revival has not been broken, it is an imaginative incitement and great example rather than an influence . . . English critics have tried to claim him for their tradition but, heard closely, his later music has that tremulous lyrical undertone which can be found in the Anglo-Irish eloquence of the eighteenth century.[27]

Thus the Irish critics of the next generation contested the claims of English obituarists to appropriate Yeats's death as a loss to 'English literature'.

There was, however, an exception. Thirty-five years before Yeats's death a profile had mischievously remarked 'Mr Yeats has probably too little coarseness in his composition ever to become a national poet – even of Ireland – in the accepted meaning of the term.'[28] The validity of Yeats's credentials as the voice of his fellow countrymen had for long been a matter of debate. In a leader celebrating his seventieth birthday nearly four years before, the *Irish Times* had confronted the question openly and rather defensively.[29] The same preoccupation was shared, for very different reasons, by old enemies who wrote for the Catholic press. For fifteen years before his death, Yeats's claims to Irishness had been vituperatively disputed; 'Pollexfen Yeats', the 'Pensioner' of the British government and unabashed celebrant of the Freemason ritual at George Pollexfen's funeral, had by these very tokens disqualified himself from claims to nationality, even without the evidence of 'the foul Swan song' and the campaign on behalf of divorce.[30] Daniel Corkery, apportioning literary citizenship in *Synge and Anglo-Irish Literature*, made much of the fact that Yeats spent a good deal of the year outside Ireland: even his residential qualifications were suspect. By 1939 the campaign against 'Anglo-Irish literature' was in full flood in the *Catholic Bulletin* (dominated by its editor, Father Timothy Corcoran, Professor of Education at University College) and the *Irish Monthly*; the death of Yeats declared open season on the enemy culture. In February 1939, discussing 'How to Oust English Literary Influence', the *Bulletin* had cause to denounce 'the Outlanders' Academy of Literary Litter, who assembled at the call of Yeats and Shaw, and who have in more than one of their alluring statements taken pains to present themselves as dabblers in dirt, scholars in the sordid succession to the Sewage School of fifteen years ago';[31] and though no obituary of the late poet appeared, his name was pulled into articles such as 'The Freedom of the Press – Should Newspapers be Controlled?'

Let us take an example of the wrong proportion which many newspapers impose upon the news of our time. During the last month the Anglo-Irish poet, William Butler Yeats, died. Immediately every newspaper on which we could lay hands, Irish and foreign, published enthusiastic accounts of this writer's work as a poet, playwright and critic. He was represented as the supreme man of letters writing in English in our time.

Now, we have no wish, when the man is newly dead, to deny him any credit to which he was entitled as an artist or a public man. We do not propose to recall in detail the many occasions on which conscientious Catholic writers were obliged to condemn his works and to warn young Ireland against his influence. It is neither our wish nor our intention to usurp the place of Yeats's judge and to strike the balance of his account. Posterity will judge him in this world and he is already judged in the next. What we do insist upon is that a completely false idea of the man and of his achievements was given by those newspapers which published enthusiastic praises of his work and said nothing at all about his quarrel with the nation and his quarrel with Christianity . . . An account of him which said nothing whatsoever about his long war upon sacred things is not a truthful portrait of the man at all.[32]

The *Bulletin* decided to redress the balance: not through a general evaluation, but by recapitulating a long-running campaign. Since the foundation of the *Irish Statesman* in 1923, the *Bulletin* had denounced AE's and Yeats's 'essay to control Irish interests', which is how it interpreted Yeats's remark that 'Ireland has been put into our hands that we may shape it.'[33] In the *Bulletin*'s view, that 'we' represented a Protestant claim on behalf of a 'New Ascendancy'. The scandal over the short-lived literary journal *To-morrow* in 1924 fixed the battle-lines.[34] The *Bulletin*'s strategy had been to claim that a Northern Protestant and the scion of Sligo Unionism had no right to speak for Ireland; much was made of the un-Irish sound of 'Pollexfen', as well as the non-Catholic nature of Yeats's and Russell's mystical beliefs. 'Some readers may have at that period felt that our emphasis on the un-Irish and utterly exotic character of these motives and aims was over-stressed,' admitted the *Bulletin*; but since the demise of the *Statesman*, they felt that publication of correspondence[35] and the nature of Yeats's later writing fully vindicated them. And the poet's death enabled them to concentrate on what had long been an obsession: the fact that the greatest Irish poet was not, in point of fact, Irish at all.

The pieces by Higgins and Clarke in the *Arrow* indicate that Irish opinion in other quarters had already been slightly irritated by the way that English obituarists annexed Yeats for their own; even David Garnett's perceptive tribute had ended 'his death is the greatest loss English literature could suffer'. Sean O'Faolain took a characteristically larger line in the *Spectator*: 'though he is by minor definition an Irish poet, he is by major definition a world poet'.[36] Even the *Irish Press*, while admitting Yeats's frequent absences from Ireland, made clear that 'not all the flattery of the outside world, not even the conferring of a Nobel Prize, could tempt this poet away from his preoccupation with the life of his own country . . . As a mystic he may have followed doubtful gleams and hovered on the verge of dim frontiers, but sooner or later he returned to Irish soil, there to find new material and fresh inspiration.'

But the *Bulletin* took the opposite view, being all too ready to cede ownership on Ireland's behalf. In the first instalment of an article ominously entitled 'The Position of W. B. Yeats', Stephen Quinn trawled through the obituaries to find the many 'special notices of his character as an English writer, and of the formative influences which went to give him his position in England'.[37] *The Times* notice provided valuable corroboration, being 'prominent and pointed in its affirmation of the dominant note: that note was less Yeats than Pollexfen'. The statement that 'Yeats belonged by birth to the Protestant Anglo-Irish' was triumphantly quoted; moreover, the *Daily Telegraph* was 'very definite as to the proper placing of this essentially English writer'. The *Telegraph* was particularly apposite for the *Bulletin*'s purposes: its notice had begun 'English literature suffers a heavy loss in the death . . . of William Butler Yeats, the famous Irishman, who was the greatest living English poet . . . English because while he was Irish by birth and a passionate patriot, his language was English and as poet and artist he was the heir of a great English tradition.'[38] The *Autobiographies*, with their emphasis on the Pollexfen strain, and the celebration of Anglo-Irishry in the later poetry, provided further grist to the mill. Instancing the early influences of pre-Raphaelitism, Coleridge, Keats, Blake and Morris added up to only one thing: 'in no vital way was Mr Yeats entitled to be designated an Irish writer'. Better still, from the *Bulletin*'s point of view, was an ill-judged tribute by Lennox Robinson (whose own Satanic record as the author of the short story 'The

Madonna of Slieve Dun' in *To-morrow* was well known). In an interview Robinson remarked obscurely that Yeats 'was certainly among our Irish poets the equal of Moore, Mangan and Ferguson'.[39] Stephen Quinn took this to be an unintentional but cruelly accurate cutting down to size: '[Robinson] ranked the poetry of W. B. Yeats with the poetry of – Thomas Moore, Esquire! No such note of discord, assuredly, would have been struck in the English literary world. That world knew its Yeats better than to mete out to him such cruel candour of appraisal.' But as far as Catholic Ireland went, the evaluation was just about right.[40]

All this was too good to leave alone, and a month later Quinn returned with 'Further Placings for W. B. Yeats'.[41] The same issue contained an enraged article, 'The Sham Literature of the Anglo-Irish', sparked off by Father Stephen Brown, who, at the University College Literature Society, had dared to take the affirmative side in debating 'Do We Owe Something to Anglo-Irish Literature?'.[42] Perhaps incensed by this, Quinn threw all caution to the winds, denouncing the late poet for 'aping an aristocratic attitude, combining as its basis the Cromwellian foxhunter and other weird specimens such as the intrusive picture-jobber'. By now, moreover, a similar tone was heard elsewhere. Probably spurred on by the publication of Yeats's letters to AE,[43] Aodh de Blácam published a long denunciation of Yeats's unnational credentials in the *Irish Monthly* of March 1939. At the outset of Yeats's career 'we did account him one with our masters'; he had apparently devoted himself to Ireland; his great personality cast a magnetic spell; he was 'the most consummate of advertising agents' (notably on behalf of 'the grotesque Synge'); but in the end, his actual achievement was no more than that of a minor poet. In fact, he was corrupted by morbidity and supernaturalism. 'He was delicate in youth, he was not "a man's man", and his over-introspective nature made him aloof from the wholesome world.' Finally he emerged as 'the repudiator of the Gael'. De Blácam instanced damning evidence such as his arrogant letters issued from the Ascendancy fastness of Coole, and his 'mock-mysticism' ('he liked symbols as a child likes coloured stones: not for meaning but for sensuous effects'). His philosophical work was 'worthless'.

For one golden moment in the early 1920s he appeared to be

influenced by the new French Catholic writers Charles Péguy and Francis Jammes. 'It almost seemed that Yeats, the man we had loved long since, was turning towards the Catholic Faith.' But it was not to be, and de Blácam's record of the poet's latter years presented him in a light more sulphurous than that of Aleister Crowley:

Yeats became more bitter than ever before, against what we hold most sacred. The indecency which marred so many of his past books now grew more horrid, and the latest book, which he published less than a year ago, was a repulsive play that we can excuse only by assuming that the mind which conceived it was unstrung. His poems, in the last dozen years, were morbid. He wrote of the blood of Calvary some lines so horrible that I could not quote them: one wonders how a publisher printed them. He described Bethlehem as the birthplace of a monster, and lamented the coming of Christianity. How ill this became the poet who had once charmed us with lines about the child that the Little People stole, the mice bobbing round the oatmeal chest in a country house, and the merry playing of the Fiddler of Dooney!

In such exposures, the *Bulletin* felt, 'good service has already been done'. But it was less satisfied with the record of the liberal Jesuit journal, *Studies*. In previous battles, the Jesuits had weighed in on what Professor Corcoran conceived to be the side of the angels; though the magazine had published a eulogy of AE in September 1935, this had been neutralized by a debunking article by Michael Tierney, and one of the weightiest contributions to the long-running debate about the un-Irishness of Yeats was Father Shaw's two-part article on 'The Celtic Twilight'. Shaw asserted that Yeats's supposedly Irish inspiration found its basis in a pseudo-Oriental dream-world, far removed from anything properly called Celtic, and based on 'much mutual borrowing and uninspired imitation'.[44] Shaw had taken particular issue with F. R. Leavis's assertion that Yeats's Irishness made 'his dream-world something more than private, personal and literary', and conferred on it 'an external validation'.[45] In contrast, Shaw denounced Yeats for turning upstanding Irish heroes into effeminate dreamers and Anglicized lotus-eaters. He further demonstrated Yeats's inability to appreciate not only the reality of the Celtic experience, but the achievements of medieval Christianity in Ireland. His vision of a dim

and narcoleptic otherworld owed much to Renan and Arnold, but had
nothing to do with 'expressing national character and feeling . . . The
fact of the matter is that while Mr Yeats went to O'Grady and Lady
Gregory for his heroes, he went to the "Brahmin philosopher" and
Madame Blavatsky for his inspiration. Is it not a little surprising to
find "the great fountain of Gaelic Ireland" pouring forth, by some
strange perversion, a pure stream of Oriental theosophy?'

However, at the time of Yeats's death *Studies* chose not to denounce
the poet for 'perversion', but to celebrate him as an Irishman. The
issue for March 1939 carried two long and sympathetic articles about
the poet and his work. Mary Macken's affectionate recollections of
Yeats, O'Leary and the Contemporary Club,[46] which summoned up
the world of Protestant Home Rulers like C. H. Oldham and John
Butler Yeats, were roundly anathematized by the *Bulletin*; even worse,
to Corcoran's suspicious eye, was J. J. Hogan's evaluation of the poet
and his times.[47] Hogan took a judicious and fairly critical line about
some of the work, making an interesting comparison to d'Annunzio,
'the great poet of insolence, cruelty and lust – the prophet, incidentally,
of certain current philosophies of life'. (Those who ran, might read.[48])
At his best, however, Hogan judged that Yeats's true European peer
was Goethe. His kind of Irishness was carefully defined: 'Yeats is
specially the poet of the Anglo-Irish. But he has lived in Ireland and
taken part in every Irish cause and quarrel for nearly forty years. He
has fallen in with Nationalist movements, and has fallen out with them
and lashed them from the Anglo-Irish, the planter's side.' But this did
not go nearly far enough for the *Bulletin*, which could not forbear to
quote Hogan's summing-up with apposite italicization: 'The first great
poet of modern Ireland; the poet who will command our literature as
long as we use the English tongue. He was great, too, in other literary
fields; a fine prose-writer and critic, a dramatist, and the chief creator
of our theatre. He was perhaps also, though this cannot be said with
certainty yet, a great public man, and a principal shaper of our recent
history.' That 'our' rankled badly enough; but even worse was Hogan's
innocent remark that in some of his early work Yeats 'catches the very
mind of the simple Catholic people'. At this assertion, the *Bulletin*
could not restrain itself.

Yes; he was always an adept at that. Why, not little short of a score of years ago, that man was enabled to place himself before a public audience, in a Catholic hall, for an expressly Catholic cultural cause, to discourse on that most characteristic theme, his own style, himself. He there held forth before an audience mainly fetched from their strict suburban seclusion, convoyed by a stream of taxicabs.[49] Readers will find themselves in full agreement with Professor J. J. Hogan's engaging ingenuousness of descriptive phrase. The Professor's second statement, some four pages later, is still more apposite, were that possible. It is a couplet, 'W. B. Yeats, his very own', a couplet printed in italics for Professor Hogan,

> We the great gazebo built;
> They convicted us of guilt.

What gazebo? None other than that gross imposture, that the mouthings of the two Mahatmas, Russell and Yeats, were in any way compatible with the mind of this Catholic and Irish people of Ireland, and a fit theme to be fostered by the young adorers at the Merrion Square shrine, the holders-forth of the Plunkett House eleemosynary hat, the promoters of the Plunkett policy of self-help from the public pocket, of cash from the seekers of social titles of honour, diverted into the Organization coffers by the crafty crew of calculating cadgers. The story has been told in full, has been treated with complacent pen as well as on the air, by a well-satisfied performer on the Plunkett platforms. It will soon be time for *Studies* to secure once more the services of Professor Tierney, MA, with another set of four selected slingstones. The gazebo of Yeats should be saluted with a salvo in these sedate pages of *Studies*, as fully effective as those launched, after undue delay, against the gazebo of Russellism and of Plunkettism.

Studies did not rise to this challenge.[50] Discussion of the dead giant shifted to his inheritance. Sean O'Faolain published a coruscating essay in the 1942 Irish number of *Horizon*,[51] 'Yeats and the Younger Generation'; to read his analysis of Yeats's intellectual origins is to realize how much Joseph Hone missed, and to regret the biography of Yeats which O'Faolain began but abandoned unwritten. Within the same covers Frank O'Connor wrote on the significance of Yeats's death.[52] A year before, in *The Bell*, O'Connor had drawn an unforgettable portrait of the Yeats he knew.[53] The images are those of a high priest, his rooms characterized by 'the long orderly table, the silver candlesticks, the dim light', 'the touch of dandyism in the lofty ecclesiastical stare, the vital motion of the hands, the unction of the voice'. But O'Connor also affirmed the poet's blazing enthusiasm and incandescent excitement, contradicting 'the pomposity and arrogance Dublin people never tired of talking of '. O'Connor went on to identify Yeats (in contrast to AE) as 'a rabid Tory; he professed himself a member of the Church of Ireland, though he had much more of the Catholic in him; he was a fascist and authoritarian, seeing in world crises only the break-up of the "damned liberalism" he hated; an old IRB man, passionate nationalist, lover of tradition, hater of reason, popular education, and "mechanical logic".' This is a partial view, based on public performances of the late 1930s and reflecting the perspective of 1941; but it deliberately identified Yeats's artistic personality as not only Irish but objectively Catholic. Moreover, Hogan's assertion that Yeats could catch the mind of native Irish Catholics was reaffirmed: O'Connor finally stated that, faced with the uniquely Irish note present in Yeats's poetic voice, 'generations of country blood in me responds and I am ashamed of writing as I seem to do in a foreign language'. Thus for all the poet's hieratic, snobbish, exotic affectations, not to mention his Protestant background and unionist family, he emerged as more Irish than the Irish themselves.

By then, in any case, the *Catholic Bulletin* was no more. Through 1939 it had continued its campaign against such 'sinister moves' as 'the curious effort to impose the "study" of the pointless outpourings of William B. Yeats on all schools',[54] but on 4 December 1939 the sudden death was announced of its editor and proprietor, Senator Patrick T. Keohane (motto: 'We stand by our friends – living or dead'). In a special appendix the journal extolled his staunchness: 'Senator Keohane's mind stood where the mind of the Gael always stood. For him the schismatic island which lies between our island and the Continent might be said not to exist.'[55] However, that was the last number of the *Bulletin*. Discussion of the late poet's reputation in the journals had been displaced by analysis of the schismatic island's Continental war which would – among other effects – ensure that he lay buried in Roquebrune eight years longer than intended.

Meanwhile discussion of his reputation had been reclaimed from the realm of squabbling obituarists by the disciplines of biography and literary criticism, though another effect of the war was to put most of his books out of print.[56] What is most arresting about the reactions immediately after his death is the concentration on the issue of who owned his literary body, the fierceness with which the claim was contested and the prominence of religious criteria in the argument. 'Outside of Ireland his place is safe on Parnassus,' wrote Robert Speaight; 'but inside of it he would perhaps prefer a place in the memory of his people's soul.'[57] That place would not yet be unanimously awarded, though it was ceded in full measure when the occasion of his reinterment at Drumcliffe in 1948 was made a great national celebration. The battle over his literary remains, however, would not have surprised the poet's shade; he had already had the last word, in the *General Introduction to my Work* left behind him for posthumous publication.

no people hate as we do in whom [the] past is always alive. There are moments when hatred poisons my life and I accuse myself of effeminacy because I have not given it adequate expression . . . Then I remind myself that though mine is the first English marriage I know of in the direct line, all my family names are English; that I owe my soul to Shakespeare, to Spenser, to Blake, perhaps to William Morris, and to the English language in which I think, speak and write; that everything I love has come to me through English. My hatred tortures me with love, my love with hate.[58]

6

The Normal and the National:
Yeats and the Boundaries of
Irish Writing

Struggling in the tragic grip of Alzheimer's disease, the novelist Iris Murdoch asked a perplexed group of friends: 'Who am I?' To their surprise, she herself went on to answer: 'Well, I'm Irish anyway – *that's something*.'[1] Is it? The prescribed boundaries enclosing 'an Irish writer' are both national and intellectual, intimately associated with the way political conceptions of identity relate to the imposition of boundaries of acceptable expression: in other words, and less politely, censorship. While 'official' censorship is more or less a thing of the past, a long history of disputation anticipates the way we position Irish writing within Irish borders in the current literary boom: sometimes generously – or opportunistically – lax, sometimes strictly exclusive. 'Censoring' can have more than one meaning, and the notion of decontamination that lay behind outlawing 'obscenity' in the 1920s also influenced the idea that to leave Ireland, or to write from outside it, diluted or debased the essence that made a writer Irish. Living in Paris or Trieste was bad enough, but living and writing in England raised very particular problems indeed. It would be nice to think that Europeanization and globalization have cleared all this up, but the difficulty of labelling Irish writing is still somehow with us.

To understand this requires returning to the era before independence. The condition of being 'an Irish writer' is at the centre of the Irish Literary Revival, and intimately connected with the politics of the day. Thus for many years Joyce was put in a rather different critical box to Yeats and Synge, until the recent shift in interpretation of his politics, or inferred politics. In the general sweep of Modernism, self-conscious national identity tends to go out the window. Joyce clearly conceived of himself as belonging within the borders of Irish writing, while at the same time he wanted to extend those borders into 'world literature'. But how far Pound saw himself as an American writer, or Wyndham Lewis as an English one, is an interesting question: even if we may think they fit into American and English traditions as recognizable respectively as apple-pie or roast beef. (Eliot's American-ism is another issue, put in sharper perspective by his apparent decision to be English.) The pre-independence era in Ireland is of course marked by writers who cross the water and stay there – Wilde, Shaw, Joyce, intermittently Yeats; while O'Casey and Beckett continue the theme after independence, in the 1920s.

It is superficially tempting to opt for the simple line that creative writers inhabit a sort of Fifth Province of the mind, above nationality, and that attaining it is a mark of passage, like the absence of thought in Transcendental Meditation or 'Getting Clear' in Scientology. But a great deal of Irish literary criticism and literary history has concen-trated on how the border of Irishness remains a reality, even while we have been most energetically exporting people. In fact, the idea that writers leave their natural borders and yet remain within them, con-tinuing to inhabit the mental territory of home, is not peculiar to Joyce: Cavafy, living in Alexandria, put it gloomily:

> You won't find a new country, won't find another shore.
> This city will always pursue you.
> You'll walk the same streets, grow old
> in the same neighbourhoods, turn grey in these same houses.[2]

The way emigrant writers keep up with missing places by an act of imagination is different from what other emigrants do. Albert Memmi has described North African colonists' attitude to France as 'requiring that she constitute a different, never intimately known ideal, an ideal immutable and sheltered from time'.[3] Many Irish emigrants take that line, but writers as a general rule escape it. None the less, they do not – generally – escape writing about Ireland – even Shaw, though he tried. (Luckily, for those of us who think that *John Bull's Other Island*, taken with its 'Preface for Politicians', is a masterpiece.) Joyce and Yeats kept Ireland at the centre of their inspiration, and the Yeats of the 'Innisfree' period may be seen, from some angles, as a quintessential 'exile' writer.

There is, of course, a literary language of exile which relies on the sense of displacement from Eden, and intensifies with distance. It is reflected in the popular and populist literature of what President Robinson taught us to call the 'diaspora' and President McAleese (whose style is less dramatic and more sentimental) has christened the 'Irish global family'. It is a language that has to be learnt. David Fitzpatrick has interestingly compared the records of what determined the decision to emigrate from Ireland with the memories of the emigrants themselves decades later. Contemporary records emphasize anger and frustration at the daily lot in Ireland – neighbours, debts, weather, bad luck. Memory, however, prioritizes the sense that cruel England drove them from their home.[4] By then, the emigrants have learned the language of exile, inculcated through a long history of border-crossing, from the religious poetry associated with the cult of Colum Cille to the romance of the Wild Geese. But popular exile literature becomes more and more of a reflex-action, bearing less and less similarity to the emigrant existence as lived in the second and third generations, and simultaneously diverging more and more from the reality of life as lived in the old country. And that demotic exile literature, especially in nineteenth-century America, was very often an expression by professional intermediaries on behalf of the supposedly inarticulate. They provided the formal expression of 'remembered' experiences (often actually lived by parents or even grandparents) which, by a strange symbiosis, would often feed back into the construction of nationalist consciousness back home. Once again, we may remember Namier's remark that through judging history on precedents, by a double process of 'symmetry and repetition', we imagine the past and remember the future.[5]

Creative writers, however, carry a certain inoculation against this process, partly because their equipment contains a radar for scanning received ideas and often rejecting them. Writers who have left 'home' are also advantaged by the duality of the emigrant existence, inhabiting, at least initially, two worlds: the unfamiliar, adopted one, and the remembered, imbibed one of home. Emigrants learn to manipulate language, and this is especially true of nineteenth-century emigrants from Irish-speaking areas. But even today the ability to ventriloquize persists, if only to try to evade the stereotyping and the excluding jokes. The Irish novelist Colm Tóibín has written a feline essay called 'Fecking Off to England', in which he describes encountering a compatriot in the house of English friends and talking to her. They quiz him afterwards.

Did I know that my accent had changed completely . . . Did I know that I had spoken one way to her and another to them? They were amused and anxious. Of course I knew, I said. Did they, too, not change their accent and tone, dependent on whom they were speaking to? No, they looked horrified at the idea, no, never.

It then strikes him that all his life he has been operating 'in stereo', while the English were 'mono'.[6]

There is a serious point here. Tóibín is pointing out that political borders and national identities are expressed in linguistic ways which are subtler than simply speaking one language or another. Irish history, preoccupied by definitions, has unfolded against a background of shifting borders and changing names. A language has been lost or abandoned; an official effort has been made to win it back; and another language has been recolonized into a flexible and hybrid thing. Tóibín's anecdote pinpoints the dual relationship with audiences. This is very much a theme of Irish literature under the Union: but it is characteristic of independent Ireland too. (The plays of Martin McDonagh, and their success with English audiences, spring to mind, or Edna O'Brien's novels in her late-high-hokum period – Irish melodrama for non-Irish audiences, leaving Irish readers rather nonplussed.)

A far more subtle relativism, shifting notions of truth and reality, inflects the literary voices of William Carleton or Maria Edgeworth, and many others; this is linked to strategies for survival at one level, and the great Irish literary tradition of subverting the recognized and accepted form of things on another (Joyce, Wilde, Flann O'Brien). That tactic is politically expressed too (the Land League's alternative structures of rural government, or Sinn Féin abstentionism, or Articles 2 and 3 of de Valera's constitution). Dualism persists, along with an interest in crossing borders between reality and non-reality, death and life, worlds and otherworlds – from Celtic voyage poems to the supernaturalism of Yeats. It was put memorably in the early nineteenth century by Charles Maturin, creator of Melmoth the Wanderer (the great border-crosser, carrying various historical guilts with him). In one of his novels (called, in a very Irish way, *Women; or, Pour et Contre*), Maturin referred to 'that terrible sensation, so common in the imagination of the Irish, of a being whom we believe not to be alive, yet know not to be dead, who holds a kind of hovering intermediate existence between both worlds and combines the passions of human existence with the power of a spirit'.[7] That is one way of describing the ideal Irish writer.

During the Literary Revival, the question of borders came sharply into focus, perhaps because the idea of invasion was so central to the work of writers like O'Grady, upon which the cultural reclamation project of Yeats and his contemporaries was built.[8] At the same time, one forgotten aspect of the great phenomenon was an attempt to widen out the borders of 'Celticism' into Cornwall, Brittany, the Scots Highlands – reasserting the truth of John Stuart Mill's dictum that Ireland is in the mainstream of European developments, and England an eccentric tributary. But in Ireland the Celtic Revival became the Gaelic Revival, and was rapidly politicized; so was the revival of the spoken language, which had initially been happily embraced by several Ascendancy intellectuals and underemployed Church of Ireland clergymen, anxious to prove that St Patrick was a Protestant.[9] In the process, old borders were reaffirmed. In 1908 Father Peadar Ó Laoghaire, a great influence in the Gaelic League, made the point that speaking English was incompatible with faith and patriotism, and the use of the English language sapped 'the very fibres of mental and moral nature ... growth in the understanding of English speech ... means only a more complete obliteration of the historic faith and patriotism of Ireland'.[10] This was exactly what the nationalist Yeats wanted to prove untrue.

Like several of his most influential contemporaries, who would make the new Ireland, Yeats was born astride many of the borders which separate Irish people. His early life was lived against a background not only of marginalization as a *déclassé* Protestant, but as a representative of the syndrome of temporary (and recurrent) emigration. He and his family take their place among the flow of middle-class Irish people who colonized the worlds of journalism, letters and artistic endeavour in Britain, America and Australia: a group to whom emigration did not automatically mean loss and exile. Yeats's irrepressible father proved this when he departed to New York in old age and simply refused to come back, declaring that he had come to an enormous fair where at every turn there was the chance of some tremendous stroke of luck.[11]

His son carried on the habit of crossing borders all his life – always transgressive, always bent on breaking out of genre, always bent on liberation. Just at the stage when Father Ó Laoghaire was deciding that writing in English could not be patriotic, Yeats had decided that the borders of acceptable nationalist expression needed to be redrawn. For the next few years he would look for his own inspiration in places like European avant-garde theatre and Japanese ghost stories. But, like the exile in Cavafy's poem, he took the city with him. I have already looked at the way he brilliantly wrote himself back into the Irish revolution of 1916–22. But after the dust had settled, Irish nationalist intellectuals were, as remarked earlier, like the disorientated civilians of another Cavafy poem, whose ancient enemy had evaporated: caught between a remembered, colourful, emotion-laden past and the necessary compromises of a new order. When writers tried to take it on, they usually did so obliquely. O'Casey's plays about recent revolutionary history, Eimar O'Duffy's mordant fantasy novels, the literature of heroic autobiography (whether reflecting life in the Western Islands or in a flying column), short stories in Gaelic-pastoral mode – all avoid dealing with the present realities of the Free State. The central character in Elizabeth Bowen's 1929 novel, *The Last September*, thinks of Ireland – Anglo-Irishly – in terms of separation and incomprehension: 'a way of living, abstract of several landscapes, or an oblique, frayed island moored at the north but with an air of being detached and drawn out west from the British coast'.[12] Here the question of borders raises, obliquely, that of partition. But already Irish writers were looking beyond. What bothered Daniel Corkery, when he took to issuing literary visas a few years later, was the uncomfortable thought that the 'colonial ethos' which he had denounced in Edgeworth, Griffin and other nineteenth-century Anglo-Irish writers was creeping back: Irish writers were writing to be read in England, 'with the insolence of Ascendancy-minded literature', instead of 'belonging' to the Irish world.[13]

A large part of the reason was the censorship imposed by the Free State itself. Just when Bowen was writing *The Last September*, a bill to introduce literary censorship was being fought over in the Dáil and Senate. The issue had been looming since independence: presented as a way of reinforcing the border against 'the great mental invader', as one pro-censorship organization described Britain. But there was also an argument that ran directly counter to this: the idea that Ireland, by encouraging intellectual freedom, could affirm and emphasize intellectual and cultural difference from England. This was, above all, the argument of the chief opponent of a censorship bill – W. B. Yeats, again.

As early as 1903 Yeats had linked intellectual and political boundaries in an aggressive essay called 'The National Theatre and Three Kinds of Ignorance'. Here he claimed that 'extreme politics in Ireland were once the politics of intellectual freedom also', but now, thanks to the polemics of Arthur Griffith, 'extreme politics seem about to unite themselves to hatred of ideas'.[14] This was, in his view, the distance travelled from Fenianism to Sinn Féin. He went on to attack the ignorance of Gaelic propagandists, rural politicians and country priests, thus breaking the taboo of Irish politeness whereby Protestant nationalists usually left anti-clericalism to their Catholic allies. But he knew perfectly well that censorship could come from the other side of politics too, and when Dublin Castle tried to interfere with the Abbey programme over Shaw's plays *The Shewing-Up of Blanco Posnet* (1909) and *O'Flaherty VC* (1915), Yeats seized the chance to take as publicly adversarial a position as possible and to emphasize the border between the cultures of Britain and Ireland. The Lord Chamberlain's writ of censorship did not run in Ireland, and *Blanco Posnet* gave Yeats the perfect opportunity to face down the government, as the play contained nothing to offend either Irish nationalists or the Catholic Church – even if the English censor had deemed it 'profane'.[15] Yeats would later decide to put on *Oedipus Rex* for the same reason: to show that Irish opinion was, or could be, less hidebound than in England. He put this memorably in his speech before the Abbey's production of *Blanco Posnet*:

The root of the whole difference between us and England in such matters [as censorship] is that though there might be some truth in the old charge that we are not truthful to one another here in Ireland, we are certainly always truthful to ourselves. In England they have learned from commerce to be truthful to one another, but they are great liars when alone. The English censor exists to keep them from finding out the fact. He gives them incomplete arguments, sentimental half-truths, and above all he keeps dramatists from giving them anything in sudden phrases that would startle them into the perception of reality.[16]

But with independence from 1922 he was forced to consider the imposition of borders within Ireland. As a senator, a public man, and a friend and associate of several members of the Cumann na nGaedheal government, Yeats kept a keen eye to the dangers of thought control in the new dispensation. He particularly cultivated one of the few new ministers with avant-garde intellectual interests – Desmond Fitz-Gerald, an Imagist poet and a friend of Ezra Pound. The friendship with FitzGerald was, for instance, a key counter in Yeats's long and canny campaign to make the Abbey Theatre state-subsidized without compromising its artistic independence. 'The only condition we could not accept,' he told Gregory (who wanted to hand the whole thing over) 'would be some interference with our artistic freedom – we could refuse and would then face a rival theatre with the advantage of standing for intellectual independence. A situation would have been created which, even though we were finally beaten – and we might not be beaten – would be a fine definition of our position and our work.'[17]

In 1925 he had his way, after much bluff and moral blackmail. The position the Abbey had achieved by that year influenced Yeats's aggressive support for the plays written by Sean O'Casey, Synge's apparent successor. O'Casey's trilogy of plays about the Irish revolution are full of echoes of Synge, not least in their baroque language and determined anti-heroics, but their controversial effect lay in his view of what politics meant to ordinary people. O'Casey was not only influenced by socialism and scepticism about aspects of nationalism; he was determined to put prostitutes, drunks and unmarried mothers on the stage. All this testing of boundaries was a recipe for trouble, as Yeats well knew. He also knew that, as with Synge's work, the enterprise would raise at once the issue of acceptable definitions of Irishness. And though he never got on well personally with O'Casey, he took his stand on defending *The Plough and the Stars* both because it questioned accepted pieties, and because it was a marvellous chance to demonstrate the Abbey's independence in spite of its government-aided status. The government nominee on the Board of Directors, George O'Brien, had been distinctly unhappy with the play in rehearsal, but Yeats managed to bear him along. The theatre would always be a forum for controversy – all the more so because it was now a 'national' theatre. And there was much about the new national state – to which Yeats was deeply committed – that made him worry about the prospects for intellectual freedom. For him, censorship meant a loss of independence in a political sense as well as a cultural one.

Many of these ominous tremors about artistic expression would be concentrated around one Irish writer, and one Irish book: James Joyce and *Ulysses*, appropriately published just as the new Free State came into being. Yeats had been an early champion of Joyce, introducing him to literary contacts, arranging a Royal Literary Fund pension for him, putting him in touch with Ezra Pound; and from the establishment of independence he was determined to bring Joyce back within the fold and have him proclaimed a great contemporary Irish writer. He pressed his candidacy for the projected Irish Academy of Letters; he instanced the genius of *Ulysses* whenever he could (and read far more of it than is sometimes thought); and when the Free State instituted Aonach Tailteann in 1924, a sort of mixture of a national Olympic Games and a world's fair, Yeats tried his best to have Joyce invited as one of the honoured guests. All this when *Ulysses* had become, in the two years since its publication, a byword for obscenity and indecency among Irish conservative opinion. It also focused the question of censorship – as both Yeats and Pound were very aware.

The Free State's ethos was inevitably Catholic; confessionalism was implicit in the legislation for censoring films introduced in 1923 after aggressive lobbying from the Catholic Truth Society and the Vigilance Associations. The same was true for the ensuing campaign against 'evil literature' – especially as it included literature advocating or even explaining non-Catholic methods of birth control. But the core issue, for Yeats and his opponents, was the expression of sexual feeling in creative literature. He consistently argued that this was central to ancient Irish literary tradition, and that Joyce was, therefore, distinctively Irish. Moreover, Yeats claimed Joyce as an Irish writer because his creative energy was a result of recent Irish history. He put this forcefully when replying to a quintessentially pompous undergraduate address on 'The Modern Novel' at the Trinity Philosophical Society. Yeats disagreed that *Ulysses* was 'open to the charge of dullness', the *Irish Times* reported:

James Joyce was certainly as voluminous as Johnson's dictionary and as foul as Rabelais; but he was the only Irishman who had the intensity of the great novelist. The novel was not his [Yeats's] forte. All he could say was there was the intensity of the great writer in Joyce. The miracle was possibly there; that was all he felt he had the right to say; and, perhaps, the intensity was there for the same reason as the intensity of Tolstoi and Balzac.

When James Joyce began to write in Ireland they had not come to their recent peril – or the robbery and the murder and the things that came with it – but he thought that the shadow of peril was over everyone when men were driven to intensity. The book *Ulysses* was a description of a single day in Dublin twenty years ago. He thought it was possible that Ireland had had that intensity out of which great literature might arise and it was possible James Joyce was merely the first drop of a shower.[18]

Thus Yeats claimed Joyce both as a great European and a modern Irishman. The difficulty was that for official opinion in the new Free State, *Ulysses* represented a border that was not to be crossed. As long as there was no censorship Act in Ireland, the book could not be formally banned; thus when copies were seized at Folkestone in May 1924, Yeats did not want to provoke a similar reaction in Ireland. This point was not appreciated by Joyce's champion Ezra Pound. Though Yeats pointed out to Pound that 'all our liberties are surreptitious', Pound took the line that Irish independence must mean freedom from censorship. Yeats's inquiry whether the Folkestone seizure was made under the League of Nations charter provoked Pound into putting the point about Irish difference in his own inimitable way.

???? I know that England, her ministers, her academic committees, are a mass of moribund filth and that the League of Nations was invented by one of the worst fahrts Nature ever let loose from her copious and inexhaustable arse-hole.

WOT I wanted to know from you was whether free and assassinous Ireland was still under Hengland's bloody thumb: or whether she acted for her evergreen and bhlossoming self in these little matters;

Does a manifestation of bigoted idiocy on the part of Gawd's own boss of the traffic in Southampton [recte Folkestone], imply an identical or DIFFERENT idiocy from that of Mikky Grogann boss of the port of Cork?? Or wd, the noted conthrariety of yr. esteemed comphatriots incline them to insist on having something because england thought it unsuitable to their consumption?[19]

Pound's idea, like Yeats's, was that Irish writers might be defined by censorship in England, and celebration in Ireland: indeed, when Yeats was awarding gold medals for literary achievement at the Tailteann Games in 1924, he lauded Joyce *in absentia*, very much in the same terms as at Trinity a year before. His campaign, however, incensed conservative academics at both Trinity and UCD; while the *Catholic Bulletin* took up at once the issue of Joyce's Irishness. Admiration for the pariah was

confined to the petty little field of the Anglo-Irish; and there is no use now in attempting to impose that on the mass of the Irish people as being at all a genuine article worth preserving in Irish culture. It is an upstart of yesterday, alien in source, in models, and in such little inspiration as it can boast; and many of its avowed leaders are simply exhibits of literary putrescence.[20]

From the other side, Professor W. F. Trench of the Trinity English Department called on Yeats to stop 'proclaiming Joyce a genius in and out of season' and to 'cry halt to the aesthete's publicity campaign on behalf of that which is so foul'.[21] Yeats's response was to raise the bidding, only a few weeks later, by throwing heavy support behind the scandalous literary journal *To-morrow*, started by Francis and Iseult Stuart, together with Liam O'Flaherty and F. R. Higgins: Yeats wrote an inflammatory editorial claiming that the puritanism of 'bad writers and the Bishops of all denominations' made them essentially atheists, while a true Christian art celebrated 'the whole handiwork of God'. To prove the point, *To-morrow* printed Yeats's 'Leda and the Swan' and Lennox Robinson's short story 'The Madonna of Slieve Dun', dealing with a country girl who is raped and subsequently believes she has been chosen to re-enact the Incarnation. Both these pieces had been published already in the USA but was Ireland ready for them? Or for a short story by Margaret Barrington, 'Colour', dealing with a love affair between a black man and a white woman?

Certainly not. The fury of the *Catholic Bulletin* at this 'foul fruition' was predictable. More ominously, Cosgrave contemplated suppressing the journal by government order, stopped only by Kevin O'Higgins, who pointed out that a prosecution 'would merely represent the moral attitude of a certain people and place and time'.[22] This sophisticated relativism was all very well, but the outrage of that particular place at that particular time inflamed the provost of Trinity and the Carnegie Library Committee (which employed Robinson) as well as the Catholic press. Yeats threw himself into the discussion, telling Robinson to stand firm on the ground of Flaubert, Tolstoy, Dostoevsky, Balzac and Anatole France: 'Ireland must not be allowed any special privilege of ignorance or cowardice'.[23]

But this was exactly contrary to the official view. It should also be pointed out that his own endorsement of intellectual freedom and the artist's traditional right to experiment were at odds with his increasing tendency – at this very time – to repudiate apparently outworn forms of democracy, and to dream nervously of an authoritarian, coherent rule of life as mediated through politics, invoking an inherited aura of tradition. (Simultaneously he wrote, recalling the intellectual searches and struggles of his youth: 'I wished for a system of thought that would leave my imagination free to create as it chose and yet make all that it created, or could create, part of the one history, and that the Soul's.'[24]) Pound, his ally in defending Joyce's right to speak, would in the end opt for political extremism and thought control; Yeats, for all his interest in Mussolini and doubts about liberalism, defended free speech as part of his ideal Irish cultural project.

He also continued his campaign against Irish literary censorship through the drafting and passing of a bill in 1928–9. His essay 'The

Need for Audacity of Thought' (refused by Russell for the *Irish Statesman*) recurred to the arguments about Irishness, religious orthodoxy and European traditions which he had aired during the *To-morrow* controversy.

The intellect of Ireland is irreligious, it is not possible to select from any Irish writer of the last two hundred years until the present generation, a solitary sentence that might be included in a reputable anthology of religious thought. Ireland has not produced a religious genius since Johannes Scotus Origena, who wrote in all probability under the influence of philosophical Greek and Roman refugees of the fourth and fifth centuries; and its moral system being without intellectual roots has shown of late that it cannot resist the onset of modern life. We have had murders, authorized and 'unauthorized', burnings and robberies; we are quick to hate and slow to love; and we have never lacked a Press to excite the most evil passions. To some extent Ireland but shows in an acute form the European problem, and must seek a remedy where the best minds of Europe seek it – in audacity of speculation and creation.[25]

It was a losing battle, though he fought it with several more broadsides, forecasting that by endorsing censorship Ireland would cut itself off from Europe, and that a bill designed to exclude pornography would be invoked against Darwin, Marx, Flaubert, Balzac and Proust.[26] By 1929, even though some government members were as embarrassed by the bill as Yeats and Russell, they had lost the support of intellectuals like Desmond FitzGerald – who wrote angrily to Pound that 'Uncle William' understood nothing about Catholic doctrine or Irish opinion.[27] As for Yeats, the Rabelaisian directness with which he addresses sex in his poetry from the late 1920s is certainly – as so often outlined – associated with preoccupations in his personal life: but it has too rarely been associated (except by Elizabeth Butler Cullingford[28]) with his lost battle against censorship, and his determination to assert an indigenous, salty Irishness against puritanical impositions from outside. 'Crazy Jane' mischievously subverts and eroticizes all the transactions of life: and when she talks with a bishop, it should not be forgotten that Yeats had been making a practice of setting his own opinions against bishops since the *Countess Cathleen* row of

1899. As far as he was concerned, it was all part of defining modern Irish literature against essentially un-Irish limitations.

By the time of Yeats's death, however, the definition of an 'Irish writer' had been tightened to exclude those who lived or wrote abroad, a process that carried the implication that foreign travel, like sexual frankness, acted as a disqualifier for Irish status. The most influential statement of the case was Daniel Corkery's: so-called 'Anglo-Irish' literature tried to break across a border that could not be crossed, since it was 'not national and therefore not normal . . . for normal and national are synonymous in literary criticism'.[29] Corkery embarked, therefore, on restricting entry to the Irish literary canon. Careerist expatriates like Shaw and Goldsmith were turned back at the border. Echt-Irish people like Colum and O'Flaherty voluntarily ruled themselves out by emigration. Yeats presented a problem but eventually had his literary passport stamped because 'it was not his habit to spend the whole of any year abroad'.[30]

However, by 1940, a year after Yeats's death, there was a concerted attempt to redraw the borders by the dissident writers who set up a new literary journal, some of them ex-pupils of Corkery, others the object of his anathemas. *The Bell* began with a manifesto for reconciliation of the different traditions within Ireland, a crossing of internal borders, by Elizabeth Bowen;[31] it was accompanied by the first of many pieces by Sean O'Faolain, making the uncomfortable case that Ireland – unique as its cultural sensibility was – was still inescapably affected by its trafficking with Britain and that this cross-border intellectual commerce, tragic and exploitative in many ways, could be enriching in others. Given O'Faolain's difficulties with the censorship board, this might also be read as an argument against censorship. *The Bell*, under Peadar O'Donnell's editorship a decade later, printed a symposium on the direction – or directionlessness – of Irish writing. All the contributors attacked the censorship of the Church, the paucity of literary magazines in the Republic, the relative absence of Irish publishers. But the two most forceful pieces were from Northerners. Mary Beckett wrote a witty piece about the obscure senses of guilt that inhibited Irish Catholic writers in Northern Ireland, and declared the need to write of life as a whole, without embarrassment. And the most thoughtful and angry contribution came from John Montague, who called for the urbanization of Irish writing, or for works dealing with the life of the individual against the background of the 'semi-urban' ethos which was replacing provincialism. Montague also worried that the effort to create a specifically Irish literature, through the emphasis on borders, had exhausted itself, leaving Irish writing cut off from contemporary European literature.[32]

In this he was both looking back to Yeats's argument, and demonstrating critical prescience; and when the borders were pushed out, a process beginning ten or so years later, the impetus came from the North. I remember in the early 1960s reading a short story of Montague's, 'The Cry', about a police beating in Belfast, and being powerfully struck by the sense that something new was being said.[33] In 1975, reading Seamus Heaney's *North* (one of those books indelibly marked by the where and the when of discovery), I thought, 'So this is how it can be written about.' 'It' was, I suppose, Ireland without intellectual boundaries.

By then, censorship was in retreat, and the Northern border coming sharply into focus. What has happened since has been a generation of literary border-crossing, in the dazzling achievement of poets like Paul Muldoon, Derek Mahon, Michael Longley, Tom Paulin, Seamus Heaney and John Montague, and more recently with the ferocious panache of novelists like Robert McLiam Wilson and Glenn Patterson. Ireland as a whole is even blessed, or plagued, with writers who want to be Irish (a question on which the Irish people do not, apparently, have a veto). One aspect of our recent literary renaissance has been the prospecting of Irish themes even in the most ostensibly *déraciné* of our writers. Responding to a Trinity College Dublin graduate long resident in Canada, who had devoted much of his expatriate career to valiantly trying to build up a network of scattered Trinity people with enthusiastic and interminable newsletters and requests, Samuel Beckett thanked him for offering enlightenment about his Irish connections and background but added: 'I'd rather not know.'[34] This is not a privilege he will be allowed. Fintan O'Toole has recently given us a dazzling portrait of the playwright Sheridan as someone who – though he left Ireland young and never returned – remained resolutely and increasingly Irish; Wilde has been re-Hibernicized as a 'Fenian' and even 'the first gay nationalist martyr'. This begs a number of questions as to what Wilde saw as his country and his cause, but it is significant that the Irish are so energetically repatriating this most transgressive of writers: the centenary of his death was marked by endless oblations, including a toast proposed by President McAleese in the British Library.

As for Joyce, he has become a patron saint of Dublin with his own Saint's Day and his meditations flashed up (a couple of years ago) in neon on prominent Dublin buildings. Thus not only have the banned been reclaimed as Irish, but the reductive way that the canon of 'English Literature' used to colonize Irish writers has been reversed (a process that not only deliberately denied Irish culture its separate place, but also reflected the traditionally careless attitude of English literary criticism towards historical context). At the same time, the old Free State effort to make physical and metaphorical borders coincide, in the frantic pursuit of a kind of congruent literary geography, may not yet be quite gone. Later in this book, the question of claiming or rejecting a writer like Elizabeth Bowen arises – still apparently an issue after all these years. Rather like Isaiah Berlin's historic distinction between the 'freedom from doing things' and the 'freedom to do things', the question of being an Irish writer is apparently susceptible to two methods of definition, one positive and one negative. Into the negative definition, the questions of race, religion and political belief can still obtrude, even if dressed up in new clothes – reminding us of the efforts a century ago of D. P. Moran and others to sanitize the definition of Irishness into a simple congruence rather than a graded palimpsest. Yet history, and not only Irish history, shows some disastrous precedents when borders of nations, states, peoples and geography are drawn to fit some preconceived theory or prejudice.

More happily, the people in Cork who organize a regular symposium celebrating Bowen as both an Irish and also a Cork writer apparently agree. And she is just one Irish writer who has been reclaimed by her place in the summer school industry. Annually the cavalcade moves from Synge's Wicklow to Kate O'Brien's Limerick to Carleton's Clogher Valley to Hewitt's Antrim coast to Merriman's Clare to Hopkins's Monasterevan to Swift's Celbridge to Yeats's Sligo. Wilde is for some reason celebrated in Bray, for an entire week. Does it matter whether Wilde could, or would, have spent a week in Bray? Or that O'Brien lived away from Limerick most of her life, as Carleton did from his valley, or that Hewitt's *locus classicus* is Belfast rather than Garron Tower, or that Hopkins was unhappy in Ireland generally and Monasterevan particularly? Probably not. The point is not so much (or not only) that these writers belong in, or were inspired by, these places. They are reclaimed on behalf of those places, and on behalf of Ireland's newly asserted identification with them. As Ireland becomes a nation of immigrants rather than emigrants, it is repatriating its writers. They are being reinserted within what is conceived of as their appropriate borders: celebrated in the same way as people are often mourned, for the sake of the bereaved rather than the dead. This is both therapeutic and perfectly rational, but perhaps the reasons – historical and literary – behind the process deserve re-examination.

It is easier to leave the issue there than to look for reasons why Irish writing, and Irish culture at large, at the outset of the twenty-first century seems less preoccupied by imposing its own borders, and readier to cross borders into world culture. Irish fiction, poetry and drama need to be placed in contexts of economic prosperity, post-nationalism, our own brand of postmodernism, the globalization of communications and the self-perpetuating idea of another Irish literary renaissance. For a start, looking at the issue through the prism of our own literary and political history since independence can be enlightening; the apparent contradictions explored by the Yeats generation persist. Did the attempt to dictate acceptable boundaries and norms for the content of 'Irish' culture, from the 1920s to the 1960s, actually have the reverse effect of that intended – by inhibiting an autonomous cultural expression, as Yeats foretold? From the first explosions in the North to the recent peace process, what effect has the dilution of the political border within the island (culturally and politically) had upon the way Irish writers conceive of themselves? Is this process parallel to, and linked with, a dilution of the self-consciously maintained borders between Ireland and Britain, and Ireland and the USA? And when will the different kind of self-consciousness that has replaced the old 'exclusivity' – the self-consciousness of being internationally fashionable – create inhibitions for Irish writers as it has, perhaps, for certain genres of Indian and South American writers? Some of the answers to these questions may already be emerging. But is it also possible that regarding the answers to some of them, like Beckett, we would rather not know?

7

Square-built Power and Fiery Shorthand: Yeats, Carleton and the Irish Nineteenth Century

William Carleton described himself, in one of his thinly disguised autobiographical stories, as a 'poor scholar'. This is a long and distinguished identification in Irish literary history, and Carleton's position in his fellow countrymen's affections is partly based on the honour which accrues to such a position. At the same time, he was a determined careerist, who left a poor rural background to conquer the metropolis, and made a reputation in London as well as Dublin. If his background was not quite as poor as he made out, and if part of his careerist armoury included a readiness to play to Irish stereotypes, these attributes have a long history behind – and ahead of – them too. It is, however, a less endearing tradition, and Carleton has always attracted his share of ambivalent reactions. In all this, the complexities of claiming and rejecting Irishness, discussed in the last essay, arise again. The profession of literary Irishness (and the profession of Irishness itself) carries a special resonance in Carleton's case: most of all because of his fierce reaction to the Catholicism of his youth, and the ensuing controversy about how deep this actually went. His best work also carries a supercharged quality that seems to appeal to poets: Gerald Dawe has written illuminatingly about him in *Stray Dogs and Dark Horses* (2000), and Carleton's ghost invades one of the most powerful sections of Seamus Heaney's masterwork, 'Station Island'. Above all, he appealed profoundly to the young Yeats; but the ambivalence that surrounds Carleton's reputation in Ireland also explains why Yeats strategically denied the debt in later life.

If being a 'poor scholar' constituted a qualification for the esteem of Irish people, the young Yeats should have been held in more affection than he was. In 1889, when he published his now-forgotten *Stories from Carleton*, the 24-year-old poet was both extremely poor and embarked on a desperate search for scholarship. The family had moved back to London two years before and were all in their separate ways trying to live as artists. An autodidact all his life, he was immersing himself in the Irish fiction of the early nineteenth century, which he thought would provide material for a series of editorial works to keep the wolf from the door without descending to hack journalism. But he was also genuinely excited by what he was finding. In early December 1889 he wrote to the literary-minded Jesuit Father Matthew Russell about his plans for an anthology of nineteenth-century Irish writing.

I am trying to make all the stories illustrative of some phase of Irish life meaning the collection to be a kind of social history ... The heroines of Carleton and Banim could only have been raised under Irish thatch. One might say the same in less degree of Griffen [*sic*] and Kickham but Kickham is at times, once or twice only & (merely in his peasent heroines I think), marred by having read Dickens, and Griffen most facile of all one feels is Irish on purpose rather than out of the necessity of his blood. He could have written like an English man had he chosen. But all these writers had a square built power no later Irishman or Irish woman has approached. Above all Carleton & Banim had it. They saw the whole of every thing they looked at, (Carleton and Banim I mean) the brutal with the tender, the coarse with the refined. In Griffen & Kickham the tide began to ebb. Kickham had other things to do and is not to be blamed in the matter. It has quite gone out now – our little tide. The writers who make Irish stories sail the sea of common English fiction. It pleases them to hoist Irish colours – and that is well. The Irish manner has gone out of them though. Like common English fiction they want too much to make pleasent tales – and that's not at all well. The old men tried to make one see life plainly but all written down in a kind of fiery shorthand that it might never be forgotten.[1]

There is so much here that it is easy to forget that Yeats had only that summer embarked upon a crash course of reading the people whom he analysed so authoritatively. He now knew the problematic reputation of Carleton; Father Russell felt very ambivalently about him as an apostate, and Yeats's own recently published selection of *Stories from Carleton* would draw a violent attack on the writer from the

Nation.[2] But in this letter Yeats is defending the novelist as truly Irish, as an uncompromising artist, and, in the process, defending not only the whole tradition of early nineteenth-century fiction, but the nationalist politics which it helped inspire. Charles Kickham, after all, 'had other things to do and is not to be blamed in the matter' – the 'other' things being no less than his duties as supremo of the Irish Republican Brotherhood, or the Fenians.

So Yeats's discovery and celebration of Carleton must be linked to his discovery of the Irish national achievement of fifty years before: the Young Ireland era, in which the old Fenian John O'Leary had been acting as his tutor and providing a lending library over the past five years or so. To this must be added Yeats's discovery of Irish Catholicism – or, more accurately, of the opportunity of easy intellectual friendship with Catholic nationalists, a possibility which was far removed from his Sligo Unionist background. His father had obliquely remarked on this in a letter to O'Leary. 'If you will allow me to say so, when I met you & your friends I for the first time met people in Dublin who were not entirely absorbed in the temporal and eternal welfare of themselves ... It was meeting you all that has left an impression on my young people that will never be quite lost.'[3] The distinction from Irish Protestants, who in the Yeats family's view were a caste determined above all on getting on in the world, could not be clearer, or more refreshing. And O'Leary had held the keys to the Catholic nationalist literature of the heroic period. When Yeats took on the job of editing stories from Carleton for the Walter Scott publishing house, it was partly (as he said) to get his friend Ernest Rhys (the editor of the series) out of a scrape;[4] but it was also a way of stepping further into the national culture of the Irish nineteenth century. It contributed essentially to his wider enterprise of rejection.

This should be borne in mind when we note how often Yeats tells us that Carleton is a *historian*. He is not only excusing and explaining what might be seen as the over-inclusiveness and circumstantial detail of Carleton's fiction; he is also clarifying Carleton's importance to Yeats himself at this stage of his life. He was determined to discover a tradition for himself, from the doubly marginalized standpoint of a Protestant-bohemian background and a Hammersmith exile. Thus he tells us that Carleton, 'a peasant among peasants', is more important in this way than his only great forerunner in Irish fiction, Maria Edgeworth. She wrote of 'that section of Irish society which is, as are the upper classes everywhere, the least national of all, and was, as the upper classes have seldom been anywhere, ashamed of even the little it had of national circumstance and character'.[5] This cavalierly ignores the importance of Edgeworth's Thady and Jason Quirk, but it aligns Yeats with the company he wanted to keep, in terms of literary tradition and political identification. The autobiographical resonance is strong here; it reminds us that Yeats in the 1880s and early 1890s was in the process of repudiating his background and discovering an Ireland outside unionist Sligo or Ascendancy-clerical Dublin. Though his introduction to the world of O'Leary had in fact come through a dissident Trinity don, C. H. Oldham, Yeats in the 1880s identified the College as a centre of paralysis: the essence of that sterile-bourgeois Protestant world from which his own family had in every sense migrated. Trinity, he said, was the repository for the only instinct of veneration experienced by Irish Protestants; the professor of English Literature there, Edward Dowden (who had encouraged him at the outset of his writing career) was imagined as a kind of Cerberus guarding a kingdom of the dead. During his Fenian youth, Yeats sparred with as many Trinity representatives as he could; in later life this attitude, like many others, was moderated. But the Irish Protestant world *in toto* remained under his anathema. And Carleton's part in this was vital. As a young man he had, after all, repudiated his own background in order to be taken up by Irish Protestant luminaries, under whose influence he had written as searingly about Irish Catholic sensibilities as the young Yeats was to do about Protestant pieties. 'The Lough Derg Pilgrim' laid it out on the page with embarrassing clarity. The claims made by Yeats and others that Carleton later repented were decidedly special pleading; in a letter written shortly before his death Carleton reiterated that he 'had not belonged to the Roman Catholic religion for half a century or more'.[6] But, as years went by, Yeats made the same discovery as Carleton: that your background, and what has made you, survives repudiation and can return to claim you in strange ways at the end.

Yeats came to Carleton at a stage when he and his friends (gathered in the O'Leary circle) were trying to marshal a canon of Irish literature, which would be expressed in reading-clubs, new editions of out-of-print Irish authors and publicized lists of 'Best Books'. The writers who appealed included the Banims, Gerald Griffin and others whose 'square built power' seemed to Yeats a different level of achievement from either the apparent frivolities of Charles Lever or the Anglo-Irish identification of Edgeworth (not to mention Swift, Goldsmith and Sheridan, still, for Yeats, beyond the Irish pale – or within the Anglo-Irish Pale). Authenticity was what was at issue, and here Carleton was vital, since authenticity is what he himself claimed (over and over again) to be his chief merit. This would be stressed in Yeats's introduction to the five stories he chose for the Walter Scott compilation ('The Poor Scholar', 'Tubber Derg; or, The Red Well', 'Wildgoose Lodge', 'Shane Fadh's Wedding' and 'The Hedge School'). The introduction was written in a hurry, which shows; it reads sentimentally and, at times, perfunctorily. But, like everything Yeats wrote, there is a complex subtext. Astutely inferring details of Carleton's life from his fiction (the *Autobiography* was not yet published), Yeats deals with the theme of violence in Irish nineteenth-century life, and at first carefully skirts the issue of Carleton's alleged conversion to Protestantism – and, indeed, of religious antipathy itself. But he knew that this could not be sustained throughout. After all, the first story in the collection, 'The Poor Scholar', begins with a powerful imprecation upon the religious basis of expropriation in the history of Irish landholding. So Yeats finally comes to the thorny question of Carleton and religion:

He began drifting slowly into Protestantism. This Lough Derg pilgrimage seems to have set him thinking on many matters – not thinking deeply, perhaps. It was not an age of deep thinking. The air was full of mere debater's notions. In course of time, however, he grew into one of the most deeply religious minds of his day – a profound mystical nature, with melancholy at its root. And his heart, anyway, soon returned to the religion of his fathers; and in him the Established Church proselytizers found their most fierce satirist.[7]

This argument was repeated by Yeats many times, as after the publication of the *Stories* the issue of Carleton's 'apostasy' naturally recurred; even for liberals like Father Russell, it was too much to take, and it took all too logical a place beside the stereotypical stage-Irishry which some of Carleton's stories veered into – the very stories that Yeats carefully excluded from his collection. Undaunted, Yeats tried to buy off some of the criticism by the audacious expedient of reviewing the book himself.[8] Much of the review centred round the question of Carleton's conversion, and the way that none the less 'his heart was northern Catholic – was Catholic made more stubborn by the near neighbourhood of Orangeism'. 'Perhaps he was thinking of himself,' Yeats wrote, 'when he makes two converts fight about their new creeds and before it is over unconsciously return to their old ones.' This ingenious speculation did not stop the *Nation* reviewer attacking Carleton's view of Irish life as 'envenomed caricature' and 'slanderous', and scoffing at Yeats's claim that the novelist was Ireland's social historian for the nineteenth century. Yeats replied in an important letter[9] returning to the question of conversion. He steadfastly argued that Carleton remained essentially Catholic; and that this was some-how part of his essential authenticity. The assumption that echt-Irishness necessitated cradle-Catholicism was in line with his own thinking in the 1880s and 1890s: all the more striking because in later life he repudiated this belief so completely.

His claim for Carleton extended beyond the assertion that he was a historian: with *Traits and Stories of the Irish Peasantry*, he said, Carleton began modern Irish literature. This is a momentous assertion. It is, in fact, the very thing that Yeats would claim for his own generation in his speech accepting the Nobel Prize in 1923. But in the 1880s his priorities were different. At his best, in *Fardorougha the Miser* and *The Black Prophet*, Yeats finds Carleton capable of the acceptance of grimness and the creation of a terrible dramatic unity; he particularly admires *Fardorougha* for its portrait of a character driven by an overpowering obsession. (Interestingly, this is just what he would later discover, and admire, in the novels of Balzac – Yeats's one consistent passion in reading fiction, apart from his addiction to English detective stories in the 1920s and 1930s). And towards the end of his introduction, Yeats confronted the question of Protestant–Catholic antipathy in the Irish nineteenth century, when he instanced *Valentine M'Clutchy* as proving Carleton's hatred of Protestant pros-elytism. From this he moves to the Young Ireland revolution in national consciousness pioneered by Thomas Davis, and relates Carleton both to Davis and – obliquely – to Kickham: an unmistakable claim for Carleton's nationalism. The conclusion to the introduction repeated that Carleton was 'a great Irish historian' as well as 'the great novelist of Ireland'. It reiterated the clarity and lack of sentimentality which Yeats found in Carleton's work, and which he was already (the year he first drafted 'Innisfree') trying to establish in his own poetry.

There is no wistfulness in the works of Carleton. I find there, especially in his longer novels, a kind of clay-cold melancholy. One is not surprised to hear, great humorist though he was, that his conversation was more mournful than humorous. He seems, like the animals in Milton, half emerged only from the earth and its brooding. When I read any portion of the 'Black Prophet', or the scenes with Raymond the Madman in 'Valentine M'Clutchy', I seem to be looking out at the wild, torn storm-clouds that lie in heaps at sundown along the western seas of Ireland; all nature, and not merely man's nature, seems to pour out for me its inbred fatalism.[10]

That conclusion, and the sputtering controversy about Carleton as apostate, was not the end of the story. Yeats's work, as it strengthened and extended its range over the next ten years or so, sets off a surprising number of echoes of Carleton. He plundered *Traits and Stories* for Irish folklore, but there are less expected resonances too. *The Countess Cathleen*, which Yeats was working upon at this very time, owes much to what Carleton had taught him about famine in 'The Poor Scholar', 'Tubber Derg' and of course *The Black Prophet* – which, as Yeats himself said, depicted 'the supernatural terror of the people, the slow decay of well-to-do folk, the bargaining with a thieving meal-seller'. And perhaps the image of Raymond-na-hatta, with what Yeats called his 'half-inspired and crazy oratory' as a mechanism for expressing his creator's profoundest truths, is an ancestor of Crazy Jane. But above all the echoes of Carleton in Yeats alert us to the future national poet's evolving relationship with the Irish nineteenth century.

The poetic imagination supposedly always conceives of itself as situated at the end of an era. As the Victorian era came to an end in 1900, Yeats's attitude towards the nationalist culture which had emerged in the Young Ireland period was changing too. By 1895, indeed, he was backtracking on the highest of his claims for Carleton; in his article 'Irish National Literature' he uses the same ideas that he had employed six years before, but substantially moderates them. The Clogher Valley storyteller's claims to being the Irish Balzac are diluted by his own primitivity.

. . . only Carleton, born and bred a peasant, was able to give us a vast multitude of grotesque, pathetic, humorous persons, misers, pig-drivers, drunkards, schoolmasters, labourers, priests, madmen, and to fill them all with abounding vitality. He was but half articulate, half emerged from Mother earth, like one of Milton's lions, but his wild Celtic melancholy gives to whole pages of 'Fardorougha' and of 'The Black Prophet' an almost spiritual grandeur. The forms of life he described, like those described with so ebullient a merriment by his contemporary Lever, passed away with the great famine, but the substance which filled those forms is the substance of Irish life, and will flow into new forms which will resemble them as one wave of the sea resembles another. In future times men will recognize that he was at his best a true historian, the peasant Chaucer of a new tradition, and that at his worst he fell into melodrama, more from imperfect criticism than imperfect inspiration. In his time only a little of Irish history, Irish folklore, Irish poetry had been got into the English tongue; he had to dig the marble for his statue out of the mountain side with his own hands, and the statue shows not seldom the clumsy chiselling of the quarryman.[11]

Still, Yeats's list of 'Best Irish Books' compiled that year included *Traits and Stories*, *Fardorougha* and *The Black Prophet*.

By the turn of the century, however, his mind was reaching elsewhere. The question of truly Irish literature was still paramount, but he was now possessed by the idea that it must be both Irish and modern; and that the way to achieve this was through the theatre. In the process, and also driven by upheavals in his private life, he was becoming distanced from some of the nationalist friends of his youth, and specifically from the Fenian companions of the 1890s. The achievements of Wagner, Edward Gordon Craig or Stanislavsky in modern European drama would suggest ways in which Irish culture could find a new and uncompromising voice; by the early 1900s that voice had made itself heard nearer home, through the plays of J. M. Synge. Synge, and all he stood for, seemed to Yeats to detonate the conventions of the nineteenth century – and not only in drama. Around Synge, and the opposition to him, crystallized Yeats's assertive new stance in politics as well as art. And to understand how potent this was, we must place Yeats – like Carleton – firmly in his own times, and perhaps see him – like Carleton – as an emblematic figure as well as an individual genius.

This is thrown into clear relief simply by considering many of the problems which preoccupy Irish historians of the later nineteenth and early twentieth centuries, and then noting how directly they intersect with Yeats and his life. The marginalization of the Protestant Ascendancy and the rise of a successor class; the importance of provincial entrepreneurs in Irish business life; the chronology of Irish nationalist revival in the 1890s; the importance (or otherwise) of Fenianism around the turn of the century; the impact of the Boer War in Irish politics; the backroom dealings of British politicians around the time of the Anglo-Irish Treaty; the replacement of the old Home Rule elite by a new class of conservative ex-revolutionaries; the Fascist content of right-wing Irish political ideology from the late 1920s – to all of these issues Yeats's experience contributes central illumination. But his historical 'placing' also raises themes specifically allied to the experience of his nineteenth-century predecessors, most notably Carleton. One concerns the marginal situation of the Irish intellectual who has made a reputation through mastering English audiences; whose emotional centre is located in Ireland, but whose professional market is attuned to the readership defined by the Union. Another syndrome which comes to mind is the attraction and repulsion of the two confessional monoliths of Irish life. For both men, the endemic restlessness of the Irish writer and the problematic relationship to location discussed in the last essay inevitably meant confronting, and partly rejecting, the beliefs of the tribe. For Yeats, it specifically meant grappling with the distinctness of Irish Protestant subculture, and the difficulties of accommodation with the overwhelmingly Catholic complexion of Irish nationalism: areas which Carleton, from radically different origins, had trespassed into before him.

Yeats's relationship to Irish Protestantism is central to his life, though oddly little looked at by scholars.[12] It helps explain the depth of his relationship to Augusta Gregory (which far transcended Mícheál Mac Liammóir's description of it as 'high priestess and sacred snake'[13]). It illuminates the stormy relationship with colleagues within the Abbey Theatre, as well as with audiences across the footlights. And here Yeats found that a culturally nationalist movement could not be above politics in the way he had initially conceived – nor above sectarian politics, when they reared their head. By the time of Synge's death in 1907, this was clear; and it made him reconsider his ideas about nineteenth-century national literature, marking the point where he diverged from his early reverence for the nineteenth-century Irish novelists whom he had spent so much of his early critical efforts resurrecting. By 1910 he had formally set up an alternative set of artistic standards. His elegiac essay on Synge formally posits the writer's individual mission against the pressures of nationalist political conformity – what Seamus Heaney (who has walked this ground) has called 'the quarrel between free creative imagination and the constraints of religious, political and domestic obligation'.[14] And this argument is constructed around a reconsideration of the quintessential icon of nineteenth-century literary nationalism, Thomas Davis.

Thomas Davis, whose life had the moral simplicity which can give to actions the lasting influence that style alone can give to words, had understood that a country which has no national institutions must show its young men images for the affections, although they be but diagrams of what should be or may be. He and his school imagined the Soldier, the Orator, the Patriot, the Poet, the Chieftain, and above all the Peasant; and these, as celebrated in essays and songs and stories, possessed so many virtues that no matter how England, who, as Mitchel said, 'had the ear of the world', might slander us, Ireland, even though she could not come to the world's other ear, might go her way unabashed. But ideas and images which have to be understood and loved by large numbers of people must appeal to no rich personal experience, no patience of study, no delicacy of sense; and if at rare moments some *Memory of the Dead* can take its strength from one, at all other moments matter and manner will be rhetorical, conventional, sentimental; and language, because it is carried beyond life perpetually, will be worn and cold like the thought, with unmeaning pedantries and silences, and a dread of all that has salt and savour.[15]

This judgement, however nuanced and skilfully manipulated, declares Yeats's repudiation of the Young Ireland canon of literature which he had imbibed in the O'Leary circle. With this 'grand refusal' he sets himself against what I have elsewhere called the 'theme-park' approach to Irish history, and announces the primacy of the creative imagination – wherever it leads. Style alone gives significance to words; national stereotypes and self-referencing images inhibit artistic expression; 'salt and savour' come from the shock of the new, epitomized by Synge's original and uncompromising art. A certain respect and affection for Davis remains – which Yeats would never lose. But the primary value of Davis's teaching now lay, for Yeats, in his commitment to free speech and liberty of conscience, and his opposition to O'Connell's alleged encouragement of confessionalism in Irish politics. This was abundantly clear when Yeats appeared on a debating platform with Patrick Pearse late in 1914, at a controversial meeting to celebrate Davis's centenary. Trinity College – so often excoriated by the youthful Yeats – had banned the meeting from taking place within its precincts, because of Pearse's anti-recruiting activities. In a masterly exhibition of balance-holding, Yeats gently chided Provost Mahaffy for failing to follow Davis's example of tolerance towards his antagonists, praised Pearse's contribution to literature, and – reverting to the nineteenth century once more – condemned Davis's ally John Mitchel for preaching hatred of England instead of love of Ireland. 'Hatred of England soon became hatred of their own countrymen as when they learned to hate one man, perhaps for a good reason, they hated probably twenty men for bad reasons.'[16] Later, at another Thomas Davis celebration, he returned to the theme, implicitly drawing a strong and antagonistic contrast with the kind of nationalism pioneered by Arthur Griffith, and now in the ascendant. Griffith and his new newspaper *Nationality* are condemned by means of Davis and the *Nation*:

All who fell under [Davis's] influence took this thought from his precept or his example: we struggle for a nation, not for a party, and our political opponents who have served Ireland in some other way may, perhaps, be better patriots. He did not, as a weak and hectic nature would have done, attack O'Connell, or parade with a new party; no venomous newspaper supported his fame, or found there its own support. When the quarrel came it was

O'Connell's own doing, and his only; and the breach was so tragical to Davis that in the midst of the only public speech he ever made he burst into tears. It is these magnanimities, I believe, that have made generations of our young men turn over the pages of an old newspaper as though it were some classic of literature, but when they have come, as some few have, to dream of another 'Nation' they do not understand their own lure, and are content to copy alone his concentration and his enthusiasm.[17]

By then he had formally – as he thought – turned his back on the literary nationalism and nationalist literature of his youth: rejecting both his mentor, O'Leary, and his mentor's library too.

Elsewhere in this book I have discussed the process whereby Yeats reinscribed himself into the nationalist political tradition from 1916 onwards – not long after this speech in which Davis is used to condemn Griffith. In any case, echoes of his early intellectual apprenticeship would continue to resonate through his later creative work too. Moreover, it is worth questioning how far repudiating the mid-nineteenth-century Irish canon in general meant repudiating Carleton in particular. On one level, he might seem to come within Yeats's imposed ban on stereotypical and unsubtle national image-making. In another way, however, Carleton was capable of his own version of the uncompromisingness, originality, rigour, 'salt and savour' which Yeats missed in the Davis school and found in Synge. Yeats himself had always distinguished between Carleton's best work and his hack productions. There is an uncertain space in between, occupied by works like *Valentine M'Clutchy* which – as Yeats said in 1889 – ruin themselves through didacticism. 'The habit of dividing men into sheep and goats for the purposes of partisan politics made havoc out of what might have been a great novel.' But this crudeness should be balanced against reflections like those in 'The Poor Scholar', where Carleton's authorial voice inveighs against 'abstracted hatred' and 'the stunted virtues of artificial life' – phrases which Yeats reuses almost word for word in 'J. M. Synge and the Ireland of his Time' (and paraphrases in 'Easter 1916'). The echoes of his Carleton reading return even as he apparently moves further and further from the Young Irelander nationalism which had inspired him during his years of apprenticeship. His speeches during the Home Rule crisis of 1912–14, when he attacked the intolerance apparently inseparable from Irish life and compared Catholic and Protestant bigotry to 'two old boots' bobbing around the stagnant pond of Irish politics, suggest an earthy image from Carleton too.[18] And Yeats's own uneasy relationship to the perceived authenticities of Irish life, as well as his ability to keep one eye on a metropolitan audience and another on the contentious critics at home, implies a fellow feeling with Carleton which went deep, and continued. The poor scholar from the Clogher Valley represented far more than just one of the over-compensating enthusiasms of Yeats's youth.

He did not always welcome reminders of the fact. When, in 1934, the young American journalist Horace Reynolds reprinted a selection of Yeats's literary journalism from the 1880s and 1890s, he received a telling communication from the poet:

The articles are much better than my memory of them, but I knew better than I wrote. I was a propagandist and hated being one. It seems to me that I remember almost the day and hour when revising for some reprint my essay upon the Celtic movement ... I saw clearly the unrealities and half-truths propaganda had involved me in, and the way out. All one's life one struggles towards reality, finding always but new veils. One knows everything in one's mind. It is the words, children of the occasion, that betray.[19]

Carleton, reviewing the false trails and opportunistic confections of his youth, might have felt no different. By then, it was clear that Yeats's literary achievement had soared to levels far beyond the capacities of those 'old men' he had delineated so appreciatively in his letter to Father Russell more than forty years before. He had also elected to place himself in the tradition of very different Irish writers in English: Berkeley, Swift, Burke, exactly those Anglo-Irish sages whose claims to Irishness he had dismissed in his youth. It is likely, however, that what he wrote in 1889 about 'The Lough Derg Pilgrim' remained as true for him as for other readers of Carleton: 'nobody who reads it forgets it'. In the anxieties of influence woven around Yeats, perhaps more anxiously than around any other Irish writer, the earthy and essentialist voice of Carleton is a continuing and discernible presence. Inscribing John Quinn's copy of *Stories from Carleton* decades later, he offhandedly contradicted this: 'I thought no end of Carleton in those days & would still I daresay if I had not forgotten him.'[20] But perhaps he remembered more than he knew, or wanted others to know.

8

Stopping the Hunt:
Trollope and the Memory
of Ireland

The person who made Trollope's novels possible was, in a sense, not Trollope himself, or his wife, or his mother, but an Irishman called Barney. Trollope acquired his services as a groom when living in Banagher as Post Office surveyor and obsessive rider to hounds; Barney came with his employer into married life, moved around Ireland with him and eventually went back to England with the household. And for all their long association, Barney's task was to awaken his employer at five-thirty in the morning with a pot of strong coffee in order to make possible the precious few hours of writing before Trollope's day's work. It is an appropriate metaphor for Trollope's relationship with Ireland which was – like that with Barney – influential, continuing, close and dependent. It also, like any master–servant relationship, raises questions of possessiveness, dependency, condescension and exploitation. Barney's surname, apparently, remains unknown.

But it goes further than that, and is more complicated. Professionally, Trollope's life was made in Ireland; he became a success there. Arriving in 1841 with a bad reputation to live down, he transformed himself (and the Irish postal services in his area: there is still an elegant octagonal post-box in Galway City which represents one of Trollope's most influential innovations). He was lucky in finding one superior (Godby) who declared he would ignore the bad reference sent by Trollope's previous boss in London; and another, George Drought, who was so lazy that Trollope had a free hand and rapidly became indispensable.[1] (Rather like Evelyn Waugh with Cruttwell, his hated college dean, Trollope took a novelist's quiet revenge by bringing the name 'Drought' into characters in his fiction.) This is all very important for the Irish postal services and for Trollope's personal history.

He met his wife there (Englishwoman though she was); his children were born there and spoke in Irish accents until they moved to England; the family even called Trollope's redoubtable mother by the quintessentially Irish nickname of 'the Mammy', supplied (like the morning coffee) by Barney. But for posterity, these details are dwarfed in importance by the massive fact that he started writing novels there; his first novel, *The Macdermots of Ballycloran*, is Irish; and so was his last, forty years and millions of words later. This was the unfinished *The Landleaguers*. Ireland saw him in as a novelist; and saw him out.

It also stayed with him all his life; witness the gallery of Irish characters even in his most English novels, the sustenance of Irish friendship, the abiding (if exasperated) interest in Ireland, and of course the evidence of his *Autobiography*. However, it is becoming clearer and clearer, with the latest clutch of highly detailed biographies, that this is a highly disingenuous text and nothing in it should be taken as read. Even the most matter-of-fact account of signing a contract for *Doctor Thorne*[2] can be checked against contemporary correspondence and seen to be so carefully tailored as to be fanciful. And here as elsewhere the point of the tailoring should be understood – not to deceive for the sake of deception, but to add one more brick into the beautifully and artistically constructed edifice of Anthony Trollope, novelist, public man and resolutely private person. One might instance the marvellously laconic line about his marriage being like the marriages of other people, and therefore of no more interest than theirs. (Or less.)[3] The matter of writers' autobiographies should be carefully considered; especially when, as with the early chapters of Trollope's, they contain some of their very best and most affecting writing. John Stuart Mill's contrives never to mention his mother; Evelyn Waugh's (as Selina Hastings has shown) misrepresents most of the background of his youth; above all, perhaps, Yeats's autobiography resembles Trollope's, in its resolutely artistic construction and its extraordinarily confiding tone, full of self-deprecation, ironic humour and confidentiality. As with Trollope's, these are danger signs, pointing to misdirections; events are moulded together, dates given which are wildly inappropriate, people eliminated, characters genially assassinated, and all to create a central character who, like Trollope, struggles with adversity and overcomes it. Of course, they both did; but was it the kind of adversity they describe?

The key to writers' autobiographies is that they tell us a great deal about the state of mind of the writer at the point when they were written, in terms of preoccupations, priorities, fears, obsessions and their own sense of where their reputation was going. They may tell us a lot less than we think about the actual events of the life – or at least, a lot less reliably. Trollope's *Autobiography* was constructed (like Winston Churchill's *My Early Life*) to show how a child may grow up to confound its parents' low expectations, and how a unique and individual talent can overcome disadvantages of circumstance and the cruel stereotyping of the world. In this dramatic progression, Ireland was a vital stage. All that went before it was painted in the deepest black, to show a childhood tougher than Dickens's; all that came afterwards was to show a man transformed. The butterfly that emerged from the chrysalis was to be the no-nonsense, politically *au fait*, man's man of the perfect Garrick type: the 'advanced liberal conservative' in control of his life, his fortunes, his feelings and himself, a world away from the dirty schoolboy shunned by his fellows. We know enough about Trollope's effect on other people to know that he was not at all like that. He remained passionate, sensitive and clumsy, talked too much, and annoyed people. We know from the novels that his psychological antennae were extrasensory instruments. We know from testimony of friends and fiction alike that he was an extremely close friend to women, and that his emotions were not at all the bluff, ordered, sceptical matter which he would have us believe. So how should we read all that he says of Ireland? And how should we interpret the emotionalism of his language on the subject, and the bitterness of the repudiation in that last, fragmentary novel?

'When I meet an Irishman abroad I always recognize in him more of a kinsman than I do an Englishman.' 'From the day on which I set foot in Ireland all . . . evils went away from me. Since that time who has had a happier life than mine?'[4] He was looking for a family who would make him feel at ease, since his relationship with his own 'kinsmen' was at best uneasy. And he was anxious to reassure himself that his life had been happy, that he was fortunate and blessed, and that this blessing had coincided with his arrival in a country where he was unknown and could make a new start. (In fact, a classic frontier.) Ireland in the early 1840s was not a foreign country; it was, in fact, legislatively part of the United Kingdom. But it was undeniably exotic. Irish weather, Irish landscape, the Irish use of English, Irish social modes were all different. Trollope would have added (shockingly to us) that so was Irish dirt, on which he has many disquisitions. Irish working people and menials were cleverer, sharper and funnier. Irish girls were prettier and more approachable. Irish hunting was unparalleled.

All this is the re-creation of a Golden Age, lit with the sunny optimism of energetic youth. It is also coloured up to contrast with a later descent into darkness. As literary criticism has come to emphasize the darker side of Trollope's vision, threatened paradises emerge as a recurrent theme in his work – often English, rural and time-warped, like the Thornes' establishment at Ullathorne, or Roger Carbury's country estate in *The Way We Live Now*, or the Barchester cathedral close itself. Similarly, woven through his novels, from the early *Orley Farm* to the late *Mr Scarborough's Family*, is the threat of the loss of a house, a theme whose links to Trollope's own insecure family background and marginalized social status are too obvious to need stating. Ireland is perhaps, above all, the great lost domain of Trollope's mental landscape. Here he had found both emotional security and social status, becoming a Freemason, a member of an elite, an acknowledged gentleman. His status in Ireland has been well described by Andrew Sanders as at once 'intimate and privileged'.[5] But he lost Ireland, not once but twice. The first time was when he finally returned to England in 1859, and became famous and successful. The second loss came as Irish politics radicalized from the late 1870s and the social role of the Irish landowning classes was called into question, with the rise of separatist nationalism and the advent of the land war. Above all, this meant the end of deference politics in Ireland – which had constructed the background of the Ireland Trollope knew and loved.

The sunlit Ireland of Trollope's youth may have been, on some levels, real; but the interesting thing is, how much he wanted it to be true. He certainly came to know Ireland well; living through most of the 1840s and some of the 1850s in Banagher, Clonmel, Killarney, Mallow, Belfast and Dublin; holidaying in Kerry and on the Waterford coast; accepted into local society wherever he went. Irish class was constructed along patterns other than those in England; Irish manners, Trollope always thought, were both subtler and better than the general run of manners in England. His social position there was more advantageous than it was in England; a background of debts and scruffiness was not there to be held up against him, and in the out-of-the-way places where his work took him, a new face was always welcome, especially if joined to a pair of legs that could ride and dance. (His short story, 'The O'Conors of Castle Conor', preserves this, and he claimed it was autobiographical.) He could move through the class system in Ireland in the manner he later showed Phineas Finn slipping through the interstices in great London society. He could – and did – become a friend of Sir William Gregory of Coole, who had been a gilded contemporary at school and subsequently a golden boy of Disraelian political circles; at Coole, Trollope not only heard the kind of political gossip he would later immortalize in fiction, but also actually met practising politicians and learned their language. In Ireland, where perspectives seemed altered, his past (even that ignominious schoolboy past) did not count against him.

In a way, of course, religious difference in Ireland filled the place of class consciousness in England; and Trollope early on allied himself with the party of tolerance, as shown by the treatment of religion in his early Irish novels. Perhaps the most personally revealing of his Irish texts is the short story 'Father Giles of Ballymoy'. Trollope always claimed it was autobiographical, and the narrator is 'Archibald Green', the name he often gave for such purposes. The point about 'Father Giles' is that there is no plot, only an event. Staying in a particularly dicey hotel in the west of Ireland, the narrator (a young Englishman) is woken up by a stranger in the middle of the night, determined to share his room. The Englishman throws him out, and inadvertently down the stairs, injuring him. The adversary turns out to be the much loved and respected local priest, who has told the landlady the stranger may share his own room in the hotel (which it is). The narrator spends the night in the local gaol for his own protection, but the priest befriends him the next day, and for life. Here is Trollope's essential view of Ireland: the frontier; the uneasy social relations; the effusive but devious landlady; the local knowledge denied to the incomer;

the priest's perfect manners, and intelligent defusing of a potentially dangerous situation; the reconciliation not only of the English and Irish characters, but of their countries (the priest often comes, in after years, to visit Green in England).

For Trollope's own purposes of self-esteem, and to carry through the powerful myth of himself which he sustained in his art and life, Ireland had to be a success. It had to be a frontier that he could conquer; it had to produce heroes and heroines; it had to be a happy place. For Trollope, Ireland, in fact, was to fulfil the function of the kind of happy childhood which he felt he had deserved (much as Oxford was to do for Waugh). This is the key to understanding both the sympathy of his perception and the determined obtuseness in areas where the reality diverged from his ideal. And the most spectacular illustration of this concerns the devastation which afflicted Ireland at exactly the period of Trollope's sojourn there: the Great Famine of the mid 1840s.

The potato blight was first noticed in 1845, and returned year after year to create conditions of indescribable horror, starvation and disease (which killed far more). The cheerful squalor which Trollope liked to describe in the overpopulated Irish countryside when he arrived was by the end of the decade altered for good; that population had declined by two million through death and emigration, and would decline steadily from then on. *The MacDermots* was published as the Famine took hold; its successor, *The Kellys and the O'Kellys*, was written during the height of the devastation. The former is a bleak tale of rural tragedy, which may owe a good deal to Irish realists like William Carleton, John Banim and Gerald Griffin; the latter is a cleverly counterpointed study of marital and financial politics at two social levels of Irish life (characteristically, Trollope spotted that 'O'Kelly' could be, in Irish terms, a grander name than 'Kelly'). Very deliberately, Trollope opens with a closely observed account of the trial of Daniel O'Connell in 1844. He chooses thus to capture and anatomize Irish life on the eve of the Famine, definitively before it, and thus to preserve that cheerful frontier country which he had discovered in 1841. Leisure, indulgence and indeed *eating* predominate – whether it is the unforgettable mutton meal on the canal boat, or the dinners produced in Mrs Kelly's kitchen at Dunmore, or the languid dining room of Grey Abbey. There is throughout a deliberate denial of what rural life in much of Ireland had actually become by the time he was writing it. *The MacDermots* could (and did) present a tragedy of Irish life, even providing an English villain to seduce the heroine, but this did not negate Trollope's vision of Ireland. The Famine presented a trickier problem.

The failure of the potato crop in Ireland produced an unparalleled and apocalyptic catastrophe; that much is clear. How far it could have been prophesied is controversial; but certainly in all the great weight of economic analysis brought to bear on 'the Irish question' since rural prosperity began failing after the Napoleonic Wars, a warning note is often sounded. Nutritious, easily cultivated, well suited to Irish conditions, highly compatible with the pig-rearing ecology of small-holding life, the potato was seen as interacting with a population explosion and an unsatisfactory land-tenure system to create a poten-tial disaster. Which did, of course, happen. And when this staple failed, what could be done about it?

At first, the Conservative government under Peel did what it could, interfering with the market by stealth, and relaxing several orthodoxies in order to distribute food at cost price. But when Peel was succeeded by the inflexible laissez-faire doctrinaire free marketeers of Russell's Whig government, they relied entirely on a 'free' market, an inappro-priate Poor Law on the English model and expectations that the local landlord class would do their duty in terms of supporting relief work through the rates and through running local relief committees. The government might facilitate but could not intervene. This was contem-porary orthodoxy, but in Irish conditions it did not answer. As the disaster escalated from year to year, some voices were heard to argue that the government had failed terribly in its moral and social duty to feed the starving. These voices tended to come from radical philanthro-pists, or from paternalist Tories who never subscribed to Adam Smith economics, or from Irish nationalist revolutionaries. None of these elements was very congenial to Trollope, and it is unsurprising to find him on the other side. But the nature of his response is both extreme and revealing.

He held his peace, for the moment, in his fiction, but he did write a series of letters to the *Examiner* in 1850, when the worst was over.

Trollope's initiative responded to a series of attacks by Sidney Godolphin Osborne in *The Times*; it also supported Charles Trevelyan's apologia in the *Edinburgh Review*. Like Trevelyan, Trollope argued that the government had done all they could. The state of Ireland had been misrepresented by sentimentalists. The only way to help the people was to let them help themselves through Famine works. Free distribution of basic food would have exacerbated the underlying situation. Most shocking to us, he argued that in the end the Famine would be seen as a blessing in disguise, reconstructing the unsound economic structure and enabling a better life for all.[6]

These were opinions which he shared with the majority of middle-class English clubmen and politicians – but the majority of them did not know Ireland as intimately as Trollope did. Perhaps because of this, he argued with a stridency and vehemence which suggests an underlying doubt. Certainly a suppressed sense of contradiction is borne out by the novel he did write about the Famine, *Castle Richmond*. It is a curiously absorbing though uneven work, which he left aside in order to work on *Framley Parsonage*, his first great popular success. Written in 1859, it was (he thought) his farewell to Ireland, but it also floats themes and character types which would recur. The interesting thing is that he is determined to give a direct and almost documentary account of how the Famine affected the gentry of the Cork–Kerry border; the Fitzgerald family throw themselves into relief committees and soup-kitchens, and, though their humanity incites them to give alms to the starving, they know this is not the answer. They are, moreover, counterpointed against the grander but infinitely poorer Desmond family in their crumbling house Desmond Court. Part of the lesson is that if the Fitzgeralds are the ideal Irish gentry, many are far from the ideal. (The names, as usual, should be noted: both 'Fitzgerald' and 'Desmond' suggest Norman stock, deeply integrated into Irish life as early as Elizabethan times, rather than later planter settlements.) And though the local clergy have severe reservations about each other, Protestant and Catholic come uneasily together and combine on the relief committee, agreeing to forget traditional antipathies. It is, in a sense, the blueprint for Utopia again.[7]

The other thing Trollope tries to do in *Castle Richmond*, however, is to show the Famine from below. There are the starving women who beg at the gate; there are the hopeless teams of men on the relief works; and most chillingly of all there is one of the bleakest chapters Trollope ever wrote, when Herbert Fitzgerald (at a particularly low point in his own fortunes) takes shelter in a wayside cabin and finds himself with a woman and children in the last stages of starvation. Whether he means to or not, this view of the depths negates all the prescriptions Trollope has given us before, and he as good as admits it, in the offhand way we are informed about their eventual fate. The interest of *Castle Richmond* lies in Trollope's attempt to argue, almost with himself, what should or could have been done about the Famine. By the time he wrote it, a fair degree of rural prosperity had returned, and he presented a doggedly rosy view of this. But he also argued an essentially Providentialist view of the visitation. Mary Hamer, writing recently about the novel, claims that the plots about rivals in love, and an inheritance threatened by the discovery of an unintentionally bigamous marriage, are incompatible with the effort to give a portrait of Famine-racked Ireland.[8] It could be argued instead that the Fitzgerald family fortunes revolve around the theme of behaving well, accepting the fate meted out to you and doing the right thing. The person who would benefit from a concealed bigamy refuses to do so; the disputed heir still accepts his fate, gives up all and goes to London to earn an honest living. By contrast, over in Desmond Court, the ageing Countess of Desmond stays immured in selfishness, whereas her daughter remains true to a suddenly impecunious suitor, and receives her reward for it. Thus the lives of the characters are dominated by an apparently capricious fate, which deals them a cruel blow. The person who tries to turn it away by striking a Faustian bargain, the father of the family, dies – significantly – by wasting away. Those who accept their fate with Christian fortitude will survive and eventually prosper, sadder but wiser. Surely this is intended as a Providentialist paradigm of the visitation striking desolation all around them? And the moral is implicitly to be extended, applying to the country as a whole.

With the publication of *Castle Richmond*, Trollope left Ireland in both senses. Through the 1860s and early 1870s he hit his peak of success, writing about Barsetshire and the Pallisers, celebrated for his 'cleverness' as well as his humour, and the astonishing range and depth of psychological portraiture which he brought to ordinary people.

There was also the phenomenal 'exactness' of his settings: so much so that even when his reputation was at its nadir in this century, historians still turned to him for illustration of the way people lived then. All these qualities had been heralded in the first Irish novels: the description of the social geography of Dunmore, that canal-boat, the hunting scenes (of course), the portrait of Feemy in *The MacDermots* (who endures as one of Trollope's most complex women), the Kanturk hotel in *Castle Richmond*. The clergymen in his early Irish work – bigots and liberals – reveal the early lineaments of the denizens of Barchester. And if a constant preoccupation of Trollope's was the idea and conduct of a gentleman, as displayed under pressure, Father Giles of Ballymoy stands as an archetype. Houses, again, deserve attention; the idea of a rooted place, the architecture of a house that belongs to its situation and whose inhabitants belong to it, makes his descriptions of Barchester, or Plumstead, or Allington, or Matching vividly realized. This too he learned in Ireland, where the ownership of a house, and the way it identifies you with territory insecurely held, is a resonant theme in all Anglo-Irish writing. (Note those titles: 'The O'Conors of Castle Conor', 'The Macdermots of Ballycloran', 'Castle Richmond'.) In this way, as in others, Ireland taught Trollope the importance of belonging.

All this being the case, it must surely be of prime importance that Trollope made the central figure of the early novels in the Palliser series a young Irishman. Like Owen Fitzgerald in *Castle Richmond*, Phineas Finn is physically beautiful, with natural self-possession and good manners. Like several characters in *The Kellys*, he is the product of a mixed marriage, so combines Celtic glamour with the social advantages of Protestantism. Like Trollope himself, he is an apprentice politician (though he gets much further). Like the heroes in Stendhal's novels, he is there to be *told* things, to learn lessons – often rather cynical lessons, and often taught by women of the world. His Irishness, his insider/outsider status, is important here too. And like so many of Trollope's amiable, handsome young men, he is tested with moral problems, often involving fidelity of one kind or another; and he does not come through quite intact.[9] There has been much talk about whether John Sadleir, or Chichester Fortescue, or John Pope Hennessy, or William Gregory provided the template.[10] But the important thing is that Phineas is Irish. He can ascend the social ladder in the way that an English doctor's son could not; his fluency, charm and good breeding are emblematic of all Trollope loved about Ireland; and, above all, England (and Englishwomen) make Phineas's fortune. He stands, in fact, for the ideal relationship of the two countries as Trollope wanted it to be, much as Phineas himself (as Victoria Glendinning has astutely hazarded) stands for the handsome, troubled, basically decent young heartbreaker that Trollope would have liked to be. Trollope's Irish alter ego went where he himself wanted to be, in the company of women like Laura Standish, Violet Effingham, eventually Madame Max Goesler. He was given friends like Lord Chiltern, gurus like Mr Monk (who in the original draft of the novel was to be far more obviously Irish too) and a welcome in the great Palliser drawing rooms. (And near Clonmel, where Trollope had lived, there is a well-known beauty-spot called Palliser's Rock.)

While Trollope thought that Josiah Crawley was probably the character who would make him live as a novelist, he reserved his chief love for the inhabitants of the Palliser world, and among them Phineas must take a prominent place. But in the later novels of the series, as Glencora and the Duke gain in depth and complexity, Phineas becomes a cipher, pushed out to the margins. In one way, this may reflect Trollope's increasing distance from Ireland; though he still went there for the odd holiday, his interests were now centred on England. More fundamentally, Ireland was changing. By the later 1870s, when he wrote his autobiography, it was clear that the kind of friendly reconciliation, in the senior–junior partnership that he had envisioned for his Utopia, was less and less likely. There was a Home Rule Party at Westminster, whose leadership had just been taken over by the implacable young Charles Stewart Parnell. There was an equally implacable Irish-American element in the ascendant, taught by the writings of John Mitchel that the Famine had been inflicted by England on Ireland with genocidal deliberateness. There was (from 1880) a Liberal Party under Gladstone which was, in Trollope's opinion, far too ready to truckle to Irish nationalist demands. And just from that point too there was an organization in Ireland, the Land League, which coordinated resistance to landlords and rent payments, and was closely linked to just the elements in Irish politics which most threatened Trollope's beliefs: Irish-American nationalists, the secret

Fenian movement, the Home Rule MPs and their obstructive tactics at Westminster. He was also older, crustier and in many ways more pessimistic than the young Post Office surveyor who had wrestled with the priest in Ballymoy.

It is against this background that we have to read his assertion in his *Autobiography* that it had been a mistake to make Phineas an Irishman, and that the novels would have been better if he were not.[11] And Trollope's Irish disenchantment would take him even further. The year 1882 was the last of Trollope's life. It was also a year of maximum crisis in the Irish situation: Parnell was released from gaol under the tacit terms of the Kilmainham 'treaty' with Gladstone's government. There were the operations of Gladstone's potentially radical Second Land Act of 1881, the Phoenix Park murders of Lord Frederick Cavendish and T. H. Burke by a breakaway Fenian secret society, the Invincibles, and another series of murders, of the Joyce family in County Mayo, which were seen by English conservative opinion as a lurid flash from the depths of anarchic Irish rural society. These events supplied the background to Trollope's last visits to Ireland, collecting material for the novel that became *The Landleaguers*. His last novel, like his first, dealt with Irish rural society, land hunger and violence. It is manifestly an imperfect novel, without the fascination of other unfinished works by master novelists, such as *The Mystery of Edwin Drood* or *Weir of Hermiston*. But for students of Trollope and of Ireland it supplies a commentary on how Ireland had grown away from him, and a bitter *envoi* to a part of his own past.

Trollope's reaction was to go back to the prescriptive, even polemical approach of his very first Irish novels. *The Landleaguers* was written, as he deliberately tells us in one of its chapters, to show how Ireland had come to the crisis which now gripped it. His last visits to the country were uncomfortable. Many of the old friends were gone or dead; others told him one side of the story. The novel that emerged is a violent reaction, expressing not so much the falling out of love, as the rage that comes when the love object lets you down by not being the thing that you have constructed it to be. Not the least interesting thing about Trollope's last novel – and it is a much more interesting novel than is sometimes allowed – is the way he puts in all those beloved Irish characteristics, charm, exoticism, linguistic ingenuity, intelligence, and turns them into sinister qualities. The symmetry with his first novel is obvious, and the effect can be devastating.

Forty-nine chapters of *The Landleaguers*, out of a projected sixty, had been written when Trollope succumbed to a stroke on 3 November 1882, and his son Harry refused to allow anyone to attempt a notional ending. But by then the story was well established. It moves on two tracks, between Galway and London, beginning very specifically in the autumn of 1880. The Joneses are small Galway landlords, who invested in their Irish holding under the post-Famine legislation which allowed bankrupt estates to be sold on the open market, cutting through restrictive legislation to do with mortgages and entails: their 'Castle Moroney' is in fact a modest modern house. There is a decent though unimaginative widowed father, a son – called, inevitably, Frank – and two daughters, one beautiful and gentle, the other plain, tough, witty and feisty. Thus far, it is Trollope's *ur*-family. But there is a much younger son, ten years old, called Florian. And Florian, who feels things strongly, decides to become a Catholic. He is much influenced by a formidable Father Malachi, and frequents the houses of members of local agrarian secret societies. The Joneses are not bigots: Mr Jones has both Catholic and Protestant friends and loathes Orange zealotry. But when local members of the Land League ruin Jones's land and crops by flooding them with salt water, Florian is a witness, and he refuses to testify. The situation becomes more and more tense: when he gives way and names the malefactors the family is boycotted. Their servants and workers leave, and the Joneses come under the protection of a dashing resident magistrate, who falls in love – with the wrong sister.

The other story involves a friend of the Jones girls, Rachel O'Mahony, whose Irish-American father Gerald O'Mahony is a radical land reformer, determined to do away with landlords and nationalize Irish land. He seems clearly and satirically modelled on Henry George, who had toured Ireland preaching land nationalization in 1881. Rachel and Frank Jones are in love, but Rachel goes to London to become a singer, graduating from the Charing Cross Theatre to Covent Garden. While Rachel is defending her virtue both from her impresario, Mahomet Moss, and a titled stage-door johnny, her honest but deluded father becomes an MP in Parnell's party, regularly making a fool of himself in the House of Commons. Thus the career of Phineas Finn is reversed: the anti-hero, so far from being educated through exposure to the high-political world, brings it down to his own level of burlesque.

Meanwhile things go from bad to worse in Galway. In a terrible scene Florian is shot by one of the Land Leaguers; attempts to bring the murderer to justice fail; Frank breaks off his engagement to Rachel because he will not live off her earnings; clever Edith refuses the gallant Captain Clayton because she feels her beautiful sister deserves him more. By the last completed chapters, however, it is clear that Trollope has decided the forces of law and order will prevail. Irish opinion will repudiate Parnellite nationalism and its sinister Irish-American paymasters. Rachel has lost her voice and opted for dependent marriage. Gerald O'Mahony may even see the moral necessity of paying rent. However, the increasingly perfunctory tone reflects both Trollope's own debility and his fundamental lack of conviction that things can go anywhere but down.

There is still much that is arresting in *The Landleaguers*, especially seen in the light of Trollope's characteristic preoccupations. Both Edith and Rachel are in his quasi-feminist mould, much cleverer and more articulate than the men around them. Rachel in particular owes much to Trollope's late love Kate Field, being a petite and utterly confident American girl who argues for women's economic independence, is sarcastic about the double standard and runs rings around her dim suitors. The portrait of Mr Moss casts some light on Trollope's congenital ambiguity about the place of Jewish characters in modern English life: he is superficially a villain, but his instincts are superior to many other characters, and the notion of anti-Semitism is flagged more than once. ('Papa says that hating Jews is a prejudice,' Rachel remarks to Frank. 'Loving you is a prejudice, I suppose.'[12]) Another recurring theme in this as in so many Trollope novels is the troubled relationship between fathers and sons. But here, Mr Jones's unforgiving attitude towards Florian – even after he has been shot – is all the more implacable because Florian stands for Irish corruption.

We can hardly analyse the father's mind as he went. Not a tear came to his relief. Nor during this half hour can he hardly have been said to sorrow.

An intensity of wrath filled his breast. He had spent his time for many a long year in doing all in his power for those around him, and now they had brought him to this. They had robbed him of his boy's heart. They had taught his boy to be one of them, and to be untrue to his own people. And now, because he had yielded to better teachings, they had murdered him. They had taught his boy to be a coward; for even in his bereavement he remembered poor Florian's failing. The accursed Papist people were all cowards down to their backbones. So he said of them in his rage. There was not one of them who could look any peril in the face as did Yorke Clayton or his son Frank. But they were terribly powerful in their wretched want of manliness. They could murder, and were protected in their bloodthirstiness one by another. He did not doubt but that those two girls wailing on the road knew well enough who was the murderer, but no one would tell in this accursed, unhallowed, godless country. The honour and honesty of one man did not, in these days, prompt another to abstain from vice. The only heroism left in the country was the heroism of mystery, of secret bloodshed and of hidden attacks.[13]

Above all the interest of the novel lies in its reflection of Ireland as Trollope now saw it. From the title onwards, this is made obvious. He has returned to the unambiguous names of his early books: no teasing questions about 'forgiving her', no 'knowing he was right'. The names of the characters are equally grounded in reality: it is without Peacockian jokes about the Duke of Omnium or Mr Fillgrave the undertaker or Mr Neefit the tailor: not even a Lord de Terrier or a Mr Brock. Mary Hamer has gamely tried to see the fact that Florian is called 'Florry' as evidence of gender instability,[14] but in fact in Ireland 'Florence' is traditionally a boy's name, and 'Florry' its habitual diminutive – yet another instance of Trollope's preternaturally acute ear. For the local society in *The Landleaguers* Trollope chooses actual Galway names: Blake, Morris, Bodkin, Daly. He may have known Michael Morris, an Irish Tory lawyer who became Lord Killanin and had a real-life success in London society to rival Phineas Finn's; but he also introduces a character called Persse, which was the family name of the wife of Trollope's old friend Sir William Gregory of Coole. (Augusta Persse, as Lady Gregory, would later become famous in her own right, and live a life which is like something from a late novel by Trollope.

And in the evenings at Coole forty years later she would read his by now unfashionable novels to her friend W. B. Yeats.)

Ireland was to be actualized by the use of real names in *The Land-leaguers*. Details were to be exact (he went to some trouble to find out the exact schedule of the Lough Corrib steamer, by which the young Joneses go back and forth to visit their friend Rachel[15]). All this suggests the didactic function of the novel. This purpose is made transparently clear in a late chapter called 'The State of Ireland', which is cruder propagandizing than anything he condemned in Dickens. An attack on Liberal policy in Ireland, it is written in the language of a journal article, and slots oddly into place. Its belated positioning may reflect his wish to hook the reader by the narrative first; but, more likely, it was occasioned by recent events. Trollope probably wrote this chapter in mid or late October 1882; Gladstone's second Land Act was just coming into force, and the Irish National League, the Land League's successor, was founded at a great public meeting on 17 October. In the summer Trollope had travelled round Ireland, visiting Judge O'Hagan and other members of the Land Commission, the chief secretary George Trevelyan and Clifford Lloyd, a resident magistrate who took a public role in the campaign against the Land League (and wrote a self-publicizing book about it).[16] Trollope was by now convinced that Gladstone had perpetrated an amoral and abject sell-out of Liberal principles: the government's record in Ireland fulfilled all his gloomiest expectations about the debasement of public life. *The Landleaguers* therefore illustrates another late-Trollopian preoccupation – his distrust and fear of the Americanization of English society.

Rachel, funny and clever as she is, does not always read things right, and she has the propensity to violence which links her to another American adventuress, the alarming Mrs Hurtle in *The Way We Live Now*. Mrs Hurtle, at some point in her unclear past, has shot a man; Rachel eventually fulfils her threat to stick a knife into Mr Moss, though the scene is more reminiscent of comic opera than *Tosca*. Time and again, American violence and amorality are blamed as the corrupting force in Irish politics. Gerald O'Mahony, though he is stupid and weak rather than unprincipled, stands for an insidiously spreading disease.

When he began his book he hated rent from his very soul. The difficulty he saw was this: what should you do with the property when you took it away from the landlords? He quite saw his way to taking it away; if only a new order would come from heaven for the creation of a special set of farmers who should be wedded to their land by some celestial matrimony, and should clearly be in possession of it without the perpetration of any injustice. He did not quite see his way to this by his own lights, and therefore he went to the British Museum. When a man wants to write a book full of unassailable facts, he always goes to the British Museum. In this way Mr O'Mahony purposed to spend his autumn instead of speaking at the Rotunda, because it suited him to live in London rather than in Dublin.[17]

The world is being turned upside down by careerist women and obstructionist MPs in London, by pseudo-scholars who – like Karl Marx – use the institutions of English life, such as the British Museum, to subvert it from inside, and by the boycott and the Land League in Ireland. The social integument is breaking up. For this Trollope found the perfect metaphor, in an aspect of Land League activity he had heard about on his last Irish journeys: the practice of 'stopping the hunt'. The end of deference politics in Ireland was vividly signalled by the way that fox-hunting was attacked, partly by the use of the boycott, partly by obstructing the course of the hunt (a topic keenly addressed by Irish social historians).[18] For Trollope in the 1840s, hunting in Ireland had been a passage to social integration. The sport had far fewer elitist associations than in England (and still does), entered into with excitement by any farmer who could saddle up anything that could jump a wall. None the less, it was the pastime of the propertied: access to land lay behind it, in more ways than one. Over three chapters of The Landleaguers, Trollope describes how a hunt is stopped, and the traumatic effects on Black Tom Daly, the strange, moody enthusiast who is the local Master. To compare the treatment of the hunt in Phineas Finn, or the easy give-and-take of life in the west of Ireland as portrayed in The Kellys and the O'Kellys, is to measure the distance which Trollope had put between himself and the Eden of his youth.

This was a conscious effort. Because The Landleaguers is often thinly written, crudely characterized and hastily plotted, and because he died before completing it, critical opinion has passed over the novel.

It can, however, be read as a deliberate unsaying of all Trollope had earlier said about Ireland. Small but careful connections are made back to the world of his earliest novels. When describing the horrific murders of a whole family (based on the Joyce murders at Maamtrasna, which happened during Trollope's visit in August 1882), he calls the family 'Kelly' and slams home the reference to his own early novel by stressing the name again and again, and discussing them as a 'clan'. When Florian is shot from behind a hedge, just as Lord Mountmorris was actually murdered earlier that year, Trollope meticulously relates the deed and the place to the disaster of the 1840s. 'The place was one where the commencement had been made of a cutting in the road during the potato failure of 1846.'[19] Thus the atrocity of 1882 is linked back to the horrors of the 1840s. For all his Providentialist writing afterwards, Trollope now knew that one inheritance of that nightmare was the implacable hatred sustained by Irish-American nationalism.

This is not the only way in which *The Landleaguers* is deliberately counterpointed against Trollope's earlier views of Ireland. The tolerant, gentlemanly, older Catholic priest who cannot control the corrupting zealotry of his younger colleagues is called 'Father Giles' – a direct reference to the incumbent of Ballymoy, and a sign that the old order has passed for the worse. Instead, the vulnerable convert is taught to lie. One of the oldest Protestant shibboleths about Catholicism, often put to use in Ireland's past, is that Catholics are taught it is no sin to lie to Protestants. In *The Landleaguers* Trollope defiantly adopts this ancient bigotry, pivoting the first half of the book around the attempt to make Florian tell the truth about the flooding of his father's land. The concept of truth and lies is central to the book; the words recur relentlessly to point up (intentionally or not) the English incomprehension of Ireland. In the *Irish Sketch-Book* Thackeray had asked, 'Where is the truth to be got in this country?' and answered himself that there were two truths, the Protestant truth and the Catholic truth.[20] Trollope, who revered Thackeray and had recently written his *Life*, took this a stage further. When Edith instructs her brother to 'tell the truth and be a gentleman', she is encapsulating a fundamental Trollopian principle, but it seems simplistic in a world turned upside down. And in 1882 Ireland, which had supplied so many gentlemen for Trollope's fiction, was past producing the genuine article. There was instead what Trollope called, in a chapter title, the 'new aristocracy' of the Land League.

If *The Landleaguers* is seen this way, its fractured effect may stem not from its incompleteness but from a deliberate representation of a fracturing society. It may be thought that the inconsistent way Florian talks – sometimes in a sullen brogue, sometimes like a young gentleman – is a sign of Trollope's failing concentration, but it seems more probable that he is using an instability of language to indicate an instability of character, and an effort on the boy's part to 'belong' to the native Irish. (Edith puts it sharply: 'He has got it into his head that the Catholics are a downtrodden people, and therefore he will be one of them.'[21]) Irish cadences, for which Trollope retained all his old sensitivity of ear, are used to convey deviousness and insincerity, where once they had been used to show cleverness and guile: this is particularly clear in the exchanges with the two girls by the roadside after Florian's murder. Above all, Irish intelligence, always a preoccupation of Trollope's, has now itself been corrupted, and turned to the sinister uses of the boycott:

It must be acknowledged that throughout the south and west of Ireland the quickness and perfection with which this science was understood and practised was very much to the credit of the intelligence of the people. We can understand that boycotting should be studied in Yorkshire, and practised, – after an experience of many years. Laying on one side for the moment all ideas as to the honesty and expediency of the measure, we think that Yorkshire might in half a century learn how to boycott its neighbours. A Yorkshire man might boycott a Lancashire man, or Lincoln might boycott Nottingham. It would require much teaching; – many books would have to be written, and an infinite amount of heavy slow imperfect practice would follow. But County Mayo and County Galway rose to the requirements of the art almost in a night! Gradually we Englishmen learned to know in a dull glimmering way what they were about; but at the first whisper of the word all Ireland knew how to ruin itself. This was done readily by people of the poorer class, – without any gifts of education, and certainly the immoderate practice of the science displays great national intelligence.[22]

By the time he wrote *The Landleaguers*, Trollope saw only one of Thackeray's Irish truths. Like Thackeray, he had woven Irish figures into his great tapestries of English life: in the world depicted in *Pendennis* or *Vanity Fair*, no less than in *Phineas Finn*, Ireland was an apparently inseparable part of Britain under the Union. Ireland and Irish experience were so central to Trollope's early life, and to his imagination, that he could not conceive of Englishness without it. The admission that the Union was neither ideal nor eternal was unacceptable. Hence the convolutions of Trollope's attitude to the Famine, and the way that the argument of *Castle Richmond* is destabilized and subverted by much of what the novel actually represents. Hence too his determination in *The Landleaguers* to adhere to a version of landlordism which relies alternately on the defeatism of survivalist economics, and the idealizing of a class and a caste in crisis.

Trollope had written Ireland into his panoramic vision of Victorian English life, but in his last year, and his last novel, he saw Irish nationalism beginning to write Ireland out of the Union. This would prove such a successful operation that the Irish dimension of Trollope's English identity has tended to recede: forgotten along with the British identity of the Victorian Irish middle class, Catholic as well as Protestant, who produced generations of Phineas Finns. But the vehemence of *The Landleaguers*, and also its uncharacteristically ungenerous vision, is a stark reminder of how much the possession of Ireland meant to its author, in his art and his life. It is the reaction of someone who feels that something is being taken from him: something which he discovered and possessed in his youth, something which became part of his achieved personality (that achieved personality celebrated in the *Autobiography*), something which he treasured and loved and celebrated. It is, yet again, the fear of the many heroes in his books (including his Irish books) who are threatened with the loss of their habitation. Trollope stands for many Victorian Englishmen and women who came to Ireland and found themselves excited, enthused, renewed by it.[23] Yet in his writings about Ireland, and the way Ireland refracted itself through his fiction, there is a passionate cross-flow of contradictions. One of his most pronounced personal characteristics was, perhaps, his inconsistency:[24] contemporaries who encountered him often expressed surprise that the man they met – with his loudness, embarrassingness, bluster, apparent insensitivity – could write the marvellous books they read. Perhaps in the end, it was Trollope the man who pronounced on Ireland; but at the same time Ireland did more than is often recognized to produce Trollope the writer, and this is reflected in the shade as well as the light.

9

Prints on the Scene:
Elizabeth Bowen and the
Landscape of Childhood

The effort to define congruent literary geography, as suggested earlier in this book, has been a recurring preoccupation in Irish cultural commentary – and it is not over yet. A mystifyingly crude version was produced in 1993 by the editor of the shadowy Aubane Historical Society's eccentric *North Cork Anthology*. The contents page includes the name of 'Elizabeth Dorothea Cole Bowen CBE' – with a line drawn through it. The editor explains laboriously that this is to show that though some people may think Elizabeth Bowen is an Irish writer, this is not the case. 'She was English . . . Most of her novels are still in print due to an English demand for them.' Even more damningly, 'she was not a North Cork writer either, in the sense of being a product of North Cork society, or of being interested in it or writing about it. But since the *Cork Examiner* keeps on about her, we include her in this anthology, in deleted form, in order to explain why she does not belong to it.'[1]

This approach recalls the old Irish political tradition of recording an abstaining vote in person, or one of the delectable absurdist arguments developed by Flann O'Brien. But it also reflects what Louis MacNeice called the sheep and goats approach to Irish qualifications, since Bowen is excluded from north Cork sensibilities because of her ancestry, her part-English residence and her work for the British government during the Second World War. (For good measure, the anthologist also describes Bowen's biographer Patricia Craig as English, though she was born and bred in Belfast.) Bowen herself, who crossed and re-crossed the border between Britain and Ireland constantly, said, 'I regard myself as an Irish novelist. As long as I can remember I've been intensely conscious of being Irish.' The texture, as much as the content, of her writing bears this out: an Irish ear and an Irish sensibility pervade many of her novels and – even more particularly – her short stories.[2] But for at least one self-appointed arbiter, neither her own testimony nor the nature of her fiction constitutes admissible evidence.

It might seem parochial to raise the issue at all, at a time when Bowen's reputation is worldwide and growing. Her novels have come out of the shadow of predecessors and successors alike, and she is seen for the original she was. *Pace* the Aubane Historical Society, critics like Seamus Deane, W. J. McCormack and Declan Kiberd have recently given her work detailed consideration as part of the corpus of Irish literature, and it can take its place in a distinctly Irish tradition. Her writing comes freighted with sensuous language, baroque humour, oblique psychological insights, penetrating moral issues and overall strangeness. It is also marked by an uncanny ability to re-create childhood, and a sense of place experienced with a paranormal intensity. It is, therefore, worth considering whether she is, at one level, a 'regional writer' of the kind reclaimed by summer schools all around Ireland. This may seem ironic, since her novels are often identified by their sophistication and metropolitanism. But the Cork she knew haunts her fiction: *The Last September* preserves north Cork during the Anglo-Irish War, *The House in Paris* pivots around a long section set in the city's Anglo-Irish villadom, *A World of Love* is rooted deep in the Irish rural landscape during a haunted heatwave, while short stories like 'Summer Night' should take a predominant place in any Irish collection. The key to analysing Bowen's idiosyncratic 'regionalism', however, lies in her autobiographical writing – particularly the two books she wrote in wartime, about her Cork and her Dublin. And this in turn raises the question of how far her writings about herself are – as with so many Irish writers – half-concealed meditations on Irish history.

Much the best known is *Bowen's Court*, an autobiographical history, delineating a terrain and anatomizing relationships as well as re-creating a place. The passionate feeling behind it sometimes tips it over into sentimentality, and the more risky and over-the-top passages do not always come off, but the sense of familiar life and the love of place put it in a long tradition of celebrations. As she herself knew, she was 'manifestly a writer for whom places loom large'.[3] Her location in Ireland was on one level uncertain: as seventeenth-century planters, 'my family got their position and drew their power from a situation that shows an inherent wrong'.[4] The landscape was, therefore, haunted:

though one can be callous in Ireland one cannot be wholly opaque or material. An unearthly disturbance works in the spirit; reason can never reconcile one to life; nothing allays the wants one cannot explain. In whatever direction, the spirit is always steadily moving, or rather steadily being carried as though the country were a ship. The light, the light-consumed distances, that air of intense existence about the empty country, the quick flux to decay in houses, cities and people, the great part played in society by the dead and by the idea of death and above all, the recurring futilities of hope all work for eternal against temporal things. These work for inspiration against method and make a country of loudly-professing sinners and spoiled saints.[5]

Much of her writing concerns an effort to define location and establish the illusion of permanence – in a world where she was highly conscious of being the last of a line, in insecure possession of a house. (It is, perhaps, no accident that one of her Irish books is the history of that great Dublin institution, the Shelbourne Hotel.) 'Descendancy' was not, however, an issue to whinge about, and she writes very sarcastically about people who do. *Bowen's Court* is also notable for not shirking the fact that her family history was based on dispossession and privilege, albeit three centuries before. 'It would be very presumptuous to say that the Bowens have been popular around Farahy. I can only say, we could not have been better treated if we had been popular – our hardnesses have been pardoned, our vagaries suffered, our dicta accepted with reservations so tactful that we are not aware of them and our characters thoroughly understood. (I only realize how much this is the case when I am in England, and feel lonely.)'[6]

If *Bowen's Court* is an act of pietas (and fits into the old Irish tradition of memorializing and celebrating a place), it is also an act of remembrance, located in a history and a culture where remembering can open very raw wounds. Dealing with ancestors like hers, even 'colouring their outlines in', can raise particular local problems. 'Having looked back at them steadily, I begin to notice, if I cannot define, the pattern they unconsciously went on to make. And I can see that

that pattern has its relation to the outside more definite pattern of history.' But she claims that this relation is 'unconscious', because her family was 'unhistoric'.[7] Perhaps she has to say this, as a proleptic anticipation of the Aubane Historical Society. Irish history stands silently behind a reflection of Bowen's on the impossible pain of remembering accurately:

Raw history, in its implications, is unnerving: and even so, it only chronicles the survivors. A defeat accompanied every victory: faiths failed: millions went under leaving behind no trace. If the greater part of the past had not been, mercifully, forgotten, the effect upon our modern sensibility would be unbearable; it would not be only injustice and bloodshed that we should have to remember but the dismay, the apathy, the brutalizing humiliation of people for whom there was no break.[8]

The large segments of Irish history built into *Bowen's Court*, which alternate with the family's story, are not restricted to the Ascendancy world; they owe much to her tutelage by Sean O'Faolain, and her own reading of Stephen Gwynn and Edmund Curtis. There is a deliberate attempt to be fair-minded (as she claims for herself); she manages to be both astringent and sympathetic about her own caste, while generally sarcastic about the British government. Sometimes there is an improbable echo of Daniel Corkery, possibly imbibed through O'Faolain, but finished with a Bowen twist: 'Meanwhile the Gaelic culture ran underground, with its ceaseless poetry of lament. (Gaelic was spoken in the kitchens and fields and in untouched country the settlers did not know.) It has taken the decline of the Anglo-Irish to open to them the poetry of regret; only dispossessed people know their land in the dark.'[9]

Elsewhere, in a key essay which helped launch that essential journal *The Bell*, she tried to present Bowen's Court as somewhere which could be redefined in independent Ireland – to bring people together, to be 'as never before, sociable', to 'scrap the past, with its bitterness and barriers, and all meet, throwing in what we have'.[10] In Ireland, of course, the past cannot be scrapped, as she knew. But she also knew that Irish life, like Irish literature, is a matter of diverse growths from tangled roots, and that local stocks can be equally tough and enduring even if they stem from very different origins. Indeed, any study of Irish regional society shows, besides the celebrated diversities, a pattern of similarities in cultural attitudes, social practices, agrarian habits, family structure and much else.

The permanence that Bowen sought, in writing about her Irish past (while the world exploded at war all around her), required an exploration of memory – the only place where, as Proust had taught her, permanence resides. A recognized landscape would take her there: that sheltered Farahy landscape from where, she wrote, 'personal pain evaporates, as history evaporates'[11] – the dream of forgetting again. Bowen's Court stood, she wrote in an afterword to her history, like an island of peace; but 'wave after wave of war news' broke against it from the wireless, and cloudy threats hung all around it, as they had done in the Anglo-Irish War twenty years before. Memory was to preserve the sustaining part of identity: as Bowen's Court evaporated, so she would preserve it. 'The indefinite ghosts of the past, of the dead who lived here and pursued the same routine of life in these walls add something, a sort of order, a reason for living, to every minute and hour': or so she wrote in her generalized essay 'The Big House'.[12] In the afterword to *Bowen's Court*, describing the atmosphere of the house one wartime Christmas, this idea is developed into a passage of pure Anglo-Irish Gothic: the dead family as Irish history.

The empty parts of the house, piled up in the winter darkness, palpably and powerfully existed. I was not conscious of the lives of the dead there. It may be that, like so many writers, I have not much imagination to spare. But the unconsciousness – the unknowingness, the passivity – in which so much of those finished lives had been passed did somehow reach and enter my own. What runs on most through a family living in one place is a continuous, semi-physical dream. Above this dream-level successive lives show their tips, their little conscious formations of will and thought. With the end of each generation, the lives that submerged here were absorbed again. With each death, the air of the place had thickened: it had been added to. The dead do not need to visit Bowen's Court rooms – as I said, we had no ghosts in that house – because they already permeated them. Their extinct senses were present in lights and forms. The land outside Bowen's Court windows left prints on my ancestors' eyes that looked out: perhaps their eyes left, also, prints on the scene? If so, those prints were part of the scene to me.[13]

The landscape of memory is here a consolation and a refuge, but it is also – like the bombed London streetscape which she evoked so powerfully in her contemporaneous wartime fiction – a land inhabited by the waking dead. And at the same time as writing about Cork, she was writing about Dublin, in a far shorter book called *Seven Winters*. Here, the consolations of memory fail her, and the terrain of recalled experience is markedly different – for reasons of 'raw history' as well as personal trauma.

One of Bowen's characteristically defiant pronouncements was: 'I am dead against art's being self-expression.'[14] She apparently did not apply this dictum to autobiography: twice in her life she devoted herself to extended autobiographical works, once in the early 1940s with *Bowen's Court* and *Seven Winters* and again just before her death in the early 1970s, with the unfinished *Pictures and Conversations*. In between, she reflected on the genre in an essay published in 1951:

whereas autobiography used to be based on statement, now it derives from query, being tentative rather than positive, no longer didactic but open-minded. It is mobile, exploratory. This may come from the fact that today it is less often written in old age; it is, rather, the work of early or late maturity. Is it not at this point, about halfway through the journey, that we do all have an instinct to pause, look back, and reflect? The autobiographer's impulse has synchronized with that of his fellow-man; he is speaking not only to but for his contemporaries.[15]

She was speaking about herself. She did feel the autobiographical impulse at the very end of her life, setting down a series of penetrating and self-analytical reflections when she knew she was dying of cancer. But the much more substantial surge of autobiography had come thirty years before, in the early years of the war – an experience which supercharged both her emotional and creative experience. Out of it came *Bowen's Court*, evoked with a passionate desire to belong and to claim a territory. But it was also written from a vantage of displacement, which was not only to do with the collapse of buildings around her in London: she felt she had been born and lived her life in transit. Her novels often depict women constantly on the move, armoured by a shell of worldliness which conceals a past of dammed emotions and

lost attachments. Mobility was an attribute which she characteristically used both as a strength and a disadvantage. Asking herself why
people never inquired about the importance of place in her writing,
she speculated that it might be because she was not obviously attached
to a region: Bowen terrain was thought to be the territory of displacement, somewhere where the moorings had slipped. 'Bowen topography,' she wrote, 'has so far as I know been untouched by research.
Should anyone give it a thought after I am dead, that will be too late.
To it, only I hold the key.' Yet 'since I started writing, I have been
welding together an inner landscape, assembled anything but at random. But if not at random, under the influence of what? I suppose
necessity, and what accompanies that. A writer needs to have at
command, and to have recourse to, a recognizable world, geographi-
cally consistent and having for him or her a super-reality.'[16]

Through necessity, she had constructed her own super-real inner
landscape, or so she was saying. But there are classic Bowen evasions
below the surface. The idea that she was attached to no region ignores
the 'places' she had already framed so powerfully in *Bowen's Court*
and *Seven Winters*. In those books she was in search of permanence,
and permanence, as she said, is an attribute of recalled places. She is
both present and absent; in *Seven Winters* the painful directness of,
for instance, the memories of her mother, which she recalled in the
fragments written at the end of her life, is excluded. In *Bowen's Court*
the house and the ancestors do duty for Bowen herself; in *Seven
Winters* the question of influence is left even more implicit. We are
meant, at most, to infer the ways in which that background made this
writer. Twenty years later, writing an introduction for an American
edition in 1962, she was prepared to make the connection more
directly:

Seven Winters could be called a fragment of autobiography. At the same time,
I look on it as a self-contained work, for it is as much of my life story as I
intend to write – that is, to write directly. Through most fiction is to be traced
the thread of the author's own experiences, no doubt. But the early years of
childhood contain most others: as we now know they are in part the cause of,
in part the key to, what is to follow. No years, subsequently, are so acute. The
happenings in *Seven Winters* are those I shall remain certain of till I die. Here

is the external world as I first saw it. As a marvel it was at the time sufficient. Something of the marvel, however, something of the amazement, recurs when I write or read.[17]

This tells us how we are to read it: in terms of externality, appreciating marvels that are to be sufficient within themselves. *Seven Winters* is a masterpiece of non-information: tentative, mobile, exploratory, as Bowen said autobiography should be. It is also misleading. She tells us that her childhood memories are vaguer and start later than most people's; but even that is disproved on every page. We are deliberately disorientated from the start: so simple a fact as the aspect of Herbert Place (where her parents lived) is wrong – it looks much more south than east.

But she must have thought it was east because she is mapping a winter city, where light is always low. Born in 1899, Bowen spent her first seven years, Persephone-like, between summery, abundant Cork (Demeter's kingdom: absent mothers again) and darker Dublin. Even at its most comforting, it holds a Beckettian uncertainty, reflected in language that sometimes reads like proto-Beckett. 'So having been born where I had been born in a month in which that house did not exist, I felt that I had intruded upon some no-place.' She is not going to tell us about Farahy, the 'ragged blue line of the Ballyhouras flowing towards the horizon'. She is not going to smuggle in Cork, as she does into *The House in Paris* and *The Heat of the Day*. She is going to write about Dublin, which she had described in 1938 as 'a city in which almost every subject is controversial'. And also alien. 'Dublin does not represent Ireland; she is one aspect of it; she stands, or had stood, for wealth, for the imposition of power, for the generally European element that has made itself felt but never been quite absorbed. Not for nothing is she the capital of a country in which blood runs to the head; life here has always been lived at high pressure; everybody is highly articulate; this has always been a city of "characters" where nothing gets done impersonally.'[18] And yet when Bowen writes about Dublin only a few years later, in *Seven Winters*, this dimension is eliminated.

Seven Winters is about Dublin from 1900 to 1907, as she saw it. It is – or could be – the city delineated in *Ulysses*, in the years of royal

visits, demonstrations against the Boer War, the foundation of Sinn
Féin, the Abbey Theatre and the revolutionary 1903 'Wyndham' Land
Act which gave Bowen's father his job as legal examiner of the titles
to estates which were being sold to their tenants. Henry Bowen, in the
years she describes, was devoted to a huge study of statutory land
purchase in Ireland, from its origins in the Land Acts of the 1880s
through to the time he was writing. Working for the Land Commission,
he was determined to produce the last word, the ultimate authority,
the full analysis of this process. By a superb irony, he himself outlived
his subject: because with the drastic changes after independence the
Land Commission changed its basis and was eventually wound up,
while Henry Bowen's great work became at a stroke irrelevant – 'of
historic interest only' – well before he died in 1930.[19] Thus another
narrative of Irish history became a ghost story. The symbolism is
all the more inescapable because Henry was not only recording the
workings of a system that institutionalized the decline of his own class,
but was also defining the work of the Land Commission just at the
moment it was passing on. And this is exactly what his daughter was
doing in 1941: defining and summoning up and re-creating Bowen's
Court itself, at the historical point when its symbolic continuance was
an open question. History is happening all around. But she barely
allows it in – except as an intimation of threat, in the emptiness of Upper
Mount Street and environs. 'Perhaps a child smells history without
knowing it. I did not *know* that I looked at the tomb of fashion.'[20]

So she excises even her father's Land Commission work, this perfect
metaphor for declining Ascendancy, from *Seven Winters*; the child's
eye remains beadily fixed on the patch of winter sunlight, the drawing-
room lamp, the white muff temporarily lost. Outside is irrelevant:
probably because it is (or will be) threatening. She fears that something
terrible exists at the unknown end of Sackville Street. She has a claus-
trophobic terror of unknown terrain: 'a charnel fear, of grave dust and
fungus dust . . . something might shut on me, never to let me out again,
something might fall on me, never to let me through. I had heard of
poverty-rotted houses that might at any moment crumble over one's
head.' Houses in the Dublin slums had indeed collapsed at this time,
causing a public outcry about the property investments of city council-
lors.[21] But the idea of a crumbling city of dead souls also anticipates

her fascination with Rider Haggard's fantasy novel *She*, which she wrote about and used for perhaps her greatest short story, 'Mysterious Kôr': imagining wartime London as a fabulous ruined city. And it also forecasts the destruction of London itself around her in the Blitz – happening as she wrote *Seven Winters*. Her two cities are joined. This indicates that she knew more than she let on, while maintaining the delicately distanced perspective of *Seven Winters*.

It is worth repeating what she wrote of the country around Farahy: 'from this landscape personal pain evaporates, as history evaporates'. That was not true of the streets of Dublin, as she knew. In that earlier (1938) piece on Dublin, she wrote 'Emotional memory here, has so much power that the past and the present seem to be lived simultaneously. In Dublin, as in the rest of Ireland, if you do not know the past you only know the half of anyone's mind.' Yet that is exactly what she is going to avoid: connecting past and present. We are vigorously kept out. She hears of the Russo-Japanese War, and thinks of war 'escaping from the locked strong-room of history into the present', an image that sharply recalls Lady Morgan's metaphor of the secret library where the dangerous story of Irish history lies waiting to be read.[22] But for her, history will not touch Ireland. The little girl is led by her father through Leinster House; the adult writer deliberately suppresses the reflection that it is now (1941) the seat of an independent Irish parliament. She is determined, it seems, to avoid 'raw history' and its unnerving quality: the evidence, so clearly embedded in the Irish landscape, that history forgets the losers (whether 'mercifully' or not).

Why is her sense of this so intense at the time of writing, in the early 1940s? Probably because she knew what she was doing. At this point in her public life (as an air-raid warden in central London) and in her private existence (conducting an affair with Sean O'Faolain, meeting Irish intellectuals and nationalists) she was highly conscious of raw history. After she had cleared the ground with this surge of autobiography, recalled in wartime London, she embarked upon her high-octane novel about spying and allegiance, *The Heat of the Day*, with its key section set in Ireland. And in *Bowen's Court*, written alongside *Seven Winters*, historical context is thickly drawn in: it is part of her argument that Big Houses like that one could transcend their roots in an oppressive past and be used – unashamedly – in independent Ireland to bring people together. They were islands (a favourite Bowen image): they should be connected to a mainland. The intellectual context in which she began to write about her youth, her family and Irishness should be noted. At this time too another Irish Protestant living and working in England, Louis MacNeice, confronted his own traditions and interrogated Ireland:

> One feels that here at least one can
> Do local work which is not at the world's mercy
> And that on this tiny stage with luck a man
> Might see the end of one particular action.[23]

'It is self-deception, of course,' continued MacNeice. Bowen will go on to ask, in *Bowen's Court*, 'Must an undivided Ireland be always a shadow? Must anything else be always too much to hope?' 'To meet, and throw in what we have! How long, after all, does it take to belong somewhere, without apology? Surely 300 years is enough?'[24] 'Undivided' is not a reference to the physical border with Northern Ireland, as much as to mental and social frontiers, which she wanted, at this stage, broken down. It was not a mood that lasted, but it was there in the very early 1940s. She was reading and writing about Joyce in 1941; she was close to O'Faolain and the circle round *The Bell*; she was sending back reports on neutral Ireland to the Ministry of Information (warmly defending neutrality, as an Irishwoman, despite the Aubane Historical Society's accusations of espionage for a foreign power); *Seven Winters* was published by Yeats's sisters' Cuala Press. (Its superb evasions possibly owe something to the poet's own auto-biography, as well as, obviously, to Proust, whom she had read avidly long before.) Thus the circumstances of its writing are rooted in an acutely Irish context. But all these elements are rigorously excluded from her treatment: the present, the history, the revolutions that have intervened between 1907 and 1941 are not to be mentioned. It gives the book an eerie intensity: we read it sealed inside a time-capsule that is also the self-referencing world of a seven-year-old's mind.

In fact, *Seven Winters* (much more than *Bowen's Court*) puts into practice the precepts she laid down for writing autobiography in that

1951 essay she wrote for the *Saturday Review of Literature*. It should not be 'clogged by too much analysis'. It should obey the necessary selectivity of memory – 'arbitrary, tricky, patchy'. 'Out of impressions, no less than thought and feeling, is the texture of an existence spun. To ignore sensation would be to fail in telling the whole, which is the true story.'[25]

But is this an excuse? What does she give us instead of facts and history? The child's Dublin is the model of cities, like Italo Calvino's Venice; inferior imitations are scattered around the world, just as she supposes the word 'island' is a corruption of 'Ireland'. In the Bowens' Georgian *quartier*, brass plates announce that this is where real people really live. Every house, she thinks, as a matter of course announces who lives there (and what letters they have after their name). If an occasional Dublin house lacks this attribute, it means the owner wants 'to envelop himself in mystery'. So when she goes to London, it is a great shock to find rows and rows of houses with no brass plates. Therefore no one cares who lives there; they are all nonentities. This connects, I think, to her celebrated reflection on Irish superiority:

Through a thinning of mist I just see the colonnades of the Bank of Ireland, that had been Our Own Parliament once. I never looked up Sackville Street without pleasure, for I was told it was the widest street in the world. Just as Phoenix Park, grey-green distance beyond the Zoo, was the largest park in the world. These superlatives pleased me almost too much: my earliest pride of race was attached to them. And my most endemic pride in my own country was, for some years, founded on a mistake: my failing to have a nice ear for vowel sounds, and the Anglo-Irish slurred, hurried way of speaking made me take the words 'Ireland' and 'island' to be synonymous. Thus, all other countries quite surrounded by water took (it appeared) their generic name from ours. It seemed fine to live in a country that was a prototype. England, for instance, was '*an* ireland' (or, a sub-Ireland) – an imitation. Then I learned that England was not even 'an ireland', having failed to detach herself from the flanks of Scotland and Wales. Vaguely, as a Unionist child, I conceived that our politeness to England must be a form of pity.[26]

Later, through one of her English governesses who 'vibrates a little' to all the strangeness around her, the child 'begins to perceive that Ireland was *not* the norm, the usual thing'. It is a shock, because locality is linked to knowing who you are, and who other people are: the old Bowen theme of possession. And Dublin – *her* Dublin – is an Ascendancy possession. 'Our own parliament' is Grattan's eighteenth-century College Green, not the future Leinster House. The Ascendancy know they are apart, and like it that way. Catholics are darkly, sensually different; there is an unspoken sexual aspect to it. The following passage should be read in the light of her love affair with O'Faolain and the statements she was issuing in *The Bell* and *Bowen's Court* about 'belonging' and unity in Ireland: it may sound differently then.

It was not until after the end of those seven winters that I understood that we Protestants were a minority, and that the unquestioned rules of our being came, in fact, from the closeness of a minority world. Roman Catholics were spoken of by my father and mother with a courteous detachment that gave them, even, no myth. I took the existence of Roman Catholics for granted but met few and was not interested in them. They were, simply, 'the others', whose world lay alongside ours but never touched. As to the difference between the two religions, I was too discreet to ask questions – if I wanted to know. This appeared to share a delicate, awkward aura with those two other differences – of sex, of class. So quickly, in a child's mind, does prudery seed itself and make growth that I remember, even, an almost sexual shyness on the subject of Roman Catholics. I walked with hurried step and averted cheek past porticos of churches that were 'not ours' [territory again], uncomfortably registering in my nostrils the pungent, unlikely smell that came round curtains, through swinging doors. On Sundays, the sounds of the bells of all kinds of churches rolled in a sort of unison round the Dublin sky, and the currents of people quitting their homes to worship seemed to be made alike by one human habit, such as of going to dinner. But on week-days the 'other' bells, with their (to my ear) alien, searching insistence, had the sky and the Dublin echoes all to themselves. This predisposition to frequent prayer bespoke, to me, some incontinence of the soul.[27]

Catholics are 'other', in touch with an elemental world of instinct and passion: unlike the stylish but immobile Protestants, they can dance. This childhood is as constrained as the topography of streets around Merrion Square; its Protestantism is unashamed and she is not going

– once again – to draw any explicit conclusions for the future (or the present). After all, Molesworth Hall, where those dancing lessons take place, is the centre of the Masonic Order; and the book's last note is a redoubtably Protestant hymn, her favourite, sung at the end of a winter Sunday.

It is no accident, either, that 'Shall We Gather at the River' is about reunion in paradise. This is the autobiography of a child who will lose her father to madness at seven, and her mother to cancer at thirteen; who will then make a career in 'withstood emotion'; and who compares the existence of the Anglo-Irish to that of 'only children', missing out on things.[28] *Seven Winters*, in flashes rather than sustained combustion, illuminates themes to be reprised in stories like 'The Tommy Crans' and 'Coming Home'. Insecurity and exclusion are there throughout – not so much from the other Dublin, ironically irrelevant (Bowen learned about the Irish Literary Revival only when she went to school in England), but from parents who will leave, and a landscape liable to tilt, slide, founder. No wonder that she worried, on seeing the strange new urban topography of the English south coast, '*Would* it last?'[29] Because her Dublin, though you would not guess it from *Seven Winters*, disappeared less than ten years after she left it. In 1916 one of those local canal bridges which mark out the boundaries of her childhood walks was the scene of an insurgent ambush and bloody carnage. All that followed proved that it was not true (as she thinks in *Seven Winters*) that 'children are perishable': the adult world goes under, while the child survives through what she calls elsewhere a 'campaign of not noticing'.

But she notices everything. She is not taught to read, for a sinister reason: there is a family dread of taxing the brain, because of a fear of hereditary mental instability. So she scans the streets, the tables, the chairs, the muslin slip-covers with their pattern of harps and sham-rocks, the essences of an Ascendancy Dublin now as dead as Tyre and Sidon. Hermione Lee has noted how women writers have traditionally described learning to read as a complex, secretive process, intimately linking places and associations with the act of reading; she cites Bowen's 1946 essay 'Out of a Book', but the bookless child of *Seven Winters* bears witness to this in every line.[30] Later Bowen describes her heightened state of mind during the war, when *Seven Winters* was written: 'I felt one with, and just like, everyone else. I hardly knew where I stopped and somebody else began. The violent destruction of solid things, the explosion of the illusion that prestige, power and permanence attach to bulk and weight, left all of us, equally, heady and disembodied. Walls went down; and we felt, if not knew, each other. We all lived in a state of lucid abnormality.'[31] This is highly relevant to *Seven Winters*, because it describes the consciousness in which she was enveloped during her early childhood, of being seamlessly attached to known people and a known world. But she conveys a tension, a feeling of imminent threat, of observing adults who are not, eventually, to be relied upon. With an unintended pathos, she reinvents her mother's feelings for her. And the traumatic moment in that book is when the realization comes that she is in fact not part of everyone else, but alone and different.

It is a moment she keeps trying to isolate. On one occasion, she puts it when her first governess made her understand 'that I was I'; elsewhere she names the moment as happening during the Russo-Japanese War when she is playing at the Royal Dublin Society gardens. She hears a clock strike and realizes that at that moment, elsewhere, not in Dublin, people are fighting each other. The five-year-old Bowen is climbing the grandstand; somewhere else life is continuing in another reality. It is a prevision of the parallel worlds which she will evoke in *Bowen's Court*. Finally, in *Seven Winters*, she decides that the key moment of self-differentiation comes when she sees herself in a mirror at a children's party – awkward, red-faced, tortured into a terrible and unsuitable dress, looking utterly unlike her own vision of herself. One illusion is cracked. Others follow, and at seven she and her mother flee the broken-down father and the watery winter city. The fairy-tale childhood ends with a brutal expulsion; but she will not make it a conventional closure:

How shall I write 'The End' to a book which is about the essence of a beginning? When I was seven years old, Herbert Place was given up; my father's mental illness had to be fought alone; my mother and I were ordered to England. The end of our Dublin house, in actual time, places no stop to my memories. Only a few of these have been written here. I have halted (not stopped) in the drawing-room, for it was there that, with my first comprehension of life as being other than mine, the second phase of my memories had its start.[32]

And at this point, what happens? She is at last allowed to read. Received ideas will invade the world of pure sensation. But we should remember her later reflection: 'something of the marvel, something of the amazement, recurs when I write or read'. The seven-year-old sensationalist, at once flamboyant and guarded, will endure.

So it is this book, her Dublin book, that charts the beginning. A few years after she wrote it, Bowen produced a penetrating essay on Le Fanu's *Uncle Silas*, stressing its concealed Irishness and pointing out that it 'plays on one constant factor – our childish fears': 'These leave their work at the base of our natures, and are never to be rationalized away. Two things are terrible in childhood: helplessness (being in other people's power) and apprehension – the apprehension that something is being concealed from us because it is too bad to be told.'[33] Bowen's idiosyncratic autobiographies relate the uncertain location of her childhood to the larger uncertainties of Irish life, and do so partly by suggesting, and partly by avoiding, concealed narratives of Irish historical experience. If Cork has stood for reassurance, for 'scrapping history', for the evaporation of pain, Dublin has schooled her in evasions, in negotiating fears, in analysing social stratagems and cultural oppositions, in not making impossible choices: in all the perceptions, abilities and insecurities that would make her a great Irish novelist.

10

Selling Irish Childhoods:
Frank McCourt and Gerry Adams

The recall of childhood and early youth is invariably both the most vivid and the most convincing section of any autobiography – and of any autobiographical novel, whether it is *A la recherche du temps perdu* or *Thy Tears Might Cease*. The autobiographer is not yet worried about too many hostages to fortune; memories are preserved in the surreal laser-light of first experience; over everything hovers the sense of a time that (as Flann O'Brien mercilessly mocked in *An Béal Bocht/The Poor Mouth*) will not come again. And Irish childhoods have long delivered this magic with a particular style, if also a particular deviousness. Elizabeth Bowen's *Seven Winters* has already been discussed, but one might add Frank O'Connor's *An Only Child*, Muiris Ó Súilleabháin's *Fiche Blian ag Fás/Twenty years A-Growing*, Patricia Lynch's *A Storyteller's Childhood* and W. B. Yeats's *Reveries over Childhood and Youth*, all classics of the genre.

The idea of both Ireland and the writer's youth as adjacent and interdependent lost demesnes can appeal at all social levels, even if it is most readily associated with a crumbling Big House – recently exploited by Annabel Davis-Goff's *Walled Gardens*. None the less, long ago Mary Carbery, an aristocratic young widow in a huge west Cork mansion, cleverly recast the memories of local people into a minor classic, *The Farm by Lough Gur*; and above all Alice Taylor's recollections of rural simplicity have struck a resounding chord with an Irish reading-public which possesses an endless appetite for reassurance about the verities of times past. The title of Taylor's first volume, *To School through the Fields*, perfectly and economically encapsulates a childhood where light comes from oil lamps, entertainment from church festivals, sustenance from pot-ovens and milk-churns, and locomotion by courtesy of Shank's Mare. It was followed by a series of clones rather than sequels (*Quench the Lamp, The Village, Country Days, The Night before Christmas, A Country Miscellany*), all wildly popular. In a digitally enhanced, post-religious, post-nationalist twenty-first century, Irish readers love being reminded of how different things once were. The classic countrywoman's 'crossover' apron as worn thirty years ago is now a subject for analysis in journals of social history.[1] Colm Tóibín mischievously referred to the writers of the Field Day cooperative in the 1980s as 'the pre-electric men': guardians and celebrants of an aboriginal Irish rural magic tapped through hand-pumps and holy wells, before the telephone poles and electricity pylons marched over the horizon. For Alice Taylor too time is strangely undefined; at least two reviewers of *Quench the Lamp* confidently described the book as set in different decades. While past history occasionally breaks in, invariably as cosy memories of 'safe houses' during the Troubles of 1919–21, the outside world is kept firmly absent. The farmhouse does not, apparently, have a radio, and the background of 'the war years' is mentioned only once, fleetingly, in *To School through the Fields*. Alice Taylor deliberately ignores the bitter after-taste that pervades, for instance, Brian Friel's play *Dancing at Lughnasa*, ostensibly set in that prelapsarian world. The fantasy element in Irish childhood is the essential ingredient for commercial success.

And nowadays, the proof of a bestseller is transatlantic success. Two other Irish autobiographers who have recently achieved this are Frank McCourt and Gerry Adams. Both, in their apparently different ways, turn Irish childhoods to very particular purposes and both exemplify narratives skewed through selective 'evidence', and a manoeuvred memory, in ways treated elsewhere in this book. McCourt's *Angela's Ashes*, of course, transcended bestsellerdom to become a publishing phenomenon – a million-seller, a prize-gatherer, a cult-former, a legend still ensconced in the hardback charts when it went straight to number one in paperback. Thus it joined the international company of Stephen Hawking's *A Brief History of Time*, Jung Chang's *Wild Swans*, Dava Sobel's *Longitude*: books that fulfil a felt or perceived need among people, which may have everything to do with buying a book, but very little to do with reading it to the end. The jawdropping success of such volumes testifies to the eternal human sense of gratification through self-betterment, mingled, perhaps, with the equally eternal human tendency to console ourselves by reading about the efforts and tribulations of others. Much of this applies to the *Angela's Ashes* phenomenon, with, perhaps, some peculiar variations: such as the traditional Irish readiness to commercialize the past, the complex attitude of the United States to what it expects the Irish to be, and the enduring pride and reassurance which Americans find in hot water and flush lavatories.

Thus the paperback edition of *Angela's Ashes*[2] is garlanded with pages and pages of ecstatic review-quotes. Connoisseurs of the genre may note that the heavyweight names are often there in the guise of kind friends rather than dispassionate critics, but those who nailed their colours to the mast of, say, the *Clarion-Ledger* or the *Detroit Free Press* are no less enthusiastic: 'Frank McCourt has seen hell, but found angels in his heart'; 'Frank McCourt's life, and his searing telling of it, reveal all we need to know about being human.' It may seem rather like party-pooping to ask what this kind of bilge actually means (which is less than nothing); it is perhaps fairer to look at the meaning of the book itself, and its spin-offs. These now stretch to not only the sequel, *'Tis*, but the autobiography of Frank's brother, Malachy, *A Monk Swimming*,[3] a much touted but disappointing Alan Parker film and the name of at least one pub in Limerick.

Angela's Ashes had an odd gestation, reflected in its title, which bears no relation to anything within the covers – since the cremated remains of the author's mother were, in the end, economically reserved for the sequel. In a similarly confusing shift, the volume was at first alternately identified as fiction and as autobiography, but by the time of publication it had settled down as 'a memoir'. However, it is the sort of memoir in which the protagonist can – like Tristram Shandy – retain absolutely concrete memories from the time of his conception, and retail word-for-word conversations exchanged, and letters written, from the age of three. The conventions of magical realism and post-structuralist flannel have had a decisive effect on the genre of autobiography: while this can be presented as a liberation from the tyranny of the ascertainable fact, it makes for some confusion as far as the reader is concerned. Frank McCourt is born into a poor but

feelgood immigrant community in Brooklyn, in 1931 (according to
'Tis, the sequel published to more muted acclaim three years later).
There are kind Italian shopkeepers, and wonderful Jewish neighbours:
father is a sentimental Northern Irish republican who sings rebel
ballads, mother the regulation-issue Irish Mammy. Cliché is invoked
on the first page of Angela's Ashes, in a way that seemingly promises
subversion:

Worse than the ordinary miserable childhood is the miserable Irish childhood,
and worse yet is the miserable Irish Catholic childhood. People everywhere
brag and whimper about the woes of their early years, but nothing can
compare with the Irish version: the poverty, the shiftless loquacious alcoholic
father; the pious defeated mother moaning by the fire; pompous priests;
bullying schoolmasters; the English and the terrible things they did to us for
eight hundred long years.[4]

But what we hear is exactly what we will get, from the moment the
authors' parents leave America. Both go slightly off the rails (drink,
depression) when their daughter dies, and they return to Ireland and
a cold welcome: first of all in the North, then to the slums of Limerick.

Angela's Ashes records (or at least re-imagines) Frank's youth in a
downward spiral of poverty and immiseration, until he escapes back
to America in October 1949, shortly after his nineteenth birthday
(which would actually make him born in 1930: magical realism may
have to be invoked again). It appears from 'Tis that he started using
the awful privations of his childhood quite early, in essays at NYU
night school. Certainly the vividness of certain images and events is
marvellously realized – the fleas, the mother's miscarriage, the mentally
unbalanced neighbour begging all over Limerick for flour to bake
bread for her children before she is taken away to the asylum. The
poor are not always mutually supportive. The father's Northern background is held against him, republican though he is: he drinks and
comes and goes and eventually goes for good. With incessant rain and
the rising river Shannon, the slum floods; when this happens, the family
withdraw to the upstairs room, which they call 'Italy'. There is a lot
about sex, and even more about dirt, defecation, shared privies in the
back lane, and the indignity of emptying chamber pots.

Mam goes to the door and says, Why are you emptying your bucket in our lavatory? He raises his cap to her. Your lavatory, missus? Ah, no. You're making a bit of a mistake there, ha, ha. This is not your lavatory. Sure, isn't this the lavatory for the whole lane. You'll see passing your door here the buckets of eleven families and I can tell you it gets very powerful here in the warm weather, very powerful altogether.[5]

Charity is cold, the kindness of strangers almost non-existent, and the remnants of the family end up living with a repulsive cousin, whom the passive and exhausted mother is forced to sleep with: a step for which her writer sons do not forgive her, then or – apparently – later. Simultaneously, in a parallel universe, little Alice Taylor is out there in the countryside saving the hay and milking the cows and quenching the lamp. It would all come as something of a surprise to her.

Yet for the reader, the slum is as unsatisfactory as the farm, and for similar reasons: equally played on one note, without depth or nuance, and with a beady eye fixed on the audience throughout. Why *Angela's Ashes* is not and never will be 'a classic memoir' (*pace* the *New York Times*) is because the author lacks an internal self-editor, and a sense of developing structure. The language is monotonous, the incidents repetitive, the characterization perfunctory: people are identified by formulaic strap-lines, which are trundled out again and again each time they appear. One uncle, a jovial cynic, is never introduced without declaring he 'doesn't give a fiddler's fart' for respectable opinion, which is all right once, or twice. The level of intellectual give-and-take is reassuringly high, however, and there is usually a guru at hand down the lane to descant on Cuchulain or Jonathan Swift.

Next morning Mr Timoney says, Wait till we get to *Gulliver*, Francis. You'll know Jonathan Swift is the greatest Irish writer that ever lived, no, the greatest man to put pen to parchment. A giant of a man, Francis. He laughs all through *A Modest Proposal* and you'd wonder what he's laughing at when it's all about cooking Irish babies.[6]

Yeats's invocation to Cuchulain's wife, 'great-bladdered Emer', is also common currency in the McCourt household in the 1930s. It all goes on at breathless pace and relentless length, and is actually quite a job to finish. And the reader, labouring through it, begins to feel certain nagging irritations and doubts.

One concerns the relation to fact. Frank McCourt has guaranteed in interviews that 'all the facts are true', but some incidents stretch credulity. The father's claim of an IRA pension, for instance, is presented as a venture into a strange underworld, involving trips to back rooms in seedy suburbs. But in mid 1930s Ireland, these pensions were a matter of strict and official record, done through a government department, now preserved (though not always accessible) in the National Archives. Some doubt has also been expressed in Ireland at the likelihood of quite so many boys attending Leamy's School in Limerick in bare feet in midwinter, or open sewers coursing down the streets, but this may simply be injured local pride. It is also hard to credit the urban slum boys, escaped into the countryside, being able to sustain themselves by milking cows in the fields. The cows even thoughtfully stand still enough for a small child to lie underneath them, imbibing the milk directly from the udder: a facility they never granted to Alice Taylor.

More Tayloresque is the way that the hero also talks regularly to an angel. This being is initially conjured up by Frank's father, a bewildering mixture of sensitive soul, good housekeeper and drunken layabout. The angel occupies the seventh step of the slum stairs, and strengthens Frank's resolve to confess his sins at First Communion. This puts his father straight into counsellor mode:

Isn't it better to be able to tell your father your troubles rather than an angel who is a light and a voice in your head?
'Tis, Dad.[7]

This sentimental, uncertain and fantastic element is compounded by an eerie sense that this 'memoir' has been recalled through the prism of subsequent reading. There is a Redemptorist sermon to guilt-ridden boys straight out of *Portrait of the Artist*. There is a doomed love affair with a glamorous sixteen-year-old consumptive girl, reminiscent of Mícheál Mac Liammóir's autobiography, *All for Hecuba* (where it was, given Mac Liammóir's redoubtably unabashed homosexuality, an even less likely incident). There is an aged female moneylender, for whom the young McCourt writes improbably high-flown dunning letters, who owes a literary debt to Dostoevsky and Dickens. And over it all hovers the inspiration of Sean O'Casey's autobiographies, which are – as his biographers have pointed out – notoriously unreliable as records of his early life, but which were, as McCourt himself notes, the first Irish memoirs to exploit the full potential of childhood deprivation. O'Casey's background was, however, the tenements of late-Victorian Dublin rather than the Limerick of fifty years ago. It is impossible to escape the sneaking feeling that the literary classics devoured by the youthful McCourt and used in his later career as a teacher have heavily influenced his 'memoirs'.

Perhaps this is why the sequel touched far fewer chords in a gullible reading-public. 'Tis follows straight on from Angela's Ashes, and is interdependent with it to the extent of making sense of its mysterious title, reducing the unfortunate Angela to ashes at the end.[8] In this sequel McCourt describes his education in America: a subject given classic status by Leo Rosten in The Education of Hyman Kaplan, but disappointingly handled here. He does point out, revealingly, that as he began to read more and more omniverously, situations encountered in great novels seemed oddly to parallel his own experience. He epitomizes the Irish hunger for education, and the Irish reliance on self-supporting communities and aggressive camaraderie, which makes the story of Irish America so cheering. He is also honest – and self-condemnatory – about the national predilection to seek solace and absolution in alcohol, and its effect on his own marriage, though his first wife remains among the most unreal characters in the book. His rise from floor-sweeper and lavatory-cleaner, via a spell as a GI in Germany, to high-school teacher and night-school lecturer is impressive in its own terms. But, with the best will in the world, it is not very interesting, and the weaknesses of Angela's Ashes bedevil this volume too. Characterization comes straight from central casting (paedophile priest, angry-but-noble Communist, saintly and paternal black warehouseman). There are encounters which once again strike echoes of other autobiographies (the inevitable meeting with Billie Holiday is strongly reminiscent of an incident in The Autobiography of Malcolm X). The chronological context wavers curiously: McCourt's night-school students in the early 1970s go home to watch Jane Fonda exercise videos, and 1950s Irish Americans discuss Northern Ireland in terms that suggest the situation of the 1970s. Return visits to Ireland betray equally skewed powers of observation and a fuzzy air of anachronism.

This is more important than it might seem, because there is some danger that America is ready to believe in Ireland, past and present, as interpreted through the memories of the McCourt family. Already brother Malachy has got in on the act, with a book which – it is fair to suppose – would never have seen the light of day without his brother's precedent: a literary equivalent of the demographic phenomenon known as 'chain migration'. From the awkward pun in the title of A Monk Swimming to the slack, whoozy, flatulent style, it is an embarrassment: an account of boozing, weeping, whoring and – intermittently – acting. Malachy ran a successful New York bar, after leaving Limerick unable – he says – 'to do anything but tell lies'.[9] He also went on the stage, and fell an early victim of the curse of minor celebrity and major dipsomania. His tedious memoir is a much more unattractive performance than either of his brother's volumes, as well as a far less literate one. It is maniacally class-obsessed (the New York bourgeoisie show off by 'yawning at incomprehensible operas' and 'yelping over museums', bad cess to 'em) and violently anti-British – predictable bigotries which are, by and large, absent from Frank's less jaundiced worldview. At the same time, given Frank's testimony about the family's *couche sociale*, it comes as rather a surprise to find that in his youth Malachy was a rugby star, playing for a Limerick club against posh schools: an accomplishment he put to good use when he came to America, where one of his opponents in a Harvard game was – of course – Ted Kennedy.

Moreover, given the vehemence of Malachy's anti-British credentials, one of the unintentionally interesting elements in A Monk Swimming concerns the author's relationship to the English language. The publishers have the temerity to declare that he 'makes the English language do tricks the British never intended'. (His copy-editors certainly carry the trick through, allowing a text where female lips are 'ermined' rather than – presumably – 'carmined', the legendary Fleet Street bar 'El Vino' is Americanized as 'Alvino's' and a passage of J. M. Synge is quoted in so garbled a form as to be meaningless.[10]) Malachy believes the Irish 'took a dull tongue, English, and made it roar'. Here is a sample of his own roaring:

I averred it was a sight to gladden the eyes, the heart, and the internal organs of any decent man walking the earth this day. 'Stop the yap,' sez the bould Mitchum, 'and get it inside of you.' He had done a few movies in Ireland, and therefore knew the lingo, and how it could interfere with the quaffing.[11]

In *A Monk Swimming*, the quaffing has interfered drastically with the lingo. Stage-Irishry leans heavily on a catechism of the tiredest ersatz-English archaisms: almost everything is 'ye olde', exchanges are 'quoth', things happen 'ere long', sex involves 'dipping the wick' (though masturbation is 'shaking hands with the unemployed'), the author 'hies him off' (not often enough), beer is 'the chilled amber beverage', Muhammad Ali is 'Mr M. Ali of fisticuffs fame', and Jews are 'of the Hebraic persuasion'. Malachy McCourt is a professed admirer of J. P. Donleavy and P. G. Wodehouse – neither of them a writer who should be imitated, for exactly opposite reasons. McCourt's literary voice comes through as a misheard echo, looking for sympathy and a seat on the bandwagon.

From time to time, though, he does convey something of New York in the 1950s and 1960s, as it must have appeared to a healthy and hungry young immigrant: a Manhattan at once intimate and glamorous, pre-crack, pre-Giulani, pre-fashionable SoHo and TriBeCa. By contrast, one of the strange nullities at the heart of his brother's autobiographies is the lack of a sense of place, outside the recalled actuality of Limerick. Dublin is cardboard: there is, for instance, a very odd interlude in the Shelbourne Hotel. In Frank McCourt's memory this venerable haunt of the *haute bourgeoisie* is transformed into a place where babies' prams are parked outside, and the bar is peopled by yelling Kerry farmers with red faces. Similarly, his time in Germany is never described in terms of the place itself. And no New York institution is sharply realized in *'Tis*, with the possible exception of the Staten Island Ferry. Despite wheeling on the odd mandatory jazzman or bum, the Village in the fifties could be anywhere. As memoir goes, this carries off neither a Proustian re-creation through utter internal absorption, nor the Isherwood trick of becoming an unblinking camera. The voice in the ear wavers, the focus is offbeam.

And yet – to return to the initial point – it is what millions of people want to read (or at least to buy), and it will be built into the popular interpretation of that large ingredient of Irish history-emigration. McCourt's success in Ireland says something important about where we now are. *Angela's Ashes* may have aroused some local annoyance, and provoked an exciting exchange on the *Late Late Show*; but these are comparatively minor tremors. In general, it has been overpraised by the quality press and adored by the popular market; on the promotional tour for *'Tis*, five hundred copies a day of that lacklustre volume were shifting in Limerick alone, along with a hundred paperbacks of its predecessor. And it has meant a tourism bonanza in Limerick: 'a city', according to the *Irish Times*, 'which has traditionally found it a challenge to attract visitors'.[12] It is now attracting them by revelling in misery tourism. Since 1997 an estimated 3,000 visitors have been guided, at three or four pounds a head, around the supposed site of the McCourts' long-demolished hell-hole. The local Tourism Development Manager is considering 'other visitor-related options' – pointing out merrily that people are attracted there by McCourt's Dickensian descriptions, and then find out how much everything has changed for the better. This may not be what they expected, or wanted, but it is good for business. The local Chamber of Commerce robustly agrees: 'What better way to promote the positive side of Limerick today than to get behind *Angela's Ashes* and piggy-back on the film?' The actual story told in the book, reliable or not, fades into irrelevance. And there are signs that miraculous powers are beginning to attach to the shrine. 'One woman came from England to do the tour, hoping it would inspire her to stay in her marriage to an alcoholic husband.' How? If any message is to be read out of the book, is that you have to get out as early as you can, and head west.

And this explains the other great lesson of the *Angela's Ashes* phenomenon: the way the United States took it to its capacious heart. The McCourt memoirs confirm the traditional and reassuring belief that the Old World is a sow who devours her own farrow, and everything will eventually come right in the United States, along with creature comforts, blonde women and hot running water. The oeuvre re-creates the America of the *Reader's Digest*, redolent with

Unforgettable Characters and Smilesian self-help. Simultaneously they fulfil the Irish stereotype as brawlers and boozers, excluded from the effete WASP world, at one with fellow underdogs, with the tear and the smile always at the ready, and a way with words – as Malachy McCourt must put it, 'warm words, serried words, glittering, poetic, harsh, and even blasphemous words'. He also remarks, unguardedly, 'they're all mad in America – they pay you for talking'.[13]

But they would probably not pay you very much for talking about the new Euro-Ireland, which so cheerfully milks the McCourt phenomenon for all it is worth. They would not pay you for apostrophizing the efficient, money-making, politically ruthless Irish America already broaching the country clubs when the brothers McCourt were invading the saloons, and by now firmly entrenched in the yuppie hierarchy of the Upper East Side. This could provide just as inspiring a story in its own way, but it conforms less to the comfortable old straitjackets of the stories that have gone before. Evelyn Waugh once remarked that to the Irishman there are only two ultimate realities: Hell and the United States. The McCourt version postulates that you have to experience the first in order to be redeemed by the second.

Thus the McCourt oeuvre, apparently trading on misery, actually sells on synthetic moral uplift, contributing to the genre of idealized Irish personal history. As with Alice Taylor, this partly relies on a determinedly unreal approach to present-day Ireland, and an oddly distanced view of the Northern Troubles – both in the generation of the McCourt father and of his sons. They would be unlikely to learn much from another author who has exploited his Irish childhood to reach the bestseller lists: Gerry Adams, president of Sinn Féin, MP for West Belfast and from 1999 the power behind the republican element in the power-sharing government established in Northern Ireland under the terms of the 1998 Anglo-Irish Agreement. He is, therefore, on his way to constructing a new Establishment of the kind he made his career fighting against, and a decisive amount of retrospective remodelling is necessary. His autobiography, *Before the Dawn*,[14] was published two years before this *démarche*, but had a part to play in the process.

The groundwork for the Adams version was laid in a determinedly sentimental volume called *Falls Memories*, published in 1982, and followed by tales about internment, *Cage Eleven* (1990). In between came his advance to leadership of the republican movement, and a selection of political writings, *The Politics of Irish Freedom* (1986). All these publications have been quarried for his autobiography, which succeeded *Angela's Ashes* at the top of the Irish bestseller lists in 1996, subsequently achieving a top US publisher and blanket American coverage. This coincided with widely felt curiosity about Adams's origins, as he emerged from paramilitary experience into the kind of Irish politics nervously defined in the early days of Fianna Fáil as 'slightly constitutional', and culminating – as with Fianna Fáil – in ministerial office for its members, governing a polity they had always denounced as illegitimate.

Before the Dawn brings its own surprises. Adams was born in 1948, but his book takes 263 pages to reach the year 1978; while events since then are compressed into sixty-two, many of them dealing with the hunger strikes by republican prisoners demanding 'political status' in 1981. The book effectively ends there, except for a sentimental and unrealistic epilogue about Adams's hopes for peace in 1996. This enables avoidance of an engrossing subject: the tension between his arguments as president of a peace-seeking Sinn Féin, which he would lead into coalition with unionism two years later, and the record of contemporaneous IRA activity. Those who wondered whether this dissonance was evidence of a connected policy, or a suppressed power-struggle within the republican movement, had to go on wondering. But this is unsurprising, because the book is also completely silent on what Adams's relationship with the IRA was, or is. *Before the Dawn* lives up to its title: once again, we have a version of Irish childhood which does duty for a more uncomfortable and ambiguous reality.

Born into a republican family in Belfast, much involved with the movement on his mother's as well as his father's side, Adams tells us it somehow passed him by until the politicization of the 1960s. An idyll of working-class Belfast youth is recalled, which he has already mined for his little books of sketches and stories, purveying feelgood communitarian values. The late 1960s brought ostensible political movement, a nascent civil rights organization, then the provocation of Orange bigots and the culpable collusion of the British Army; in the process the IRA was reborn as a community defence movement.

Adams leaves school prematurely (for unexplained reasons), becomes a community 'activist', is imprisoned in the early 1970s (again for no good reason, at least as given here, though an unauthorized biography has him joining the IRA in 1965[15]), mysteriously is sprung from gaol to be part of the IRA delegation negotiating with the British government in 1972, returns to community action, is subsequently rearrested – until, round about the time of the 1981 hunger strikes, he discovers the political path and persuades like-minded people to work through the ballot box as well as the 'armed struggle'. In the frantically elided last pages, he emerges as the would-be Mandela the world's press has come to know, although this is conveyed in woolly generalities, with no mention of the compromise strategy hammered out by Adams himself with John Hume which preceded the 'peace process' of the early 1990s and lies behind the astonishing compromise of Good Friday 1998.

In these pages, in fact, the subject of the autobiography remains oddly absent. This is not through self-effacement (twelve out of the twenty-one photographs feature the author, once in cowboy costume toting a six-gun); there is a deliberate structure of evasion and conflation, even in straightforward personal matters. The account of courtship and marriage is oddly perfunctory and uneven: his wife, Colette, is praised for her good republican qualities, but the autobiographer's consciousness remains determinedly pre-sexual. (He has subsequently offered the information, perhaps disingenuously, that 'all of my children have been conceived in cars', which may throw some light on the matter.[16]) While his father-in-law 'gave us his blessing', he was 'too upset to attend the wedding' – we are not told why. Adams himself is presented as a reluctant leader, hating publicity. From this account, his most passionate commitment is to the narrow world of West Belfast, a self-justifying and tightly knit community later replicated in the republican wing of internment prison.

Yet again, the personal history is implicitly presented as running in parallel to the national narrative. But it is tempting to map the story of Adams's coming-of-age against the version of the early 1960s in Northern Ireland profiled by countless academic and historical analyses: a political landscape where seismic shifts began to register themselves through a vastly increased Labour vote, the decline of the old

IRA and the evident desire of a growing Catholic middle class to engage with the institutions of the state instead of boycotting them. (Adams's assertion that sectarianism was becoming more and more evident through the mid to late 1960s flies in the face of all the evidence.[17]) Against this background, from 1963 a new prime minister, Terence O'Neill, made his moves – too ineptly as it turned out – and was outflanked by a unionist backlash. In this lay the seeds of an impatient civil rights movement, soon commandeered by the Young Turks of the next nationalist generation. Or so it seems to historians. But this is not the landscape mapped by Adams, who is determined to see things purely in the perspective framed by his mother's back window: the final insurrection of an oppressed people against dictators and collaborators.

This is one view, but, even accepting it, there is less information than might be expected. What one wants to hear more of, above all, is the life of a young 'activist' in the 1960s and 1970s. The 'activities' seem to revolve around summer camps, drilling, living on the run, being known to the police and sometimes taking part in 'tribunals' held, for safety's sake, across the border in the republic.[18] Moreover, Adams comes from a background steeped in republicanism, with many relatives (including his father) serving prison terms. Yet the name 'IRA' is rarely brought in; at the age of twelve he claims to be 'barely conscious of where the border was', and innocent of sectarian bigotry. Later, when he learns Irish history, it is a revelation. All this seems rather unlikely for someone who attended a Christian Brothers school and inhabited a home where traditions of nationalist struggle were imbibed with every cup of strong tea. In fact, the whole thing seems unnecessarily coy, given that at least three standard books on the Troubles detail Adams's progress through the ranks of the IRA from the age of seventeen: Mark Urban, Patrick Bishop, Eamonn Mallie, J. Bowyer Bell and others have specifically stated that he moved from commanding the Ballymurphy detachment of the IRA to being in charge of the Belfast Brigade in 1971, emerging as commanding officer of IRA operations in 1979 and retaining his seat on the Army Council.[19] If true, it would of course explain why he was plucked from gaol to negotiate with Whitelaw in 1972, though different stories circulate about who insisted upon it. But as it stands, it is rather like reading a biography of Field Marshal Montgomery that leaves out the British Army.

In the autobiography, Adams prefers to concentrate upon activities such as housing action committees, radicalization through the 1960s squatting movement, and a background in People's Democracy and the Northern Ireland Civil Rights Association. This is understandable, since it chimes more tunefully with his current profile, but it would surprise many who were there at the time. (His own feelings are sometimes given away: he writes contemptuously that NICRA 'yawned itself into existence'.[20]) Even when the logic of events forces him to remark that he was on terms with 'the Belfast leadership' of the IRA, and even 'found himself witness to'[21] a meeting between Official IRA members and the breakaway Provisionals, his own importance in dictating the terms of that break (alleged in several publications) is left silent. Perhaps here too is a clue towards the sudden vagueness that descends after 1978. According to Mark Urban, it was in 1979 that Adams replaced Martin McGuinness as chief of staff of the IRA Army Council.[22] But since the translation of both men into Sinn Féin MPs in the late 1990s, their war records fade into irrelevance. IRA operations against civilians during the late 1970s and early 1980s, such as the firebombing of the La Mon Hotel by the Ballymurphy brigade (twelve people burned to death) or the atrocity at Harrods (eight killed) are best left aside. McGuinness's and Adams's entries in the register of Westminster MPs are laconic in the extreme: 'previous careers' are simply entered as 'Chief Negotiator of Sinn Fein' (McGuinness) and 'Member, Northern Ireland Assembly' (Adams). It would probably be unrealistic to expect more.

The solipsistic treatment of an idealized childhood developing into idealistic adolescence enables other evasions too. One gaping hole in the book swallows up the 83 per cent of Northern Ireland's population who do not vote for Sinn Féin: unionists and moderate nationalists. Apart from a reference in the introduction to a 'small privileged sector' of the population, the first Protestants in Adams's book are encountered on p. 140; unionism, as a political element, does not look in until p. 318. Reading *Before the Dawn*, one takes away the impression of a Catholic nationalist province draconically kept in the sway of a distant empire, awaiting liberation at the hands of its untrustworthy and corrupted mother country to the south. Thus he can describe the IRA as 'an organic system of local democracy'. This may well be how Adams sees it, but in a state two-thirds unionist and Protestant it is hardly the full picture; life would be much simpler if it were. But this is a book that deals with that simple picture, from a man who has – throughout most of his career – advocated a 'solution' so simple that, if it were viable, the problem which it purports to address would not exist in the first place. Every argument in the book tends to this end, at the expense of any nuance or ambiguity. The political nature of unionism is seen (against all the evidence) as not only immutable but completely monolithic – an interpretation spectacularly disproved by Adams's new colleague, David Trimble. The Royal Ulster Constabulary, whose officers, while Adams was writing this book, were being threatened and even murdered by Orange extremists for attempting impartial policing, is seen as an unchanging entity, indistinguishable from the long-disbanded and entirely Protestant B-Special force.

Breathtakingly, there is absolutely no discussion of the evolving attitude of British governments from the mid 1960s up to the dramatic Hillsborough Accord of 1985 and the subsequent Downing Street declaration of 1993. Few would unequivocally defend the record of the British Army in Northern Ireland, and there is plenty of evidence to convict them of draconian abuses of power; but can Adams really believe that the shooting of civilians by panicky and trigger-happy paratroopers during the Bloody Sunday demonstrations was 'a deliberate military operation, planned in advance at the highest *political* level'? No evidence is given for this assertion, which flies in the face of previous analyses of that horror, and which, in terms of British government strategy, makes no sense at all; but as far as Adams is concerned, evidence is irrelevant. Similarly, a classic sectarian standoff, such as that provoked by the Provisional IRA at the Lenadoon housing estate in 1972, is 'engineered' by the British government (how?) and the Maguire children, killed by a runaway car during an IRA chase, become victims of 'British bullets'.[23] That tragedy was the beginning of the 'Peace People' movement, described by Adams elsewhere as a government front. The conspiracy theory remains self-fulfilling: the child is set against the outside world.

Adams's formation, after all, owes much to the simplicities of 1960s conspiracy-theory: but he adhered to it longer than most. His speech at Bodenstown in June 1979 is not quoted in his autobiography, but it deserves to be remembered:

We are opposed to big business, to multinationalism, to gombeenism, to sectarianism, and to the maintenance of a privileged class. We stand opposed to all forms and manifestations of imperialism and capitalism. We stand for an Ireland free, united, socialist and Gaelic . . . Our movement needs constructive and thoughtful self-criticism. We also require links with those oppressed by economic and social pressures. Today's circumstances and our objectives dictate the need for the building of an agitational struggle in the twenty-six counties, an economic resistance movement, linking up Republicans with other sections of the working class. It needs to be done now because to date our most glaring weakness lies in our failure to develop revolutionary politics and to build an alternative to so-called constitutional politics.[24]

If this was the agenda for the 1980s, it showed an impressively skewed reading of where Ireland was actually going; the obvious reaction must be that he had abandoned these simplicities by the late 1980s. But much of *Before the Dawn* leads one to wonder. The bird's-eye view of Irish history related early in the narrative, for instance, is self-evidently that handed down at his mother's knee; it contrives to leave out completely the constitutional nationalist tradition of O'Connell, Butt, Parnell and Redmond, though he himself was apparently embracing it at the time of writing. Also ignored is the argument of the SDLP, that the position of Catholic nationalists in the North is not such as to justify violence. There is no room for any kind of move towards pluralism or inclusivity – until the epilogue, when the notion of 'democratic dialogue' suddenly raises its head. And who is this 'democratic dialogue' to be with? The SDLP and the Dublin government.[25] Unionists, as usual, go unmentioned: the difficult part of the equation is simply passed over in silence. Considering what he was about to do in the 'real world', this is striking. It may have simply been a matter of sensitivity, but the evasion fits a long tradition of Irish nationalist argument. His refusal to discuss the Hume–Adams initiative could equally be an instance of elaborate tact, or the most ominous sign of all.

The Adams story is a small part of the story of modern Ireland, so the fact that it supplies – yet again – a narrative of evasions is only appropriate. The basic strategy of ending, to all intents and purposes, in 1981 avoids discussion not only of the subsequent political manoeuvres and compromises on both sides, but of civilian atrocities such as the Warrington bombing, or Adams's own endorsement (in October 1993) of Thomas Begley, who as an IRA operative murdered eleven men, women and children with a bomb in a fish-and-chip shop (a *Protestant* fish-and-chip shop). When a knotty problem comes up, such as the rationale of violence in the context of present-day Northern Ireland, he resorts to an economical device: recycling his own earlier publications. Thus the tone shifts from awkward first-person narrative to distinctly mushy fiction, where he reprints a short story of his own, dealing with the thoughts of a sniper as he kills a British soldier. The moral endorsement is unmistakable: the soldier had no right to be there, and the 'Volunteer' was only doing his noble duty.

This is the world conjured up by the *Selected Writings*, published in 1994 to coincide with Adams's American tour. Much of it reflects the basic values of that Bodenstown speech (foreign investors are carelessly listed among the national enemies who threaten the solidarity of the republican community, which should give some well-meaning American business people pause for thought). But the construction of the short stories, which he has published steadily since his prison days, deserves attention. Here too, childhood predominates. They are moral tales, relying on black-and-white values and a denouement in the last paragraph. The sentimentality is ruthless, as is the revelling in memories of prelapsarian juvenile innocence in an idyllic childhood before 'violence' spoiled it all. 'The mass of the Irish people' are prevented from admittance into Utopia by the British government's refusal to allow 'a united Republican working class' to develop. Incidents from the autobiography are in fact predicted in the short stories, notably the unintentionally hilarious Hardy Boys tale of Gerry's dog.[26] This pampered creature, hand-reared on delicacies from the family table and lovingly nursed by the hero, is stolen by British soldiers (they have already shot the family's previous pet, under circumstances which are not divulged: trying to escape?). The dog reappears, at the end of a soldier's leash, when the hero is incarcerated in prison: it has been retrained as an army operative! Naturally it recognizes its proper master, and is dragged brutally away. The recurrence of the story is interesting: can it be a metaphor for collaborationism? And which came first, the fiction or the autobiography? In some ways, *Before the Dawn* is the novel for which the short stories prepared us.

What both share is a nostalgia as firmly unrealistic as Alice Taylor's, and an evasiveness as determined as Frank McCourt's. Kneecapping, arms deals with Libya, racketeering, kangaroo courts, the targeting of civilians whose connection with 'Loyalist paramilitaries' is asserted but never proved, bombs in shopping centres, the boycotting of Protestant businesses and the effective ethnic cleansing of Protestant communities from rural areas – none of this features in the fiction or the life story. But both reiterate the author's surprise at what has been done to the city he loves so well. He is astonished at the desecration of the old working-class areas of Belfast: his childhood has been taken from him. 'I feel sick at the way in which it has been turned upside down and I regret that people throughout the course of this war have suffered so much in so many different ways.'[27] SDLP leaders like John Hume, Gerry Fitt and Paddy Devlin, victims of IRA attacks on their homes and families, might read those words with a wry smile; unionists would find it hard to raise a smile in the first place. But neither element is allowed representation in the self-referencing world of the boy who is proud of having come far from Ballymurphy but never outgrown it.

It might be said – or at least hoped – that this is a man trying to learn a new language; but echoes from the old still come awkwardly through statements about republican vigilantes using nail-studded baseball-bats against dissidents. 'I'm against punishment beatings,' Adams averred in 1997. 'I've made that clear. I do think communities have a right to defend themselves, but it must be very measured and it must be sustainable and inclusive.'[28] Whatever this means, it is not completely reassuring: nor are his statements on the long-running issue of arms decommissioning. On his world tours, he achieves a smoother synthesis: peace-process rhetoric enables him to reap the rewards of glamorized republicanism without revealing that he has ever – so to speak – inhaled. Journalists are rarely in the position to ask him uncomfortable questions, which is why it was a mistake (if an understandable one) for the Republic to ban Sinn Féin spokespeople from their airwaves for so long, and equally a mistake for the Parliament at Westminster to deny access to Adams and McGuinness for not taking the Oath of Allegiance. At certain junctures, Adams has been able to absent himself from accountability (the Warrington bomb was one such occasion). But if his writings demonstrate anything, it is the need for his frame of reference to be challenged.

This child-like solipsism enables him to identify convenient enemies in his rhetoric; and they are not, primarily, the unionists with whom he has to share the place he lives in. These he simply eliminates from the account. While he from time to time draws modish but unsound parallels with South Africa, he ignores a closer and more sinister parallel: Northern Ireland over the last quarter-century of communal conflict has, on both sides, anticipated the interfaces between fundamentalist religion, exclusivist nationalism, resegregation and terrorism so horribly demonstrated in Bosnia. And though the death-or-glory, cowboys-and-Indians passages of his fictions and memoir present the forces of the British state as the villains of the piece, the story between the lines is rather different. One reads there his visceral dislike of the actual Republic of Ireland, which is so mysteriously unlike the virtual-reality green-and-Gaelic model he has been educated to believe it should be: its noble traditions of uncomplicated history taken over by 'anti-nationalist' intellectuals, its business interests happily profiting from the Euroboom, its political establishment uninterested in the struggle of the Northern ghettos, its ministers and civil servants hobnobbing with their opposite numbers in the Evil Empire to the east. (Significantly, he admits that the old 'Official' IRA's political wing gained support in the South by giving up republicanism and reconstructing itself as the 'Worker's Party' – but he cannot accept the reasons why this was so.) As late as 1986 he believed that 'all over Ireland . . . people can show you the land that was taken from their families three or four hundred years ago and name the families that took it'.[29] To read the attitudes of south Armagh into the ranch culture of Meath or the split-level *haut*-suburban sprawl of Wicklow implies just how little he knows the transformed Ireland south of the border.

Nor would he feel at home in such places. The other implicit enemy is represented by what Adams contemptuously refers to as the 'Catholic middle classes' of Northern Ireland. Hence his ignoring of the SDLP; hence his single reference to the Sunningdale power-sharing experiment of 1974, generally accepted as one of the few bright spots in the statelet's murky recent history; hence his lack of regret at the sectarianizing of Derry politics, and the increasing apartness of the religious demography of the region; hence his denunciation (at the time) of the Hillsborough Agreement, which was seen as a victory for Hume and the SDLP and brought about a dramatic slump in the Sinn Féin vote in Northern Ireland in 1986. The apparent pan-nationalist front which emerged at the time of the 1994 ceasefire does not disguise this. If anything is now clear (and even some Sinn Féin pronouncements after the 1994 ceasefire admitted as much), it is the fact that the traditional aim of 'the republican movement' is unwinnable. The border will not magically disappear. It is branded too deeply not only into the hearts and minds of nearly a million Northern Irish people, but also into the consciousness of a Republic determined to maintain the values of its own stable, homogeneous and politically sophisticated society. The activities of Gerry Adams and the IRA have, paradoxically, helped to cement this determination, north and south. The emergence of Adams as broker of a devolved Stormont government shows that he apparently accepts the pragmatics of the situation. But should the bad old days return, there will be little evidence on paper that he ever adapted his analysis. His response, recorded in Fionnuala O'Connor's deeply absorbing book of interviews with Northern Irish Catholics in 1993, is revealing:

What revisionism has done is tell people they can't be satisfied with what they come from. That's putting things you thought of as constants under attack: the effect's like a family trauma, like discovering you've been adopted . . . all that is where revisionism has had a political effect, where people can't be contented and confident with what they are.[30]

If rethinking history means losing your family, and questioning your childhood, no wonder it does not come easily to him. A child of the 1960s to the end, his autobiography still implies that a 'long war' will bring that hoped-for dawn and still defines his enemy as a sadistic colonial power, not a large section of the Irish population. It reflects a consciousness locked into the world of his childhood. This has been his strength, and his weakness.

But those who emerge best from the sorry history of Northern Ireland over the last decades are those who were prepared to grow up and change their minds, though there are few enough of them. Reading *Before the Dawn* recalls *Straight Left*, the autobiography published by the late Paddy Devlin in 1993. Devlin, like Adams, negotiated with the British government in 1972, though he goes unmentioned in Adams's memoir. An IRA internee in the 1940s, he was subsequently a socialist, trade unionist, local politician, organizer of Catholic defence groups in the 1960s, founder member of the SDLP, and consistent scourge of the Provisional IRA – whose zero-sum game-plan he blamed for the parlous state of both politics and communal relations within the province. Devlin and his like came to place their faith not in the ruthless nostalgia of Utopians, hugging the received images of their youth, but in local cultural initiatives, rebuilding local industry and encouraging integrated education: expecting change to follow slowly in a Northern Ireland already very different from the time-warped slough of discrimination which it was in the early 1960s. If the new Northern Ireland envisioned in the Good Friday Agreement succeeds in effecting self-transformation, it will be on foundations like these. It is one of those recurrent paradoxes in Irish history that this new chapter in the story may well be overseen by Gerry Adams, whose own worldview (or province-view) is part of a very different narrative. How far he will retain the old story is an interesting question. Perhaps an additional reason why he is anxious to stress South African parallels might lie in the way that country's Truth and Reconciliation Commission has declared that 'factual and objective truth' is not enough for a traumatized society seeking absolution: 'social or dialogue truth', 'narrative truth' and 'healing truth' must be added to the mix.[31] However well meaning and therapeutic, this extended definition raises problems for historians as it provides welcome loopholes for autobiographers.

The Irish future, so suddenly 'modern' at the turn of the twenty-first century, rests on the foundations of a past which can be glimpsed only just over the shoulder. Nevertheless, the childhoods of people now in their fifties and sixties, like Gerry Adams, Frank McCourt and Alice

Taylor, were lived in a different century metaphorically as well as literally. Their autobiographies demonstrate this in ways that are not always intentional. The stories that they tell are gauged for an audience in search of reaffirmation rather than dislocation – or enlightenment. For insights into modern Ireland, we can look to the fiction of, for instance, John Banville, Colm Tóibín, Anne Enright, Sebastian Barry, Robert McLiam Wilson, Glenn Patterson and Dermot Bolger; by contrast the supposed facts of childhood, as lived by the obscure as well as the influential, seem to be marshalled in order to reconstruct the borders and defences which apparently protected our innocence before the onrush of the modern tide. Yeats, who notoriously described this incoming flood as 'filthy', also reminded us, in another mood, that innocence can be 'murderous'. His own memoir, brilliantly disingenuous and impressionistic, was at the same time written in order to explain a revolution – political as well as artistic – breaking around him as he wrote.[32] The achievement of style, as he put it elsewhere, came from the shock of new material. The memoirs that sell best in modern Ireland are marked by an utter lack of distinguished style – a shortcoming fundamentally connected to their authors' determination to avoid the shock of confronting what is new, both for their readers and themselves.

II

The Salamander and the Slap:
Hubert Butler and His Century

To live for a very long time is not in itself an achievement, though we sometimes talk as if it were: it depends what you do with your life. And what you do with it is at least partially dictated by the times you live through and the opportunities given to you. Hubert Butler entered the world with the twentieth century and nearly lived it out. On the day of his birth, 23 October 1900, Queen Victoria was on the throne of a still united Great Britain and Ireland, which she had visited a few months before. The Boer War was in progress. The Irish Parliamentary Party had just reunited under John Redmond. And two days before Butler's birth, Arthur Griffith had founded Cumann na nGaedheal, bringing together anti-war opinion and forming the lineal ancestor of Sinn Féin. On the day of his death, 5 January 1991, the news in the papers was all about Ireland's diplomatic position regarding the oncoming Gulf War, the funding of an Irish-language television station, the Common Agricultural Policy's implications for Irish farmers, and the decision to convert the seventeenth-century Royal Hospital at Kilmainham, once the home of Irish soldiers retired from the British Army, into the Irish Museum of Modern Art.

In different ways, the news stories on the day of his death reflect the way that, over Hubert Butler's century, Ireland had become independent, and in the process moved from the periphery to the core. From being part – a central part – of the British Empire, three-quarters of its land mass now constituted an independent European republic, a process Butler had observed and commented upon. The creation of 'new' countries was a particular interest of his, and he could, with unique authority, see the Free State's birth in the same conspectus as that of Czechoslovakia or, later, Yugoslavia. In December 1943, with Europe in flux, he wrote a letter to his friend Geoffrey Taylor, literary editor of *The Bell*, who had complained of the lack of 'facts' in an essay he had been sent:

Historical facts have that gritty, substantial feel about them only in the examination schools and their too-extensive purlieus. I discard them as building material because they are really too plastic to use except as ornament. For example, in a small state like Yugoslavia you could get a purely factual account of its creation from a dozen representative citizens, Croat, Bosnian, Slovene, Macedonian etc., or from representatives of the various economic and religious cross-sections, and each would give a different but quite truthful picture. When Yugoslavia comes to be reorganized, facts will be so cogent and clamorous and innumerable that they will be used just as seasonings to the theoretic puddings made by the powers. Subjective considerations will weigh the most, shaped by the views of society current at the time. In 1918 the pundits of the moment, Seton-Watson, Pares, Miss Durham and others, felt queer atavistic attractions towards primitive forms of society, and were able to ignore the irresistibly dominant Austrian culture. I feel the same attraction and so have only sympathy for this astounding tour de force, but it is due to mental gymnastics and has nothing to do with the facts. Ireland, as a state, is the same sort of intellectual concoction, emanating probably in part, like Yugoslavia, from Anglo-Saxon brains. There are such things as real human societies, *in posse* if not *in esse*, but they are masked by these political figments, not revealed.[1]

The prescience of this does not need to be emphasized. It shows Butler, at a dark and uncertain period in the history of his century, looking forward as well as back with that blend of tough realism and resilient idealism which he would come to make his own. By the time he died, the 'intellectual concoction' that was the Dominion of Ireland had reorganized its status, both constitutionally and in the eyes of the world. If Ireland had become more cosmopolitan, that was an essential part of his vision too.

But one way he made his life a unique and original achievement was by establishing that cosmopolitanism could be practised, so to speak, at home. His early commitment (at fourteen, he tells us, the year the First World War broke out[2]) was to staying and living in the place where his ancestors had lived – that part of the Nore Valley commanded (in its gentle way) by his family's house, Maidenhall. If he left it, as he did in his twenties and thirties, to live abroad, he would return with the increment of foreign experience to illuminate Irish life. That is put with inappropriate pomposity, but it is none the less what he did. And throughout his life and work, there is a running engagement with writers who left Ireland without intending to return. The celebrated review of Brian Inglis's autobiography *West Briton* and the politely savage correspondence that succeeded it provide one example.[3] But more relevant, and perhaps more characteristic in tone, is his reflection on another Irish writer who went to work in England: George Bernard Shaw. Butler admired him on one level but – very typically – manages to relate Shaw's regrettable misjudgements and shortcomings to the fact that he left Ireland:

It is a queer paradox that Shaw, whose international influence was greater than that of any other European writer, was yet incapable of international thinking. His tributes to Hitler, Mussolini, Stalin, his defence of the Italian invasion of Abyssinia, are appalling in their tasteless frivolity, unless one thinks of Shaw as a genius shaped like Joyce by a small community to be its gadfly but pitchforked by fate into being a World Figure. He was denationalized, a very different thing from being international; that is to say, he had no passionate regard for any particular land or people, so that there was no untranslatable residue which an intelligent foreigner could not assimilate. Hence he was popular abroad and yet had no understanding of foreign countries. He seems to have seen the Balkans, for example, through the eyes of Anthony Hope.

I suppose it is idle to wonder what would have happened to Shaw had he never left Ireland. No doubt his genius would have been suffocated or cruelly cramped. And yet he carried to the end some of the stigma of the *déraciné*, and latterly he suffered badly from the pseudo-cosmic disease. That crusade for reforming spelling, for instance, has surely a rootless, expatriated sound, like Joyce's learned gibberish, O'Casey's staccato Stalinism and Yeats's intercourse with Yogis. Were these really serious experiments in literature, art, politics or religion? Or were they just the symptoms of a wild, nervous recoil from the narrow loyalties of a country which criminally failed to give nourishment to their tremendous talents?[4]

The autobiographical resonance in these rather questionable judgements comes through loud and clear: the writer himself was preoccupied by *not* being 'denationalized'. One of the ways in which Butler
was ahead of his time was in his persistent emphasis that Ireland's
future would be European as well as local, that the 'tilt' towards
England must be corrected by adopting other perspectives, while
remaining centred at home. And this necessarily involved, from time
to time, standing at an angle to his local universe.

From time to time this was inaccurately interpreted as the affirmation
of an ancient and conventional Irish division. At the heart of Butler's
notion of being Irish, and declaring a commitment to Irishness, was
an equally persistent commitment to the values of Irish Protestantism
– as he saw them. It need hardly be said that this was not how some –
if not most – Irish Protestants saw them. He made this acidly clear in
an essay called 'Portrait of a Minority'[5] as well as in crossing swords
with clerics and fellow-Protestants all his life, especially those who
believed in not rocking the boat. Butler could not see a safely moored
boat without wanting to rock it, and send ripples out to the edge
of the harbour and beyond. His notion of Protestantism was not
particularly doctrinal, and is best expressed in his essay on Shaw. Butler
liked Shaw's definition of a Protestant as 'theoretically an anarchist, as
far as anarchism is practicable in human society, that is to say he is an
individualist, a freethinker, a self-helper, a Whig, a Liberal, a mistruster
and vilifier of the state, a rebel'. But he thought Shaw correctly saw
the true nature of Irish Protestantism 'distorted into conservatism and
conformity by its association with an ascendancy class'. He noted
Shaw's expectation that under Home Rule this aspect of Protestantism
would find an aggressive voice in Irish politics; but it was 'splendidly
argued and absolutely wrong'.[6] By acquiescence and silence, Butler
thought, battles which should have been fought for *all* Irish liberals
had been lost, or at least let go by default.

This special use of 'Protestant' sometimes reflected his discomfort
with the hyphenated identification 'Anglo-Irish', and his repudiation
of 'Ascendancy', because he was committed at once to affirming his
tradition and descent, and proclaiming its close connection to the life
of Ireland. Early on, he drew attention to the fact that houses like
Edgeworthstown, Coole Park, Moore Hall and Bowen's Court, which

had stood as the Big Houses of their localities, were distinct from most of their kind because they had harboured projects to create a common culture for Ireland. They connected themselves to the country at large by giving something vital to the life of Ireland, and to Irish identity. This was born out of the intellectual commitments and interests of the remarkable people who lived there: Richard and Maria Edgeworth, George Moore (father and son), Augusta Gregory, Elizabeth Bowen. In his own neighbourhood, he would have added in Desart Court and Sheestown, which had backed the experiments in cooperation and the publishing ventures which he chronicled with humour and affection in essays like 'Anglo-Irish Twilight' and 'The Auction'.[7] He also pointed out that all those houses were now tumbled into ruins.

Maidenhall survives. It is a more modest dwelling than some of these legendary houses, but its atmosphere is as distinctive and the ambition of its most famous inhabitant to contribute to the intellectual making of modern Ireland is a comparable enterprise to theirs. The fact that he used the label 'Protestant' as unashamedly as he did raised hackles and went on raising them – though by the end of his life they were a new sort of hackles, bringing, for instance, an incoherent assault from the over-sensitized 'cultural' editor of a Belfast magazine called *Fortnight*.[8] In this instance, the word 'liberal' seemed to add a particular odium: from the perspective of this critic, the combination of Protestantism and liberalism added up to something like a posh unionist. This could not be more wrong, because for Butler, the kind of Protestant values he enshrined were Bunyanesque: it meant bearing witness and affirming independent views. He must have nodded assent to Yeats's superb statement in his Senate speech on divorce in 1925: 'It is one of the glories of the Church in which I was born that we have put our Bishops in their places in discussions requiring legislation.'[9] If a bishop required putting in his place regarding projected legislation, Butler would leap into action with alacrity. But there is a Yeatsian parallel at work at another level here. Chris Agee has pinpointed well what lies at the core of Butler's work: the 'ethical imagination' that is a creative imagination too.[10]

The form Butler's creativity took was, of course, writing, and writing in a very particular way. Content was inseparable from style. In going out into the world, on his own Pilgrim's Progress, he discovered his material, and his calling. Aged sixteen, he had passed through a Dublin still smouldering after the Easter Rising, and recognized subsequently that he was an Irish nationalist. His opinions on the subject were not altogether welcome to his family, notably his formidable mother, as he has recounted in one of his consummate little set-pieces of total recall, like a scene from Turgenev. Two republicans arrived at Maiden-hall during the Troubles and demanded money for the cause:

My mother and I were in the porch and she danced about with fury. 'I know who you are,' she said to one of them. 'You're Jim Connell. Take your cigarette out of your mouth when you're talking to me.' He took it out and I began to scold my mother for interrupting what might have been a revealing conversation. It was only the second time I had seen a republican, and when I went back to Oxford I wanted at least to say what they were like and what their plans were. My mother answered me sharply and we started an angry argument. The two men looked at each other with embarrassment and slunk politely away.[11]

Why this is like Turgenev, and not Somerville and Ross, is because the scene does not resolve itself into a reassuring collusion between Big House and disaffected tenantry: the tone, while just as funny, is bleaker and more realistic. At twenty-one he returned from Oxford, inflamed with ideas, like one of the characters in *Fathers and Sons*. In the years of the Irish 'Troubles' up to and including the Civil War he was a close observer of nationalism, from an 'Anglo-Irish' standpoint that was not 'Ascendancy'; nor did his English education (Charterhouse and Oxford, ironically recalled in 'A Fragment of Autobiography'[12]) alter this. In the 1920s he came under the sway of the saintly cooperativist and pacific nationalist, George Russell (AE), and entered the world of Horace Plunkett, Lennox Robinson and the Carnegie Libraries movement; his own work in the County Libraries has been recalled at length in a thoughtful essay.[13] But, characteristically, what preoccupied him most was the controversy into which the Libraries movement was plunged when its secretary, Lennox Robinson, published his short story 'The Madonna of Slieve Dun' in *To-morrow*, a crisis outlined earlier in this book.[14] The story gave offence to some Catholic opinion-makers (though not all) and also to the provost of Trinity, who chaired the Libraries Board. In the clash of threatened resignations, the movement foundered and control of it was shifted to Scotland. Butler saw this – afterwards – as a mistake; Robinson's story was not worth the loss of what could have been a potent transmitter of culture in provincial Ireland.

I believe that if he had read Yeats's letter trying to put backbone into Robinson, Butler would perforce have agreed. It is, once again, an echo of a voice we would recognize. When Robinson wanted to resign, Yeats told him:

Your desire would be to escape from so much annoyance by that easy act but when you consider public opinion in this country I think you will stay where you are. You have done nothing needing explanation or apology. You have but claimed the same freedom every important writer of Europe has claimed. Neither Flaubert nor Tolstoy nor Dostoieffsky nor Balzac nor Anatole France would have thought your theme or your treatment of it illegitimate. Ireland must not be allowed any special privilege of ignorance or cowardice. Even if your resignation helped the Libraries for the moment it would injure them in the end perhaps irreperably because it would injure the position of literature. We must not surrender our freedom to any ecclesiastic.[15]

Perhaps if the Libraries movement had flourished in the form Butler wished, and he had taken control of it and developed it (as AE had done the agricultural cooperative societies), Irish culture would have lost one illumination in gaining another. For as the Libraries movement stultified, Butler was free to travel, to visit Eastern Europe, and to spend two vitally important sojourns there: one in St Petersburg in 1931, teaching English, and another in Zagreb from 1934. If his essay 'Riga Strand in 1930' is one of the most poignant observations of East European Jewry before the deluge, to the St Petersburg experience we owe one of his greatest essays, and one of the most moving: 'Peter's Window'. His affinities with Russian culture helped to produce his translations of *The Cherry Orchard* and Leonid Leonov's *The Thief*. But above all he came to see Ireland against a background that was distinctively European, and to believe – exactly as Yeats put it – that 'Ireland must not be allowed any special privilege of ignorance or cowardice'.

Butler's sojourn in Zagreb in the mid 1930s began the fascination with Yugoslavia which persisted all his life, and which perhaps helped draw the attention of the world to his writings in the 1990s. But as the shadows lengthened over Europe he saw the dangers of totalitarianism in Western Europe too. In the late 1930s he was working with a Quaker organization to help Austrian Jews to relocate to Ireland, an experience unforgettably described in another classic essay, 'The Kagran Gruppe': the opening words convey the essence of the essay, and the man. 'I believe one of the happiest times of my life was when I was working for the Austrian Jews in Vienna in 1938–9. It is strange to be happy when others are miserable, but all the people at the Freundeszentrum in the Singerstrasse were cheerful too. The reason surely is that we have always known of the immense unhappiness that all humanity has to suffer. We read of it in the newspapers and hear it on the radio but can do nothing about it.'[16]

Doing something about it, in an utterly un-do-gooder way, remained at Butler's moral centre. And he continued to be deeply absorbed by the question of collaboration: when people turned their attention away from the loss of others' liberties – and their own. It led him to reflect upon episodes such as that of the Jewish children shipped off from Paris to Auschwitz in the summer of 1942. It is an unflinching confrontation of a story from which many of us would turn away: a story which, as he points out, is full of uncertainties and blurrings, like a fairy tale or a myth of such horror that no one wants to confront the ur-version. There are, accordingly, several versions of the story of 'The Children of Drancy'. But it is not a myth or a fairy tale. And part of Butler's subject is why we turn away from the contemplation of evil, and what the banality of officialdom permits itself by depersonalizing issues and removing people who suffer into the realm of statistics. 'We cannot visualize them reading Babar books, having their teeth straightened, arranging dolls' tea parties. Their sufferings are too great and protracted to be imagined, and the range of human sympathy is narrowly restricted.' This remarkable essay covers an enormous range in ten pages, ending, interestingly, with Yeats. Butler rebuts C. P. Snow's rather simple-minded accusation that the sympathies of Yeats and other intellectuals with political authoritarianism lies directly behind the atrocities of Nazism.

Yeats deliberately chose the small community, moving his heart and his body and as much as he could of his mind from London to Ireland, his birthplace. For him and a dozen other well-known writers Ireland had been a large Brook Farm, a refuge whose walls were built not by some transcendental theory but by history and geography. For a few years our most parochial period became also our most creative. If there was in Yeats a Fascist streak it derived from his disillusionment with the drab unheroic Ireland in which the dreams of the visionaries of 1916 had ended. He complained that 'men of letters lived like outlaws in their own country'. When he saw that Irish Fascism promised to be as drab and demagogic as Irish democracy, he rapidly back-pedalled and rewrote the song he had composed for the Blue Shirts, making it so fantastic that no political party could sing it. He led the campaign against the Irish censorship and in everything he did and said he was a champion of intellectual and moral and social freedom.

In all this he was an isolated figure and even in Ireland the range of his influence was very small. But in my opinion personal and parochial efforts like his did form a real obstruction on the road to Auschwitz, whereas its traffic was never once interrupted by conventional weapons.[17]

In 1941 Butler's father died and he himself 'deliberately chose the small community'. He returned to Maidenhall, which became the centre of his life from then on. He focused his writing energy on *The Bell*, working as review editor for that legendary journal, and writing some marvellous pieces for it himself. But that very year he had written a short but far-seeing essay calling for an outward-looking Ireland to take its place in a new world after the war:

Just as our island is physically protected by the sea, there is an ocean of indifference and xenophobia to guard our insularity and save us from foreign entanglements. Whatever its political value, culturally this self-sufficiency has been and will be a disaster to Ireland as to the other small states . . . It is not necessary to labour the point that self-sufficiency is in fact insufficient for a national culture . . . Great cultures have always risen from the interaction of diverse societies. And where that interaction has been varied, easy and reciprocated, as between the city-states of Greece, or during the Renaissance, national genius has expressed itself most freely. Its flowering period has been briefer and less abundant where it proceeds from a long interbreeding between two peoples, often involuntary and conditioned by geography rather than by mutual attraction.

In the eighteenth century French culture was as dominant in Germany as English culture in Ireland. In both cases the ultimate result was a bitter recoil to self-sufficiency, pedantry, mythology and linguistics.[18]

Already he had – so to speak – marched with history looking over his shoulder, from Stalin's Leningrad to Hitler's Vienna to Pavelic's Croatia, and had turned to face it in his own inimitable way. Thus he traced the Jews of Europe from Riga in 1930, to Nazi Austria in 1938, to the transit station at Drancy in 1942. At the end of the war, the fall-out from Eastern Europe's tragic history claimed his attention once more; and the cloud rolled as far as Kilkenny, when Butler landed himself in hot water by calling attention, at a Dublin meeting in 1952 which included the papal nuncio, to the forced conversions of Orthodox Serbs by Croatian collaborators. In the climate of the time, Archbishop Stepinac and even the collaborator Pavelich were being loudly praised as Catholic victims of Communism, and Butler's raising the question of these atrocities was seen as deliberately provocative (and, indeed, proof that he was a crypto-Communist himself). The papal envoy walked out; there was a storm of newspaper headlines ('Government to Discuss Insult to Nuncio'). Butler was denounced for having gratuitously insulted the Catholic Church, and forced to stand down from local involvements in Kilkenny such as the Kilkenny Archaeological Society, which he had helped to re-establish.[19]

Like Lennox Robinson, or Horace Plunkett, or indeed W. B. Yeats, he had created a seismic upheaval in Irish public opinion without intending to. This did not banish him to silence. Issues like the boycott of Protestant businesses at Fethard-on-Sea in 1957, after an altercation about the education of children of a mixed marriage, galvanized him into print; in this period also he wrote perhaps his most luminous essay about Irish social history, 'The Eggman and the Fairies', dealing with the tragic story of the burning of Bridget Cleary near Slievenaman in 1895, by a husband and neighbours who believed she had been transmuted into a changeling by fairy intercession. Again, it is a story where others have followed in his footsteps; but even as masterly a treatment as Angela Bourke's luminous recent study is, to a certain extent, in Butler's debt.[20] Both these apparently unconnected essays are dissections of rural Irish society: Butler surgically removes a top layer to reveal the impulses and currents beneath. If nothing else, they triumphantly demonstrate that he did not need to travel to the metropolis to find his subjects. At the same time, in the 1960s and 1970s, he continued to travel and to write: China and America were added to his repertoire of impressions. His reputation in Ireland was earned as much through his long record of outspokenness, often in masterly letters to the *Irish Times,* as for his astonishing accumulation of essays, many of them unpublished, others in journals not widely read.

His 'discovery' at the age of eighty-five came about exactly in the manner, and by the kind of agency, which both appealed to him and vindicated his own belief in local enterprise and uncompromising intellectual standards. Antony Farrell was setting up the Lilliput Press from his bedroom in Gigginstown, County Westmeath. Earlier, as a publisher's reader in Dublin, he had come across a sheaf of Butler's essays 'with all the excitement of Schliemann uncovering Troy'. Now, with his own enterprise perilously launched, he was committed to producing a collection of Butler's essays as the firm's first book. Farrell has vividly described his initial visit to Maidenhall:

I was greeted by a serene silver-haired man, as old as the century, steadfast in gaze, erect, who welcomed me into a house of the middle size perched on a hill overlooking the Nore. Through the modestly pillared porch the darkened interior was animated by two people, Hubert Butler and Peggy, his wife. We drank sherry in a sitting-room library shelved from floor to ceiling with worn and cherished books, the freight of civilization, and the fruit of a lifetime's engagement with it. We then lunched frugally among favoured cats on produce from the garden, seated by a window under a leafing horse-chestnut in the upstairs kitchen, and began a conversation that was to last almost ten years. Food never tasted more nourishing.

That weekend – the first of many – we sketched out possibilities of publication, an *ad hoc* programme, as Peggy explained the background and isolation that Hubert had experienced since the 1950s and the time of the ban; she brought me to meet one of Hubert's oldest friends in the neighbourhood, Stanley Mosse, who spoke vividly of his feeling for the Butlers and of his support for their work. And over that spring and summer we worked on selecting and composing the material that came to make up the first book of essays, *Escape from the Anthill*, the initial batch I'd seen added to with every visit as Hubert unhurriedly drew out from desks and drawers typescript drafts and offprints of essays and compositions ranging from the local to the universal, from the flax-mills on the Nore to the Kirov Islands north of Petersburg. The essay titles alone – 'The Deserted Sun Palace', 'The Eggman and the Fairies', 'Influenza in Aran', 'New Geneva in Waterford', 'Grandmother and Wolfe Tone', 'The Invader Wore Slippers', 'In the Land of Nod' – gave hints of the riches and enchantments to come and yielded other volume titles. We borrowed 'Escape from the Anthill' from an unpublished piece, so emblematic was it of everything the work represented, and Hubert built an introduction around it.[21]

The book appeared in May 1985, to a surprising reception: indeed, what recurred in the reviews was a sense of astonishment at the revelation of such a major and original talent. The ripples went far beyond the local Irish harbour. Three widely reviewed collections followed, and two volumes of selections: accolades, prizes, interviews, critical studies. A French selection was published in Paris, with an admiring introduction by Joseph Brodsky. By the end of Butler's century, he was recognized – in the USA and Britain as well as in Ireland – as one of its key commentators, who had at once kept pace with history and kept faith with his 'ethical imagination', transmuting his observations of the great world-historical cavalcade, or the inexorable juggernaut, into beautifully worked and mercilessly clear-sighted essays which bear reading and rereading. What had also become evident was the extent to which both his preoccupations and his judgements had been vindicated by the process of history. He had tracked what Eric Hobsbawm has described as 'the age of extremes', monitoring it from the standpoint of a secular humanist (Butler might have said, 'Protestant') who had seen the value of the local and the immediate, while never losing sight of the fact that we are all a piece of the main. Nine years after his death, a symposium was held to mark the centenary of his birth, in Kilkenny Castle, a building whose restoration and public use had been one of Butler's local 'causes'. The event was attended to full capacity; homage was paid by writers and critics such as Neal Ascherson, John Banville and Edna Longley. There was even a dash of the kind of spice Butler always enjoyed, provided by two neo-Stalinists from Cork who arrived under the impression that Butler had been a Communist in the 1950s, and made up for their misapprehension by attacking him for 'racism' instead. But the most remarkable tribute came from the mayor of Kilkenny, Paul Cuddihy, who appeared in full regalia and offered an apology on behalf of the people of Kilkenny, for the ostracization of 1952: an event which he put in context, but did not excuse. The statement was directed to Butler's daughter and her family, and also to the memory of Hubert Butler himself. Neal Ascherson said that he had never heard a public official speak with such 'candour and nobility': it was a moment worthy of the occasion and the man, and marked, in a sense, the real passing of Butler's century.[22]

By the time he died he knew that his work had been valued; he also knew that it was worth valuing; but he had known that all along. In the most unpretentious way, he had become a sort of national icon. I was one of many who, after reading him and writing about him, sought him out: and always came away, down that swerving drive from Maidenhall, feeling the better for it. His voice still speaks with particular clarity to those of us conditioned (or perhaps disillusioned) by the various false dawns of the 1960s; but at the same time his work is pervaded by that dogged hope for a better world which affects so many characters in Chekhov. Ideal communities, whether at Oneidea or New Geneva, were one of his constant preoccupations. By the time the public accolades came along, his value had been recognized by his own community, and this is certainly what meant most to him. The ceremony at Kilkenny nine years after his death put the seal on it.

What he represented too, despite the gentle demeanour, the seraphic smile, the beautiful manners, was a complete preparedness to take the offensive, to carry the war into the enemy's camp, to go out and shock. There is an interesting tension here, between his chosen style of private life and his public style of engagement. And style matters, as the historian Eric Hobsbawm has pointed out; evaluating his own work at a celebratory symposium, he remarked in an engagingly un-Marxist way that it would last, not because his interpretation was correct (though of course he thought it was), but because he had taught himself to write well. The same is true of Butler. He was uncannily often in the right, but he will go on being read, perhaps for as long as Montaigne, because of the way he wrote. The beauties of his phrasing, the delicacies of his humour, the surprisingly rapid twist of the rapier make reading him a continual delight. A great deal of work went into it: he knew what he wanted to do. In that same 1943 letter to Geoffrey Taylor he described how he was developing his essay technique of 'putting an idea across and working on it at the same time' and defended an essay which Taylor had found obscure:

in fact, as I felt fairly certain where I wanted to get, and there wasn't much space, my idea was to hustle the reader (for his own good) past all the forks and turns and not picnic at each cross-roads and take him into my confidence. That would have been a different kind of journey. I was quite ready to make it, but not in that article . . . I usually find indirect methods the best and have sympathy with the man who gave his son a good slap so that he would remember having seen a salamander.[23]

This is extremely enlightening: he had nearly half a century of writing life left to him, but the approach was set out already. And for his readers, the sense of delighted approbation and agreement is invariably moderated by a well-placed slap, reminding us that we have just encountered something special.

Above all, perhaps, it is a question of voice: that direct, unpretentious, uniquely modulated tone which never falters or becomes strident, which asks questions of himself as well as of his readers. 'Peter's Window', once again, is quintessential Butler; and it is an essay that ends, pregnantly, upon a question. His life in 1931 with the Archangelsky family and their circle is described with consummate humour and psychological insight: Kolya with his passionate, flinty 'Manichaean' outlook, his mother with her agonized resentments, the Communist baroness, his friends like Lihachev and the Pole who keeps offering Butler his aunt's bed, the Mexican Communist who combats the Russian conditions by filling her room with the perfume of lilies and jasmine, 'an appalling primeval smell that was neither Slav nor Latin: Lihachev said it was Aztec'. Then there is Lihachev's father, a *ci-devant* rich doctor who since the revolution has made his home a commune for all his friends and relations, but finds it lacks the sport of the old days, when they had to travel long distances to quarrel with each other. Here, as elsewhere, Ireland and Russia seem very close.

In this one essay, a short story and a memoir all at once, the essence of distilled Butler can be tasted. The detail of life and relationships is conveyed in dialogue which might come out of a perfectly gauged novel:

One day as we were queuing up outside the offices of the Lensoviet, [Kolya] tried to explain himself to me: 'I am a Caucasian from Georgia like Stalin, with the same theological background. He was a theological student. He believes like the Manichaeans that there is Good and Evil, Black and White, a dichotomy. All this which he thinks Good is Evil.' He waved his hand at the Lensoviet and the long queue.

'Why do you like the English so much then? They are not Manichaean. They play down all the major issues of good and evil. They are loyal to small obligations, not big ones. I can't imagine an English teacher neglecting all his classes to help the friend of friends, who were once very good to him.'

He looked hurt, as if I had accused him of being un-English. But I had meant it as a compliment and I could not let the subject drop. I argued that social organization works better in England, simply because the English only made superficial impact on each other. They glide about, cannoning off each other like billiard balls. They can calculate each other's reactions accurately, because they hardly ever impinge. Perhaps the reason why the Russians are difficult to organize is because they make real contact. It's like playing billiards with bull's eyes.

'You forget I am a Caucasian. That's what I hate about the Russians, always prying and inquiring about each other.'

I found his claim to be Caucasian as irritating as he found my claim to be Irish: 'I don't think Russians could ever be detached in the tepid, unemphatic English way. You would merely isolate yourselves.'

After a pause, he said, 'Darya Andreyevna was catechizing my mother about you today. She thinks you are a spy and wants the House Committee to turn you out. She has been to the Upravdom [the president of the House Committee]. Lyubotchka did her best for you. She said she thought you were a harmless idiot because you smile when you talk to her.'

'I only meant to be friendly.'

'Yes, but real Russians only smile at jokes.'[24]

Then the searchlight swings to one of his key reflections, prompted by taking part in a march to celebrate the fifteenth anniversary of Socialist Reconstruction:

Organized in processions, those whom we have known as complex individuals shed colour and character. Also there is some unconscious tabu that we violate every time we look at our friends in their public moments, which are often the moments of deepest privacy. The violation may be easy and pleasant, but it delays us for that split second between perceiving and observing. Kolya passed close by but not till he had gone did I realize that I had seen him. A column of sailors went by and I looked in vain for Lihachev. A little later I noticed a dislocation in the procession, people moderating their step behind and on either side of the baroness. She walked slowly enough for me to watch her. Her companions on either side, keeping step, held a pole from which a banner was stretched: WE ARE MARCHING TOWARDS THE CONQUEST OF TECHNICAL EFFICIENCY IN A SOCIALIST WORLD. She did not look either ironical or embarrassed. It was as if she was half asleep but sufficiently awake to enjoy her dream. She did not seem conscious of her lameness, imposing her pace with confidence on those around her.

I have thought that just as half our physical lives passes in sleep, it is perhaps intended that our mental life should be equally distributed between the assertion of our uniqueness and its renunciation. If that trance-like state of submersion in a public or collective mood bears an analogy to sleep, it would reflect our individual and self-centred lives by very simple images and phrases in dream-like sequences. In such a way, the caricatures and slogans that floated above them would complement, like dreams, the intricate, logical natures of Kolya and the baroness. The slogans were the shadows of human thinking in which their thoughts merged restfully, just as their footsteps concurred in the broad beaten track upon the snow, and we do not expect faithfulness in tone or form or colour from shadows.[25]

I still remember reading this, in 1985, and feeling so moved, so intrigued that I read and reread the passage with mounting excitement. It remains as resonant as anything he wrote on the subject of individualism and political commitment.[26]

As the end of 'Peter's Window', the searchlight swings forward again – or one might vary the metaphor and say 'telescope', because that is the image used by Butler himself, as he revisits the heroic city twenty-odd years later, finds all his friends disappeared, and is taken by an Intourist guide, Anna, to survey the rebuilt city through a telescope in a viewing-park above the Gulf of Finland.

I traced the Neva till it veered southwards by the Finland Station and the Summer Palace. To the north I saw the islands where I had walked with Yegunov and his dog. They were now called the Kirov Islands, Anna told me, and the great highway that led to them was called Kirov Avenue. Thousands of honest men and women died because of Kirov, but their names are nowhere recorded.

I have forgotten much of what Anna told me but I am more inclined to apologize for writing about great events, which touched me not at all, than for tracing again the tiny snail track which I made myself.

Is it not obvious that when through the modern media far things are brought near, the near things must be pushed far to make room for them? Imperceptibly, we become Lilliputians wandering in a Brobdingnag of our own contrivances and persuading ourselves that through contact with greatness we ourselves become greater. Then something happens to jerk us back to thoughts and people of our own size and significance. Most of the time when I was looking through that telescope, I was thinking not of the tremendous disasters that had befallen Leningrad and all Russia, but of the small stupidities, the acts of laziness or greed I had committed myself. Why had I not given the blue rug to Kolya's mother instead of leaving it behind by mistake? Why hadn't I sent Guzelimian his fishing-rod?[27]

Great themes of Russian history, of Irish consciousness, and of human destiny focus down to the blue travelling-rug and the fishing-rod. It is worth, perhaps, quoting an unpublished reaction to this essay, from Isaiah Berlin – who knew as much about the sacrifices of humanity to abstract principle, and the scars of Russian history, as anyone. After reading 'Peter's Window' in 1990, Berlin described it, with a characteristic blend of enthusiasm and sombreness, as

absolutely delightful – touching, charming, unlike anything else, and the atmosphere is conveyed marvellously. His Russian was obviously adequate, though from time to time he does produce some non-existent forms of the language, as you might imagine. The relationships of the people living in the house are wonderfully described – I see them before me, and so do you. I fully understand why he did not send Guzelimian his fishing-rod. I think that, like me in 1945, he lived to some degree in a fool's paradise, and that his visit probably did do some of these people a certain degree of harm, which is why he didn't find them again in 1956. I was in Leningrad in the same year but did not seek anyone out – I thought I had probably done enough harm – certain[ly] Akhmatova thought I had. The only thing which astonishes me is that in spite of his foreign currency black roubles, the people he lived with had as much food and good things for their parties and lived in such relative comfort as in fact they did; by 1945, I can assure you, none of this was any longer possible, and not just because of the war; 1956 was no better. One doesn't know now. What he came across were the last relics of the old regime, lurking in the nooks and crannies of the new.[28]

It is apposite to invoke Isaiah Berlin, and indeed Eric Hobsbawm, because they share with Butler a preoccupation with nationalism in the modern age. Berlin has written more illuminatingly than anyone about the philosophic roots of nationalism in German Romanticism; Hobsbawm has, more and more, directed his scholarly attention to the development of twentieth-century nationalism rather than the progress of labour relations, as one of the forces driving us to the age of extremes. Butler was, in sense, ahead of them. Early on he grappled with the relationship of religion to nationalism in Central Europe, and though he was at first over-optimistic about the fading of fundamental-ist values, by the end of his life he had revised his opinion. 'Religion,' he had written in 1958, 'which once rampaged like a shark, devouring everything which could not escape, now feeds itself like some non-poisonous jellyfish groping for plankton with sensitive tentacles'.[29] In the age of the rediscovered jihad, east and west, this was a bit too much to hope. By an appealing coincidence, at exactly the time of the publication of *Escape from the Anthill* (May 1985), Hobsbawm was delivering the Wiles Lectures at Queen's University, Belfast, on the subject of nationalism. Here, he speculated that we were coming to understand nationalism, Hegelian-style, because it was now a phenom-enon that was passing: but he too would shortly have to change his mind.[30] Butler's relationship to nationalism was always more realistic than this. It is woven through his commentaries, autobiographical and philosophical as well as political. In 'The Auction', for instance, there is a feline passage in which he presents the Anglo-Irish gentry's interest in tuberculosis as a strategy for defusing nationalism in Edwardian Ireland, and implies that they saw them both as parallel infections:

[Tuberculosis] was one of those rare and blessed battle-cries, like cooperative creameries and village halls, which appeared to have no political or religious implications. Indeed it was better than either, for often a priest wanted to consecrate a village hall or put a crucifix instead of a clock above the rostrum, and there were rumours that the creameries were used for political agitation when the farmers' boys for miles around, having taken their milk-churns from their donkey-carts, had leisure for exchanging views. But nobody could say anything of the kind about tuberculosis. When my mother had started a branch of the Women's National Health Association in Bennettsbridge, Lady Aberdeen [crusader against tuberculosis and wife of the lord-lieutenant] had come down and talked to the Association and driven round the neighbourhood. My sister had sat on one side of her and Miss Foley, the priest's sister, on the other, and Mrs Cuffe beside the chauffeur. It was an immensely amiable, non-political, non-religious occasion. Tuberculosis acted like a love-potion, and at the end of it we children had distinctly heard Miss Foley say, 'A thousand thanks, Countess, for my most delightful drive.' With the savage snobbery of children, learning for the first time the exciting art of speaking in inverted commas, we had pestered each other for months and months with poor Miss Foley's over-unctuous gratitude. So now tuberculosis, which had once seemed a sordid, almost shameful secret between the doctors and the dying, was invested with dignity and importance. Now that it was made everybody's business, it attracted to itself not only the tender and the charitable, but also the ambitious and the interfering and the timid, who saw that sympathy for the sick might be interposed as a fluffy bolster between themselves and Home Rule which they saw irrevocably approaching.[31]

This is a pointed critique of those who take to do-gooding in order to take shelter from a coming – and necessary – deluge: in this case the national independence which Butler believed essential. Where 'nationalism' might be taken to mean 'national commitment', his support is unequivocal, and this stringency pervades his attack on Brian Inglis's autobiography. It is one of his most passionate pieces of polemic. After a fair appreciation of Inglis's description of old Malahide Protestant 'society', the atmosphere of the *Irish Times*, and so on, he excoriates Inglis for leaving Ireland to become 'an important London journalist' instead of staying in Ireland and showing that the Southern Protestant tradition could provide more exemplars of an Irish way of life than 'the handful of old country crocks, retired British servicemen, civil servants and suburban car salesmen in whom the spirit of contemporary Anglo-Ireland has its incarnation'.[32] Inglis is a 'defeatist', in Butler's view, because he believes that in the overwhelmingly Catholic Republic, the large issues of Church–state relations, and the moral law as expressed through political legislation, are 'barred' from discussion by the tiny Protestant minority:

Irish Protestants constitute 25 per cent of the population of Ireland, north and south, yet those of the Republic enjoy telling each other and being told either that they have no stamina or that they would 'only do harm by interfering'. In this way they can free their minds from the unglamorous complications of Ireland and the dreary forms of bloodshed which they foresee. They have an excuse for whatever form of disengagement may be comfortable and for devoting themselves agreeably to what they call 'wider issues' in a larger society. But for a small historic community can there be any issue wider than survival and the prevention of bloodshed?

'Outsiders only make things worse by intervening.' Chicago gangsters have grown fat on this repulsive old sophistry . . . moral cowardice dressing itself up in a diplomat's bemedalled frock-coat. The great Protestant nationalists did and said what they thought to be right and never argued that they could help their friends best by withholding their support from them. Nor did they consider themselves 'outsiders'.[33]

It is Butler at his most fire-breathing, and it is not entirely fair. Not only does he elide 'Protestant' and 'Anglo-Irish', in a way that he scrupulously avoids as a rule, but he carries out a piece of fancy statistical footwork by suddenly compressing the Protestant populations of North and South to arrive at 25 per cent of the whole (1962 figures), whereas Inglis's point is that he is reflecting the position of Protestants in the Republic alone. Inglis has, of course, committed most of the cardinal sins in Butler's canon, so it is open season. The arguments are unjustly skewed, but they reflect Butler's deep-rooted commitment to fighting for a secular constitution, and his belief that the more separate Northern Ireland became from the rest of the island, the more it would resemble what George Bernard Shaw had prophesied at its inception, 'an autonomous political lunatic asylum'.[34]

Again, on the subject of national culture, Butler was ahead of his time. In 'The Barriers', written in 1941, he argued for exchange of ideas, celebration of diversity and acknowledgement of difference:

The problem of a struggling national culture is thus an international one. It can preserve itself only if the spiritual channels by which it can communicate with foreign cultures are kept free and its intercourse is equal and reciprocal. In Ireland intercourse with England only was possible and that could not be on equal terms. Anglo-Irish culture, which should comprehend all literature from Swift to Edgar Wallace in translation, could never become the focus of a nation. The same might be said of the old Austrian civilization, on which the Succession States of Eastern Europe tried to base their new national cultures. It was too strong and powerful to be assimilated. As soon as this was apparent, they dedicated themselves, like Ireland and the new states of the Baltic, to cultural self-sufficiency. Their only contact with each other was through consuls and diplomats, tourists and bagmen, and always in the interests of politics or commerce. There was none of that easy social inter-course by means of which the cultural centres of the Middle Ages were nourished. These little states were formed to protect and foster small cultural units. They failed. Everything that was unique and spontaneous in their national life was smothered behind the barriers reared to protect it.[35]

Hubert Butler's century is over now, but in post-millennium Ireland there is no shortage of issues which reflect closely upon his preoccu-pations and which he, in a sense, taught us to think about. One need go no further than a speech of Síle de Valera, Fianna Fáil minister of the arts, delivered in Boston in September 2000. Here, she argued for the erection of just the kind of cultural barriers, and expressed just the kind of suspicion of European influences, which Butler unwearyingly combated. And, for all the supposed secularization of the state, it was still possible, in the Ireland of 2000, for a Dublin institution of higher education to give first-year history students extracts from current history textbooks and ask them to guess the religion of the author – and therefore their supposed 'bias'. Butler's work may be coming into the kind of recognition it deserves, but the controversies and problems in Irish life which he went out and jousted with remain around us.

Some come dressed in the old fustian, like Ms de Valera or that confessionally minded Dublin history lecturer; others appear in new ways. There are questions like the civil rights of refugees, the reversal of emigration, the future of 'green' politics, the revelations of political corruption and the contested ideas of 'national memory' that have been discussed elsewhere in this book. Butler's own memory stretched over this turbulent century both in personal and historic terms. His sense of the need for secularism, his observations of fundamentalist politics, his redefinition of the real message of Wolfe Tone deserve to be remembered as we confront the most immediate of all those crises which loom around the Irish 'small community' – the state of what used to be called the national question as the peace process staggers into the twenty-first century. Butler was very conscious of 'the border', which supplies a recurring image in his writing. In 1955 he wrote about it, in a manifesto that was never published for a magazine that never got off the ground:

A pessimistic Ulsterman once told me that there were not enough borders and that in his opinion we should make a few more down South. A period of appalling cosmic boredom was ahead of us and the only hope was to diversify it a bit by interposing frontiers. They might delay the passage of the mass-produced standardized ideas and emotions with which we are being over-whelmed.

I think he was wrong. Borders do not keep out vulgarity and stupidity. The only way of keeping them at bay is to have an intelligent and vigorous public opinion. At present there is, south and north of the border, an almost unbelievable spiritual stagnation. A dumb stupid antagonism breaks into an occasional muffled snarl or jeer. Where there is disagreement there should, at least, be the stimulus of conflict. It is from challenge and response that civilizations have risen in the past. Why are our differences so unfruitful?

Here is one reason. Too many people would sooner be silent or untruthful than disloyal to their side. From cowardice they keep their private opinions suppressed till they have a chance of becoming public ones. Then they burst out with the force of an explosion. What should be said is blurted. There are clarion calls and crusades and political landslides and united fronts, but the art of free controversy was never so neglected. Timid or stupid people often enjoy times of crisis. They can suspend, for the country or the cause, those careful discriminations which tire the brain and do no good to the career.[36]

These are among the most characteristic words he ever wrote. Constitutionally incapable of being either timid or stupid, he devoted himself to thinking tirelessly about careful discriminations and cared very little about his career. He broke taboos, notably the taboo whereby criticism of official thought-control in Ireland was so often left to liberal Catholics because Protestants felt it was bad form – like poor Brian Inglis – to refer to the public position of the Catholic Church in independent Ireland. But in that same 1955 essay, Butler was equally scathing about Catholics within Northern Ireland who preferred to bide their time and hope for a quiet takeover through demographic change – instead of confronting the nature of the state and its potential for pluralism:

'Time is on our side,' they are saying. 'We breed faster than they do, and Ulstermen with imperial responsibilities are leaving Ulster or neglecting it. The Province has the artificial vitality of the garrison town and no organic life. If ever the pipeline were cut, it would perish. Fermoy is ours today, Enniskillen will be ours tomorrow.' That, no doubt, is how the Britons exulted when, after the Romans left and for a few short years before the Saxons came, they surged back into Verulam and Caerleon. It is an argument as sound as it is hateful. Yet few southern Irishmen would wish to absorb Ulster like greenfly invading a neglected tree, like Poles pouring into German Silesia or Czechs into Sudetenland. Ulster would no longer be of value to Ireland if she were robbed of her rich history, her varied traditions. If she gives up these, which link her to the rest of Ireland, and becomes a mere imperial outpost, she will deserve the fate of Breslau and Fiume and Königsberg . . . On the other hand if she keeps her Irish character the border will slowly cease to be a menace and an anxiety. Either it will become meaningless and will drop off painlessly like a strip of sticking-plaster from a wound that has healed, or else it will survive in some modified form as a definition which distinguishes but does not divide.[37]

Nearly half a century later, the time has come to pay attention to this, as to so many of Butler's formulations. His acuteness and prescience about Ireland, about Europe, about Ireland in Europe will ensure his continuing influence, but that perception, and those preoccupations, are based on philosophic foundations and literary genius which put him in a far greater tradition than simply that of political commentator or historian. In an age when the intellectual market is dominated by vast, distended, catch-all histories dealing with 'millennia' or 'civilizations', churning out words which say nothing at all, Hubert Butler stayed in his fields along the Nore, and in essays which often covered fewer than ten pages said more about world history than the most inflated blockbuster or television series. The view from the front porch of Maidenhall is emblematically Irish, but it stretches far beyond the water-meadows, the river, the distant ruined Norman castle and much older Celtic church: west to American Utopias, east to Sarajevo and Riga Strand, sweeping through lost memory, failed aspirations and great hopes, like the telescope trained on the Nevsky Prospekt in 'Peter's Window'.

12

Remembering 1798

I

In 1972, as a postgraduate student working on Charles Stewart Parnell and Wicklow, I went to visit Mr Robert Barton of Glendalough House in County Wicklow. He was then over ninety, and his father had been an exact contemporary and close friend of his neighbour Parnell, though politics sundered them. Among much else, Robert Barton told me that the two friends, both owners of well-timbered demesnes, cooperated in the 1870s on building sawmills. Barton's father decided that one particularly large and aged beech should be scheduled for the mills, as its impressive circumference would test the new machinery. But none of the men on the place would agree to cut it down, without saying why: except that it was 'unlucky'. Barton's father brought in workers from somewhere else, who began to saw it down. The blade of their saw was unable to get through the trunk without grinding to a halt, because the wood was densely peppered with lead. The tree stood for more than bad luck. In the 1798 Rising, particularly bloody in County Wicklow, local rebels had been tied to it and shot. The memory persisted, and the taboo: the actual association was suppressed, whether for reasons of tactfulness or trauma. Or both.

The folk memory of 1798, like that of the Famine, the next traumatic caesura in Irish history, tends to be repressed: it often takes the form of re-remembering in the following generation. The most famous commemorative ballad was published anonymously in the *Nation* on 1 April 1843 (and reprinted in *The Spirit of the Nation* anthology later that year). It was called 'The Memory of the Dead', but is inevitably known by its first line 'Who Fears to Speak of '98'. It was written ironically, by an idealistic twenty-year-old who subsequently became a notably conservative vice-provost of Trinity College Dublin.[1] 'Fearing to speak' or not, it is a truism that historical understanding and suppressed or re-edited memory are closely interwoven: a recent study on the subject refers sweepingly to 'History as an Art of Memory'.[2] Commemoration of 1798, two hundred years later, has shaken off any fear; it has, indeed, run like a riptide. There have been dozens of books, yards of newsprint, countless conferences, even – in the most harmless possible way – attempted re-enactments of key junctures.[3]

But this is not new. 1798 has, in fact, a history of commemoration, as well as a history of itself. The impetus behind this is obvious: an astonishing historical crisis, a moment when the Irish – and possibly European – future could have been decisively changed, demands attention. There is also the wished-for association with the evident heroism of the United Irishmen and their admirable, and still relevant, principles. Wolfe Tone's charismatic insouciance ('the *beau-ideal* of Irish rebels' as Sean O'Faolain put it[4]), Lord Edward Fitzgerald's self-sacrifice, Bartholomew Teeling's address at the foot of the gallows – all these demand a certain empathy as well as respect. 'If to have been active in endeavouring to put a stop to the blood-thirsty policy of an oppressive government has been treason,' said Teeling, 'I am guilty. If to have endeavoured to give my native country a place among the nations of the earth was treason, then am I guilty indeed. If to have been active in endeavouring to remove the fangs of oppression from off the heads of the devoted Irish peasant was treason, I am guilty. Finally if I [recte to] have strove [sic] to make my fellow men love each other was guilt, then I am guilty.'[5] Two hundred years later, these sentiments make him seem more innocent than his prosecutors; and the United Irishmen remain, in Ian McBride's word, spellbinding.[6]

But commemoration is, of course, always present-minded; and future historians will be interested in how we remembered to remember 1798, and what was forgotten in the process. It is tempting to quote a memorable postcard sent by George Bernard Shaw, in response to an invitation to join the commemorationists in 1898: 'It was proposed to me that I should help to uplift my downtrodden country by assembling with other Irishmen to romance about 1798. I do not take the slightest interest in 1798. Until Irishmen apply themselves seriously to what the condition of Ireland is to be in 1998 they will get very little patriotism out of yours sincerely GBS.'[7]

What happened in 1798? The year comes as the climax of a decade of radical activity – which changed ideological direction, and political strategy, after Britain went to war with France in 1793, and government policy towards British and Irish radicals became accordingly severe and eventually violently oppressive. Behind the savage episodes of 1798 lay a complex recent history of parliamentary reform, short-circuited from the early 1790s, agitation for the lifting of all disabilities against Catholics, mounting tension in the countryside and, most influentially of all, the foundation and transformation of the Society of United Irishmen: French-inspired radicals, embracing modern, egalitarian, secular ideals. A founder member, the cautious Ulsterman William Drennan, had called for 'the establishment of societies of liberal and ingenious men, uniting their labours, without regard to nation, sect or party, in one grand pursuit, alike interesting to all, by which mental prejudice may be worn off, a humane and truly philosophic spirit may be cherished in the heart as well as the head, in practice as well as theory'. The 'general end', he said, was 'real Independence to Ireland' and republicanism 'the general purpose'.[8]

Drennan rather withdrew later, and he was a less fashionable icon in 1998 than Teeling.[9] But this quotation, as inspiring in its way as Teeling's, serves as a reminder that the United Irishmen represented the Dissenter (mostly Presbyterian) merchant classes of Belfast as well as the middle classes of Dublin and some liberal-minded gentry. With the change in government policy, they too radicalized. Their exclusion by the Anglican Establishment gave them a certain sense of fellow grievance with Catholics, though their ideology remained resolutely anti-papal. Their links with France, brilliantly investigated by Marianne Elliott,[10] were strengthened as they went underground. By 1796 French invasion forces were planned, and in December there was the cliffhanging episode of a huge French fleet in Bantry Bay, with Wolfe Tone on board. Simultaneously, the United Irishmen were moving towards rapprochement with a more shadowy strand of the Irish subversive tradition: the Defenders, a rurally based secret society with roots in the ancient radical-agrarian tradition, who had been involved in confrontational activity since the early 1790s.

By late 1797 revolutionary plans were so clearly afoot that the government commenced a deliberate policy of aggression, through newly raised forces of yeomanry and militia. And they also used the growing network of the Orange Order, formed after the 1795 Battle of the Diamond, to drive home the identification of loyalism and Protestantism. While the United Irishmen conspired with their French allies, a stream of information came to the government from a wide range of informers. Ulster was ruthlessly 'pacified', with martial law and sweeping arrests, from the spring of 1797. None the less, in February 1798 there were still about 500,000 sworn United Irishmen, with perhaps 280,000 in possession of arms. By March 1798 Ireland was proclaimed as in a state of rebellion, and draconian measures were inflicted far and wide. The insurrection of that summer happened as a series of disparate episodes, beginning in Leinster on 23 May. Until the Battle of Vinegar Hill outside Enniscorthy, County Wexford, on 21 June, Wexford and Wicklow were ablaze, despite severe checks such as the Battle of Ross on 5 June. In early June a belated rising broke out in Ulster, but lasted only a week. The percussion of incidents ended with (at last) a French landing in Mayo, too little and too late, in August. By then, the only rebels holding out from the first wave were some bands of skirmishers in the Wicklow mountains. In all these linked outbreaks, perhaps 30,000 died (3,000 alone at the Battle of Ross on 5 June). But numbers remain conjectural, and it stands as the most concentrated outbreak of violence in recorded Irish history.

That staggered nature of the outbreak was one reason for the revolutionaries' failure; another was the incoherence of the cause for which so many fought so bravely, at least when compared to the firm revolutionary theory of the United Irishmen before its outbreak. And another was the unexpected geographical dispersal of the activity. Hearing of the Wexford conflagration, Wolfe Tone (in Paris) was astounded, and wondered at once what had happened to the North, where it had been expected (in the south-east – as records subsequently seemed to show – the United Irishmen network was tenuous in the extreme). All these imbalances have been examined anew over the past few years, but a certain sense of disparateness remains (especially as so many of the studies are, by intention and definition, local).

There is another imbalance too, which concerns the amount of material surviving. Records are vastly disproportionate on each side, the governmental archive far outweighing that reflecting the rebels. Thomas Pakenham, writing in *The Year of Liberty* thirty years ago, pointed out that there were 10,000-odd documents in the Rebellion Papers then at Dublin Castle, of which all but about a hundred originated from the government side; they are now in the admirable new National Archives, and have been added to, but a recent analysis by Deirdre Lindsay comes to much the same conclusion.[11] Only a few first-hand records from the rebel side are more or less contemporary, notably Thomas Croney's and Joseph Holt's, and even these did not see the light of day until 1832 and 1838 respectively. Other materials were gathered in R. R. Madden's great seven-volume collection about the United Irishmen, published from 1842 to 1846, which fixed the men of '98 in the mould of heroic nationalism, nineteenth-century style. Perhaps the most useful first-hand account of all, the remarkable three-volume reminiscences of Miles Byrne, was not published until 1863. Byrne, a United Irishman in his teens in 1798, subsequently became an experienced soldier in France, and Parisian correspondent for the *Nation*; his account, dictated to his wife, denied any sectarian input in Wexford and stressed the coherence of United Irish organization there. Both these issues were already the subjects of hot debate, and remained so.

Madden's first volume had stated a case generally followed until very recently, regarding the relationship between the Wexford Rising and the rest of the island. It was 'sufficiently established by the universal acknowledgement of all the inhabitants of the county of Wexford', he wrote, 'officers and men, who bore a part in this insurrection, that there was no concert between this rising and the plan of a general insurrection in and about Dublin, and that it was no more than a tumultuary and momentary exertion of popular resistance to a state of things found or considered insupportable, the sole object of which was an attempt to get rid of oppression, and to retaliate with equal violence what they had been for some time experiencing'; this was not, in other words, an ideologically inspired United Irishman revolution, and there was in fact only a sketchy United Irish organization in the county.[12]

At any rate, the rising went wrong; few would disagree about that.

In the image of a later radical, James Fintan Lalor, the metaphorical wolfdog lying chained in every Irish peasant's cabin did not slip his leash: or at least too few of them did, and at different times. Notable dogs that did not bark, or were quickly muzzled, included the Dublin dog, that resilient urban mongrel; the city did not act as the nerve-centre of revolt. The local United Irishmen were thrown off course by the early arrest of Lord Edward Fitzgerald and others, by insufficient arms and by a fatally effective ring of informers. The plan had been for Dublin to give the signal when United Irish organization in the city was ready – which it never was. Though planned for 23 May, the outbreak was rapidly suppressed by the Yeomanry, and liaison with groups outside the capital was never effectively established.[13]

The Western dog was equally quiet – or at least only woke up when the French finally arrived, apart from some unrest around Leitrim in 1795 which was apparently agrarian and Defenderist in inspiration.[14] And a dog who barked early but then fell notably silent was the noble, secular-minded dog of French revolutionary idealism, as mediated through the merchants and intellectuals of Belfast. There, in a sense, the inspiration had all begun; there, it faded most quickly into oblivion, as early-nineteenth-century Ulster solidified into confessional mode and sectarian patterns were etched yet further into economic, social and political life. The subsequent historiography reflected these silences and embodied fixed positions of partisanship. The historical treatments of the rising set hard into orthodoxy during the nineteenth century. From the unionist side (epitomized by the enormous collections of material published by the rabidly partisan Richard Musgrave), it was a bloodthirsty religious war for the expropriation of Protestants, led by priests and fuelled by the memories of the seventeenth century. Moreover, writers like Tom Moore had early on established the nobility of the enterprise. So did the cult of Robert Emmet. Much as the resistance struggle waged by Hugh O'Neill and Red Hugh O'Donnell against the Elizabethan Conquest was praised by Irish Tory romantics like Samuel Ferguson and Standish O'Grady, the glamour of Lord Edward Fitzgerald and Emmet (young, handsome, articulate, liberal, Protestant) was covertly celebrated by some unlikely protagonists from the mid nineteenth century. For the radical nationalist tradition (at least from the growth of the Young Ireland movement in the late

1830s, and further bolstered by the Fenian journalism of the 1860s[15]), 1798 was a heroic rising against oppression, after a series of reverses for the cause of Catholic equality, precipitated by government agents provocateurs.

Both sides rather played down the French input, and the pre-existing tensions in the countryside at large. Both put the events of 1798 firmly into a continuum of linked struggles for 'freedom', an interpretation greatly boosted by the 'faith-and-fatherland' version popularized from the 1870s by the Wexford Franciscan Patrick Kavanagh and the nationalist journalist A. M. Sullivan, and apostrophized in a more mystical way by Patrick Pearse when he hailed Tone as the greatest apostle of Irish nationalism because 'he died for us'.[16] The original ideas of the United Irishmen were rather downgraded in the process. For Wexford, the 'faith-and-fatherland' interpretation seemed logical enough: there was Father Murphy, the priest who led the rebels, and there were not, apparently, many United men; moreover, that pleasant south-eastern corner was a prosperous and largely English-speaking area, with a long history of colonization. From the late 1970s, however, the distinguished social historian Louis Cullen (himself a Wexford man) began analysing this interpretation, from two angles. In a series of pioneering articles, he established a prehistory of social and agrarian conflict in the county, breaking along lines of land settlement and helping to explain the savagery of intercommunal violence there. From another angle, he examined the state of United Irish organization in Wexford, and radically revised the picture which up to then had been readily accepted from fortuitously assembled government records.[17] More recently, others have shown how far these rely upon chance survivals. Kevin Whelan, for instance, repeating Miles Byrne, has laid great emphasis on the fact that a United Irishmen delegate from Wexford, through dallying with a girl in a pub, failed to turn up at the meeting subsequently raided in Dublin – so a list of the Wexford membership of the organization did not fall into the hands of Dublin Castle, and subsequently of no less rapacious historians. It should be said, however, that cold water was poured on this attractive idea by Charles Dickson over forty years ago.[18]

Still, with the gathering momentum through the 1990s towards the long-awaited bicentenary, other lacunae were addressed. Most of all, and sparked perhaps by the bicentenary of 1789 a decade ago, the French were welcomed back into the picture. Their inspirational, secularist ideal has been re-established, displacing the interpretation of a brave, tragic but essentially reactive and atavistic jacquerie asserted by Dickson in the 1950s and Thomas Pakenham in the 1960s.[19] In the process, what the French could have done for the Irish future has been framed as one of the most tragic might-have-beens of Irish history – a hypothesis, it might be added, first advanced some time ago, and with considerably more irony, by that good friend to Ireland, John Stuart Mill. It should be said that another strain of heavyweight historical research from the 1980s on, pre-eminently Marianne Elliott, preserved more of the older interpretation, notably regarding the sectarian input of the Defenders; and in 1994 Nancy Curtin published a study of the United Irishmen which is a classic of its kind and which echoes Elliott more closely than the commemorationists.[20] Tom Dunne also produced an interpretative short study of Wolfe Tone as a 'colonial outsider' which sits rather athwart the general drift.[21] But it is fair to say that the new wave of 1798 historians are all United Irishmen now. The appeal of their bracing Northern vision of egalitarianism has been re-established; the notion of 'the Republic in the Irish Village', paraphrasing Maurice Agulhon, has been put at the centre of their enterprise. A recent article on 1798 even took this very title in homage, though the actual content contained nothing at all to bear the parallel out.[22] More convincingly, James Livesey's thought-provoking edition of the United Irishman Arthur O'Connor's 1798 pamphlet *The State of Ireland* shows how adventitiously 'French Ideas' were grafted on to the rather antiquated forms of Irish oppositionism.[23] To be French is to be radically fashionable, historiographically speaking; it is also to be European, and Modern, and non-Anglocentric.

Thus the Wexford Rising has been reinterpreted as forward-looking rather than atavistic. The fact that it broke out in an Anglophone area makes sense, if it is seen as epitomizing the avant-garde secularist ideals of the United Irishmen. The relation of this elite group to 'popular culture' has been the subject of cheery if inconsistent generalization.[24] For a current generation of historians, lively, *engagé* and above all imaginative, 1798 represents the moment when the North came South, and opened up a 'space' for an 'inclusive, democratic, non-sectarian' united Ireland. We are told briskly by more than one historian that 'Understanding the reason for its momentous defeat in the 1790s can help us to ensure that history does not tragically repeat itself in the 1990s.'[25] To scent a whiff of dangerous anachronism about this can only mark one down as a spoilsport.

II

Still, if this is where we stand now, it may be interesting to look back a hundred years to the first centenary of the rising, because commemoration for the purposes of present politics is nothing new. In September 1898 the Irish Quaker Alfred Webb, nationalist, printer, ex-secretary of the Land League and currently treasurer of the Evicted Tenants' Fund, wrote to a colleague: 'The country appears *memorial mad*'. He complained about 'no less than 4' monuments to the United Irishmen in County Wexford and remarked caustically that this expenditure was 'absorbing the funds that should go to supporting a Home Rule fight and toward relieving the evicted . . . What is going on is *talk* about the past, and inaction regarding the present.'[26] Certainly the period from 1880 to 1914 was a great age of jubilees and commemoration, and squarely in the middle came the centenary of 1798, by now firmly established as an episode in the continuing struggle for faith-and-fatherland against the Saxon. Father Kavanagh was the accepted historian of the rising, rather than others more or less forgotten now; much less the partisan Musgrave, who was after all seen as a crank even in his own day, as latter-day commentators tend to forget. (Although Jonah Barrington's 'character' of him bears repeating: 'a man who (except on the abstract topics of politics, religion, martial law, his wife, the pope, the Pretender, the Jesuits, Napper Tandy, and the whipping post) was generally in his senses'.[27]) Certainly by the late 1890s Father Kavanagh held the field. Laying the Foundation Stone of the Wexford '98 Monument, he announced that it was 'proof to future generations that we were imbued with the spirit of the men of '98 . . . The men whose memory we honour today, died for a persecuted creed as well as an oppressed country . . . Their blood was not poured forth in vain. It made the earth which drank it ever sacred to freedom;

with their expiring breath they kindled the embers of a fire which burnt still.'[28] The creed mentioned was clearly not that of the French Revolution. A fellow historian who worked with Kavanagh on the commemorations rather nervously described him as a fanatic in matters of religion, who wanted to impose a boycott on Protestant businesses in Wexford town, which would certainly have been one method of commemoration. By now 1798 had been firmly annexed, and would be celebrated accordingly.

The centennial movement had probably begun in 1879, when a group of Wexford men in Dublin formed the '98 Club', with a view to commemorating the rising; two years before, commemorative meetings had been convened in Wexford. The 1879 initiative should probably be seen as part of the enterprise which produced the Young Ireland Clubs a few years later, in the mid 1880s. Both represent the colonization by Fenian elements of aspects of cultural politics, at a time when the IRB was prospecting other strategies than the traditional one. (This is a process that coincides with the apparent success of the constitutional movement, rather than succeeding it after the fall of Parnell, as so influentially claimed by Yeats.) It was therefore highly politicized, as people expected it to be – on the unionist side as well. Inspired by the early-warning commemorationists, the sardonic Ulsterman Alexander Donovan published in 1893 an only-just-futuristic pamphlet, a sort of Irish *Battle of Dorking*, called *The Irish Rebellion of 1898*. Set in post-Home Rule anarchy five years on, this cod-historical squib grafted memories of massacres in Wexford a century before on to the idea of an insurrection helped by Britain's enemies during a future war, quelled only by loyal Ulster.[29]

What began in the literary societies soon spread to the politicians, inside and outside the system. On the one hand, the movement for commemoration was seized by old Fenians like John O'Leary and his younger acolytes, including William Rooney, Maud Gonne and Yeats; on the other hand, the separated wings of the Irish Parliamentary Party, floundering in the wilderness after the shattering fall and death of Parnell, decided to climb on the bandwagon too. John Redmond, after all, was a Wexford man *pur sang*, whose ancestors had been much involved; in 1886 he had published a pamphlet, *The Truth about '98*, and lectured prolifically on the subject on both sides of the

Atlantic, usually with the aim of demonstrating the illegitimacy of the Union, as well as invoking neo-Fenian rhetoric for fundraising purposes. However, for several months the organizing committee remained firmly in the hands of 'advanced nationalists', who managed to exclude both the Redmondite and Dillonite wings of the Parliamentary Party from any part in their deliberations.

Thus 1898 became the high point of Irish 'demo' politics, coming between the anti-Jubilee of 1897 and the agitation against the Boer War.[30] In the end, the enterprise of commemorating 1798 a hundred years later helped bring about the reunion of the constitutional nationalists. But it also, I believe, helped spark the revival of the IRB, usually placed some years later, after the anti-war elements had regrouped as Sinn Féin in the early 1900s.

1898 was important in many underground ways; it intersected decisively with the projects of the young W. B. Yeats, public and private. He was one of the founder members of the Young Ireland League in 1891, a Fenian cultural society which took a leading part in the 1898 organizations. It came at a time when, after a brief estrangement, he was once more determined to win the beautiful revolutionary Maud Gonne; but simultaneously he was moving into the orbit of Augusta Gregory and planning the Irish Literary Theatre. And it coincided with a high point of mystical involvements and astrological frenzy, for Yeats and his circle of occultist would-be adepts. Their schemes to commemorate 1798 are inextricably mixed with plans for the creation of a Celtic Mystical Order, based in a Castle of Heroes on a lake isle in Connacht (Richard Wagner meets Standish O'Grady): if, Yeats cautioned, it could be done for thirty shillings a week. He was determined to seize control of this and other enterprises, and actually became president of the '98 Centennial Committee for Great Britain and France, while Gonne set herself to collecting money in the USA for a Wolfe Tone Memorial, and bringing in revolutionaries as diverse as the Garibaldi veteran Amilcari Cipriani, and sundry English hangers-on like the deranged Vicar of Plumstead. She was better at it than Yeats, whose determined adherence to the cause was at least partly inspired by astrological calculations which promised that 1898 was a year of historic conjunctions, in his personal as well as his public life.[31] But neither of them, in the end, was a match for the hard-headed politicos, from the extreme and the constitutional wings of the nationalist movement, who eventually took over proceedings. Either way, the project seems to have had less and less connection with anything that 1798 had actually been about.

Nor were they the only ones. From Ulster, commemorative plans were launched by the influential nationalist Alice Milligan, not without opposition. Convivial visits to the graves of dead rebels were organized and societies founded in their honour. Here too the constitutional nationalists (organized by the young Joseph Devlin) tried to outflank the Fenians, and effectively took over, while the centenary parade sparked off riots in the Shankill.[32] Those who recalled the Presbyterian radical tradition did so by emphasizing how different it appeared to the sectarian republicanism which they now perceived in the South. Moreover, the Union had – it was claimed – given the Northern heirs of the United Irish tradition exactly the freedoms their ancestors had fought for a hundred years before.

An interestingly ambivalent note sounded through the *Belfast Newsletter*: it opposed a Wolfe Tone Memorial, but cautiously admitted there was a case for commemorating William Drennan. In fact, ambiguity dogged the 1898 activities. Even that essential Fenian John O'Leary can be found reading a message from it that faces both ways. Before the stone-laying ceremony he told the Lord Mayor's Banquet that 'he infinitely preferred that Ireland should be under her own laws and not under English laws, and he did not mind whether it was a republic, an absolute monarchy or a limited monarchy; however he was not an impractical [man], and he could conceive Ireland accepting something short of that'.[33]

As O'Leary's speech hints, politics were breaking in all round. Yeats and Maud Gonne had ended up in the camp of the Irish National Alliance, a breakaway Fenian group, and were accordingly distanced from their patron O'Leary. They found themselves the targets of an ex-comrade, the unbalanced firebrand Frank Hugh O'Donnell, whose pamphlets denouncing their revolutionary agitprop and commemorative activities still burn off the page – as when he accused 'the Daughter of Erin from Essex' of aligning Ireland's holy cause with a secret plan to destroy the Vatican, funded by Parisian stock-jobbers.[34] Yeats's own ambivalence came through more and more clearly, as Maud

Gonne dragged him round committee rooms from Limerick to Liverpool. 'We tare each others character in peices for things that don't matter to anybody,' he lamented to Lady Gregory, who riposted with a firm public statement that anyone who wanted to commemorate the men of 1798 should simply plant a tree, and then get on with their lives.[35] Maud Gonne's money-raising efforts also caused bitter antipathy among the revolutionaries, and by the high point of the celebrations in August 1898 there was a campaign to squeeze her out of the picture. Meanwhile the rival parliamentary leaders Redmond and Dillon managed, from their different sides, to get the constitutional nationalists in on the act (rather as Redmond, an underrated political operator, would later effect a takeover of the Irish Volunteers in 1913–14). This required aligning themselves with Fenian rhetoric, and other complicated manoeuvres. Their rival commemorative organizations only just came uncomfortably together in time for the great day, 15 August 1898.[36]

The commemorations attracted great publicity and were closely watched by the authorities, but they were effectively colonized by mainstream Irish nationalism and the clerical establishment. Detectives noted that Gonne was excluded from the platforms, and the socialist James Connolly mordantly attacked the conventional direction things had taken, denying 'that the United Irishmen had anything to do with a union of classes' and attacking the commemoration committees for choosing Lady Day, a festival of the Catholic Church, 'and therefore, if not absolutely prohibitive to, at least bound to raise grave suspicion in the minds of our non-Catholic fellow-countrymen'.[37] Nevertheless, he sold the first copies of his new Marxist–nationalist magazine, the Workers' Republic, to the crowds assembling for the celebrations on 15 August.

The commemorations had made their mark. During the confused period of Yeats's life when he found his way back to advanced nationalism, after the Easter Rising of 1916, his correspondence shows that he was preoccupied by his memories of 1898 and what had happened then, when the millennium was deferred. The whole episode was a prophetic demonstration of the potent fission when politics meet history in Ireland. It also proved the inherent tourist appeal of such conjunctions. The 'diaspora' (or, as the phrase then went, the 'Irish race worldwide') were warmly encouraged to participate, and much was hoped for from this injection of 'wealth and influence'.[38] The '98 Centennial Association of America offered a 'Grand Pilgrimage' tour to Ireland, France and England – which included, as an unexpected highlight for the republican pilgrims, a visit to Shakespeare's home at Stratford.[39] However, Kevin Whelan's claim that the 1898 commemorations 'knitted together' strands of Irish nationalism[40] is hard to sustain; all the evidence seems to be – as Timothy O'Keefe has made clear – that it did the opposite.[41] While the two wings of the post-Parnellite Parliamentary Party came together two years later, this was in response to the challenge posed by William O'Brien's United Irish League rather than the uneasy cooperation on commemorative platforms: O'Brien, in fact, had sharply disapproved of the political narrowness of the '98 organizations.[42]

As for the Fenian element, they were further distanced than ever. Superficially, the movement for commemoration had been 'parliamentarized' by the constitutionalists. The site at the top of Grafton Street in Dublin where the foundation stone had been laid for a monument to Wolfe Tone remained unoccupied. There was an embarrassing amount of trouble about the money,[43] and it was finally used for an arch to commemorate the Dublin Fusiliers at the end of the Boer War.

Down in Wexford, it was different. When Oliver Sheppard's impressive statue to the United Wexford men of '98 was finally unveiled in 1905, the language used was notable: 'it was the duty of everyone claiming to be an Irishman', said the mayor, 'not to waver until the aspirations of those brave men had been fulfilled'.[44] This could be read as a safe call for Home Rule, and the proceedings were described as 'a model of constitutional propriety'. But 1898 had all the same reintroduced a certain tone. Perhaps the most potent results of the 1898 project lay in the experience gained by William Rooney (a prominent organizer) and Arthur Griffith, later channelled into the movement against the Boer War, the significantly named *United Irishman* and the creation of Sinn Féin. Even more prophetic was the creation of the 'Dungannon Clubs', whereby the IRB was reconstructed from the inside. All this took its rise from the 1898 activities. Timothy O'Keefe has engrossingly analysed the quasi-religious and hagiographical format of organizations named for United Irishmen, like the Oliver Bond Club;[45] and the secretary of that club, the Sinn Féiner George Lyons, would long afterwards trace the pedigree of the 1916 Rising back, not (as Yeats did) to Parnell's death in 1891, but to the 1898 commemorations, which began 'all our modern efforts towards an ideal of independence'.[46] And though the subsequent years saw a considerable stir of polemical and political activity in Irish nationalist circles, Fenians and constitutionalists were not particularly 'knitted together' by the memory of the dead United Irishmen. The most influential nationalist ideologue of the early twentieth century, D. P. Moran, liked to deny that Wolfe Tone was Irish at all, since he was born of English parents, became a Frenchman, and was an atheist to boot.

III

With the slightly divisive example of 1898 in mind, it is time to turn to the present day and consider how the 1798 Rising was remembered two hundred years later. This has not been left to chance. The Irish government appointed a '1798 Commemoration Committee', based at the office of the minister of state at the department of the Taoiseach.[17] On 10 April 1997 this issued a six-point 'Mission Statement on 1798' to relevant civil servants and diplomats:

1. To commemorate the ideals of the United Irishmen and the 'Fellowship of Freedom' that inspired them in 1798.
2. The recognition of the 1798 rebellion as a forward-looking, popular movement aspiring to unity; acknowledging that what happened in Dublin and Wexford was part of what happened in Antrim and Down.
3. Attention should shift from the military aspects of 1798 and be directed towards the principles of democracy and pluralism which the United Irishmen advocated.
4. A focus on the international perspective of the United Irishmen and the enduring links which 1798 forged with America, France and Australia.

5. To acknowledge the Ulster dimension and particularly the contribution of the Presbyterian tradition, with its emphasis on justice, equality and civil liberty.
6. To focus attention on the ideals of the leaders of 1798 which still live in Irish history.

It is tempting to add a seventh: 'Don't talk about the war.' Certainly, the historians retained by the government for the purposes of commemoration, and sent forth on the mission, acted up to the mark. There was a good deal of rather self-congratulatory commentary, to the effect that we had learned from the mistakes of our great-grandparents. Instead of stridently remembering '98 as a festival of faith-and-fatherland (*one* faith, *one* fatherland), the Irish were enjoined to embrace '98 as a confluence of traditions in a pluralist, secular 'space'. Certainly there was a profuse outpouring of research and commentary, much of it highly suggestive. The canonical accounts were investigated, and pursued back to their sources – leading to the restoration of General Holt's memoirs before Croker bowdlerized them, and the reassessment of Miles Byrne's evocative account.[48] The disingenuous reasons behind, for instance, Edward Hay's contemporary claims that the Wexford Rising had no plan or structure have been clarified, and the collections of local historians like Luke Cullen given their full due. The European dynamic has been re-established at this juncture of Irish history, as at others; the local texture of events, people, alliances, kinships has, following the pioneering work of Louis Cullen, been built upon by several scholars. The intended connections between what happened in the North and the South have been reasserted, and the structure of the United Irishmen and their intentions more clearly delineated than ever before. All this is extremely interesting and self-evidently worth while.

But in the process 1798 has been repackaged, and the intentions of the principal actors prioritized above the actual outcome of events. The language used is heavily loaded. 'The United Irishmen,' according to one historian, 'were trying to negotiate a political structure here and with Britain, capable of representing Irish people in all their inherited complexities and allegiances; the peace process today is trying to do the same thing.'[49] A pluralist, Europeanized, dynamic Ireland was proleptically asserted for the 1790s, as for the 1990s: today's 'Republic', declared in 1948, was described as a lineal descendant of what is called, in rather gingerly fashion, the 'embryonic Republic of Wexford'.[50] Others, less evasive, proclaimed the actual Republic as established in Wexford, and even the ecumenical 'Senate' which allegedly ran that Republic during its existence.[51] This rather ignored the debate over whether the term 'Republic' was ever used for Wexford, except by one antagonistic commentator determined to raise the spectre of French Revolutionism. Daniel Gahan, author of the most recent history of the rising in that county, specifically denied that the rebels declared a 'Republic of Wexford', and Tom Dunne sharply dismissed the actuality of either Republic or Senate in terms which were not effectively rebuffed.[52] None the less, as commercialized theme-park history took over, that 'Senate' was set up in the town as a sort of fancy-dress exhibit for 1998, manned by local – and other – worthies prepared to pay £2,000 for the privilege. 'It was like what John Hume calls "an agreed Ireland" today,' explained one over-excited local historian.[53] Senate membership, like entry to the Rose of Tralee competition, was open to anyone of 'Irish extraction', so the diaspora were welcomed in too.

The senatorial fees, where they were forthcoming, went to fund the Enniscorthy 1798 Memorial Centre, built at a cost of £2.3m; visitors walked over a Bridge of Democracy, past plaques commemorating the great republics from Athens onwards, when history could – it is implied – have changed for the better. (These sportingly include the English Republic of 1649, thus providing Ireland's only monument celebrating Oliver Cromwell.) There was a lot of dressing up and posing with pikes. There were exhibitions all over: some, like the one in the Ulster Museum, utterly admirable; others, like the ongoing 'Puppet Show of '98' in Fingal, less intellectually demanding. In the old Wicklow gaol, reopened by President McAleese as the 'National Centre for Convict Transportation to Australia', tape-recordings were played of suggestive gaol-rape scenes, and actors dressed as gaolers threatened tourists with hanging; visitors were promised the further frisson of 'meeting some of the Wicklow men of '98' (on the Other Side, presumably – an aspect which Yeats and his friends would have thoroughly approved). Re-enactment took ever more surreal forms, with the 're-creation' of the battles of Ballinamuck and Carrignagat – complete with muskets.[54] Best of all, in 1998 the French returned in force – though in the form of squadrons of Lycra-clad bicyclists taking part in the first leg of the Tour de France, which took place, by a happy chance, in Ireland that summer.

Historical memory was bewilderingly recycled into spectator sport and tourist attraction. This may not seem to matter; tourism is one thing, the demands of current politics another, and the practice of history yet another.[55] But what gives one pause for thought is the extent to which professional historians were involved in the repackaging and alterations of emphasis. There seemed, in some quarters at least, to be an agreed agenda, which owed more to perceived late-twentieth-century needs than to a close reading of events and attitudes two hundred years ago. Firstly, sectarianism in Wexford in 1798 was to be skimmed over – or, even more damagingly, attributed to one side only. It may have been self-evidently in operation in Armagh and Down during the disturbances of 1796–7, but, for these purposes, North and South are to be kept firmly apart. The leadership of the Wexford and Wicklow rebels was retrospectively removed from Father John Murphy and handed back to supposedly liberal Protestants like Bagenal Harvey or General Holt. Historians whose work a decade ago dealt with the sectarian aspects of local society in the county revised themselves with surprising completeness.[56] Most strikingly of all, the burning alive of about a hundred Protestant civilians locked into a barn by rebel forces at Scullabogue, which passed into history as one of the worst atrocities on either side, was repainted. There were Catholics there too (if only eight, who were there as servants of the imprisoned Protestants); moreover, it was claimed, the government forces had already burnt down a rebel hospital, so Scullabogue was the understandable if regrettable riposte. Tom Dunne, again, working closely from local sources, has shown that this 'hospital' is an invention, and the story represents a confusion with a similar atrocity which happened a fortnight *after* Scullabogue, in Enniscorthy:[57] separate incidents were elided, and chronology reversed, in order to provide some sort of rationalization for what otherwise seems a clearly sectarian outrage. Dunne was not thanked for his pains, but accused of engaging in 'scullaboguery'. This new coinage appears to mean asserting that sectarian atrocities and communal antipathies are a deep-laid and unavoidable theme in Irish history. To 'scullabogue' could also, at the moment, be taken to mean drawing attention to the fact that a new-look Emperor has no clothes on.[58]

Here, again, the politicians had their say: whatever party they belonged to, they read from the same script. Thus the Fine Gael minister, Avril Doyle, on 24 November 1995 announcing future plans for commemoration: 'Firstly we must discard the now discredited sectarian version of '98, which was merely a polemical post-rebellion falsification. Secondly, we must stress the modernity of the United Irish project, its forward-looking, democratic dimension, and abandon the outdated agrarian or peasant interpretation. Thirdly, we must emphasize the essential unity of the 1798 insurrection: what happened in Wexford was of a piece with what happened in Antrim and Down.' Two and a half years later a politician from the opposing Fianna Fáil Party, Síle de Valera, delivered herself of the following remarks: 'Firstly, we must continue never to entertain a sectarian version of '98. Secondly, we must stress the modernity of the United Irish project, its forward-looking, democratic dimension. Thirdly, we must emphasize the essential unity of the 1798 insurrection: what happened in Wexford was of a piece with what happened in Antrim and Down.'[59] Actually, each of these three cardinal points is, in historical terms, vigorously disputed, but the Mission Statement continued to provide the government songsheet, whoever was singing.

Thus the idea that sectarianism was an artificial invention of the government moved back into fashion.[60] Sectarianism was certainly encouraged by the authorities in some areas, especially through the Orange Order; but it was not invented. In much of the current historiography, 'atavistic visceral appeal' is – correctly – attributed to popular Protestantism, but not to popular Catholicism. By the same token, the revolutionaries are allowed their Jacobinism, but not their Jacobitism: the ancient memory of dispossession, and the ancient belief in driving out the heretic invader with foreign aid. In fact, much of this is evident in the contemporary literature of poem and ballad associated with the rising. Colonial confiscations are a raw wound, and the enemy are described as 'Luther's clan' rather than Pitt's creatures. But commemorationist history glided over these motivations, preferring to stress that the Catholic hierarchy were pro-government, and that Catholic loyalism has been critically underestimated – which is true; and going on to imply that active rebels were all French-minded secularists – which seems dubious. Similarly, much was made of the fact that the rising happened in the modernized, English-speaking areas of the east, and therefore supposedly looked forward, to French ideas, rather than backwards, to Stuart or Gaelic inspirations. The reminder that the rebels who fought at Ross were Irish-speaking (which came, again, from the splendidly tactless Tom Dunne) was, to say the least, unwelcome.[61] The most that commemorationist historians like Brian Cleary would allow was that this demonstrated 'the complex political, cultural and social effects of imperialism',[62] which does not get us very far. Too often an easy accommodation was made between 1790s 'republicanism' and an implicit 'nationalism' – forgetting, as James Livesey has put it, that Arthur O'Connor, for instance, was an Irish republican but not an Irish nationalist.[63]

This is a pity, because this trend goes against much of what has been most stimulating in eighteenth-century studies over the last ten years or so: the study of the rise of Catholic consciousness from about 1770, the importance (and complexity) of confessional identification, the nature and development of the Defender network, the revival of Whiteboyism in the early 1790s, the establishment by Louis Cullen of what he discerned as sectarian 'frontiers' in the social geography of the south-east well before the outbreak of the rising. Similarly, the desire to merge the rising in Ulster into that in Wexford (in obedience to the guidelines from the Taoiseach's office) meant ignoring the drift of Northern opinion against the French Republic by the later 1790s, and basic structural differences too. The first-hand description by David Baillie Fox of Northern United Irishmen after the brutal government 'pacification' of 1797 is worth remembering, though not much quoted by commemorationists. 'Instead of the forces meeting at any point in collected and organized bodies, they met rather by accident than by design; and they were in no better order than *a mere country mob*.'[64] The mobilization of 1798 in Ulster, in Ian McBride's authoritative treatment, was keyed closely to 'the basic categories of ethnic and denominational identity . . . [and] shaped by the magnetic pull of the settlement-patterns created by seventeenth-century colonization'.

The tensions that came to the fore were those between Protestant, Catholic and Dissenter. Nancy Curtin's work confirms this. Musgrave's picture of Presbyterian United Irishmen (still often called 'the Scotch' by contemporaries) never quite coalescing with Catholic Defenders is borne out by many witnesses.[65] And after their failed rising, there is a different record of victimization and violence compared to the south-east: there were proportionately ten times as many claims for compensation in Wexford and Wicklow as in Antrim and Down, and Presbyterians were in no way harassed like Catholics. The elision of what was happening in Ulster and Wexford in the summer of 1798 required cutting a good many corners.

It is true that too much has been made of the Presbyterian United Irishman James Dickey's supposed statement on the scaffold, that the 'eyes of the Presbyterians had been opened too late' to the sectarian nature of the Wexford Rising. Like other such statements, it may have been orchestrated by the authorities.[66] But the speed with which Presbyterian radicals shifted their ground from 1798 still tells its own story. They were heavily influenced by negotiations with the government over their *regium donum* grant, and by the attractions of a Union which did away with a parliament in which they had not been represented. First survivalism, and then respectability, enforced a deliberate distancing from the Protestant United Irishman tradition. The reaction to O'Connellism, and the rise of the Presbyterian leader Henry Cooke, would solidify the process.[67] But there is also the fact, not mentioned by commemorationists but comprehensively demonstrated by Ian McBride in *Scripture Politics*, that for the Presbyterian radicals the new French dawn had seemed to promise the twilight of Roman Catholic 'superstition'. Their own millennial surge had therefore very different roots from the Jacobite tradition clearly discernible in the polemic of the Southern rebels, and their civic republicanism was far from being proto-nationalism. Certainly when the old Presbyterian radical Henry Joy, in his *Historical Collections* of 1817, advanced the case that Wexford had shown 'all the bigotry and intolerance of the Middle Ages', he was not saying so on government orders. Nor was the heroic United Irishman Samuel Neilson, when in 1802 he wrote that Christ's true morality would win through 'in spite of superstition and priestcraft'. Here, he was simply following William

Steel Dickson's three sermons on 'scripture politics' in 1793, which claimed the Bible as 'almost entirely political', being devoted to 'denouncing the tyranny of kings, the corruption of governments, and the unprincipled connivance and rapacity of priests and prophets'.[68] As James Livesey has put it, for thinkers like these, 'Catholics might be given political rights because history had transformed them into Protestants'.[69] Early on, the movement was set in process whereby – as Ian McBride has neatly put it – left-wing intellectuals in modern Ulster 'would value Presbyterian radicalism not so much as a bridge to mainstream republicanism as a non-sectarian alternative to it'.[70]

Above all, commemorationist history tended to avoid the implications of the uncomfortable fact that so much of the evidence from this tragic era comes from informers; indeed, the nature of the evidence in courts martial indicates much about the intimate resentments of local relations.[71] The idea, firmly held in the North, that the rising in Wexford had taken a sectarian turn is not just an invention of Musgrave and other polemicists.[72] Wexford may have sustained religiously 'mixed' communities in the eighteenth century and been notably prosperous. But this is, tragically, no reason why, under circumstances of crisis and oppression, sectarian passions cannot spiral into a whirlwind of paranoia and brutality – as Mostar and Sarajevo have demonstrated all too recently.

It is worth looking at the tone employed by commemorationist historians to address these worrying issues. Ruan O'Donnell, for instance, describes the Wicklow rebels under Holt 'venting their frustration' by 'burning over twenty loyalist homes in the Roundwood area which were singled out from the general citizenry with great discipline and discrimination'.[73] Leaving aside the question as to how this discipline and discrimination must have appeared to those thus singled out, the implication that the 'loyalists' were not part of the general citizenry is ominous. Stressing that 'on the issue of rape the rebels occupied the moral high ground' and respected women and children, Whelan provides the consoling rationalization that the women and children none the less burned at Scullabogue were, after all, attached to members of the North Cork Militia. Recollections that say what the commemorationists want are prioritized, like Miles Byrne's memoirs; the fact that these were dictated half a century later is taken as specific evidence of 'detachment'.[74] This approach is exemplified by the introduction to Whelan's interesting collection of reprinted essays, *The Tree of Liberty*, which makes a present-minded agenda triumphantly clear, boasts 'a non-talmudic irreverence to textual authority', trumpets the credentials of 'radical history' and claims for the author the description 'croppy' – the appellation given to the rebels of '98 by their adversaries. This kind of feelgood identification, while no doubt uplifting for the writer in question, suggests a certain limitation of approach. It is also significant that the same author moves smoothly to attacking Daniel O'Connell, traditionally seen by a certain tradition in Irish historiography (beginning with John Mitchel and climaxing with Patrick Pearse) as a worse enemy to Irish nationalism than even perfidious Albion: partly because he accepted confessional realities, and partly because he operated within a pacifist framework. In this, as in some other ways, the redefinition of 1798 seems to have brought us back to a familiar resting place. What Hubert Butler wrote of Irish history sometimes seems true of Irish historiography as well. It is all like a journey on 'a scenic railway in a funfair: we pass through towering cardboard mountains and over raging torrents and come to rest in the same well-trodden field from which we got on board'.[75]

The point is, of course, that what happened in Ireland in 1798 was not a cardboard simulacrum, and the raging torrents were both real and bloody. It has now become part of historical memory, and been fictionalized and poeticized: retrospectively inspired creations, like Seamus Heaney's moving 'Lament for the Croppies' or Brian Friel's play *Translations* with its elegiac memory of marching to '98, become treated as sources which somehow stand in for the painful reassembling of material about that bloodsoaked summer, while modern Wexford treats commemoration as re-enactment (of the nice bits). Memory, as the mother of the Muses, is creatively selective.

There is a sequel to my visit to Robert Barton, the story of that bullet-riddled tree, and why no one wanted to remember why it was 'unlucky'. Mr Barton, as it happens, knew about remembering and forgetting. When I went to talk to him about Parnell and Wicklow, I was less focused on the fact that he had been a revolutionary guerrilla in 1919–21 (despite an Ascendancy family and a British Army background), had gone to London to negotiate the Anglo-Irish Treaty, had signed but later reneged on it, fought in the brutal Civil War on the side of the anti-Treaty republicans – probably influenced by his cousin Erskine Childers, who was subsequently executed without mercy by the Free State. After our Parnell conversation, I longed to go back and ask him about his own life, but I was courteously told that he never discussed the Civil War. He was probably right: it was a terrible time, his own position must have been agonized, and he retired to private life at the cessation of hostilities. For politicians, scrupulous silence about the past is sometimes the right course. Historians *have* to remember, even – or especially – the most unwelcome aspects. But as Bernard Shaw and Alfred Webb suggested in 1898, others would do better to look to the future than to a past which has been romanticized and sanitized for present purposes. It might be salutary to remember G. M. Young's dictum that the historian must 'read until you hear the people talking'. True, and admirable: but the trouble with commemorative history is that, if those distant people were saying unwelcome things, it is all too tempting to put words in their mouths.

Notes

Introduction

1. P. N. Furbank, *Behalf* (London, 1999), pp. 38–9.
2. Stephen Howe, *Ireland and Empire: Colonial Legacies in Irish History and Culture* (Oxford, 2000), pp. 94–5.
3. Though we may not all put it quite like David Lloyd:

Constituted in simultaneity with, and different from, modern civil society, and representing in a certain sense the 'constitutive other' of modernity, these spaces that are the object of 'new histories' are not, we have argued, to be conceived as alternative continuities, parallel to dominant narratives and only awaiting, in Gramsci's sense, to attain hegemony in order to be completed. On the contrary, and at the risk of deliberate hypostasization, the apparent discontinuity of popular or non-elite history furnishes indications of alternative social formations, difficult as these may be to document and decipher for the disciplined historian; the same discontinuity as well as the formal grounds for the persistent inassimilability of non-elite formations to the state. (*Ireland after History*, Cork, 1999, p. 84.)

4. Richard Haslam, ' "A Race Bashed in the Face": Imagining Ireland as a Damaged Child', *Jouvert: A Journal of Postcolonial Studies*, vol. 4, no. 1 (Fall 1999).
5. *If the Irish Ran the World: Montserrat 1630–1730* (Liverpool, 1997), pp. 174–5.
6. Bill Rolston, 'The Training Ground: Ireland, Conquest and Decolonization' in *Race and Class*, vol. 34, no. 4, p. 19; quoted in Howe, op. cit., pp. 59–60.
7. See Haslam, op. cit., for the 'nation-child' in fictions by Joyce, Plunkett, MacLaverty, Trevor and Doyle.
8. Quoted in Furbank, op. cit., p. 6.
9. Thus Lloyd, op. cit., pp. 11, 12, 107, presents arguments that rely on the exactly opposite situation regarding emigration than is actually the case.

10. See Simon James, *The Atlantic Celts: Ancient People or Modern Invention?* (London, 1999). David Brett, *The Construction of Heritage* (Cork, 1996), also provides some germane reflections on the subject.

11. Interview with Patrick McCabe, *Irish Times*, 10 June 2000.

12. Gerald Dawe, *Stray Dogs and Dark Horses* (Newry, 2000), p. 81.

13. *The Break-up of Britain: Crisis and Neo-nationalism* (London, 1977), p. 340.

14. Lloyd, op. cit., pp. 43–5.

15. Ibid., p. 22.

16. Two recent books making a start on this are Senia Paseta's *Before the Revolution: Nationalism, Social Change and Ireland's Catholic Elite 1879–1922* (Cork, 1999) and Patrick Maume's *The Long Gestation: Irish Nationalist Life 1891–1918* (Dublin, 1999).

17. Lloyd, op. cit., p. 80.

18. Furbank, op. cit., p. 40.

19. *Recollections* (London, 1897), pp. 353–4.

20. *Irish Weekly Independent*, 16 May 1896.

21. Cheryl Herr, 'The Erotics of Irishness', *Critical Inquiry*, no. 1 (Autumn 1990); Joep Leerssen, *Remembrance and Imagination: Patterns in the Historical and Literary Representation of Ireland in the Nineteenth Century* (Cork, 1997), pp. 35–8.

22. See John Waters, quoting the Native American artist Jimmie Durham, in *Irish Times*, 11 October 1994.

23. *Men in Dark Times* (1968), quoted in Dawe, op. cit., p. 100.

1 The Story of Ireland

1. For example, Paul Ricoeur, *Time and Narrative* (translated by Kathleen McLaughlin and David Pellamer, London, 1984–8); Hayden White, *Metahistory: The Historical Imagination in Nineteenth-century Europe* (Baltimore, Md, 1973) and 'The Historical Text as Literary Artefact' in R. H. Canary and H. Kozicki (eds.), *The Writing of History: Literary Form and Historical Understanding* (Milwaukee, Wis., 1978); Frederic Jameson, *The Political Unconscious: Narrative as a Socially Symbolic Act* (London, 1981); Northrop Frye, *The Secular Scripture* (Cambridge, Mass., 1976); Michel de Certeau, *The Practice of Everyday Life* (translated by Steven Randall, London, 1984), especially Chapter 6, 'Story Time'.

2. Cf. Paul Ricoeur, 'Personal Identity and Narrative Identity' in *Oneself as Another* (translated by Kathleen Blaney, London, 1992), p. 114n. Also see

Jameson, op. cit., p. 30, on how collective history is iconized into an individual life by a strategy of 'repressive simplification'.

3. Cf. Frederick Jameson, op. cit., p. 35. 'History is not a text, not a narrative, master or otherwise, but ... as an absent cause it is inaccessible to us except in textual form and ... our approach to it and to the real itself necessarily passes through its prior textualization, its narrativization in the political unconscious.' Also see Lynn Hunt's comments on how the historical events of the French Revolution conformed (at least in the telling) to the narrative conventions of comedy, romance and tragedy in succession: *Politics, Culture and Class in the French Revolution* (Berkeley, Calif., 1984).

4. Interestingly, O'Faolain's volume (London, 1946) is one of a series called 'Britain in Pictures: The British People in Pictures', and both Lawless's and McCarthy's are in an 'imperial' series too.

5. For another aspect of this, see Clodagh Brennan Harvey, *Contemporary Irish Traditional Narrative: The English Language Tradition* (Oxford, 1992).

6. 'The Storyteller' in Hannah Arendt (ed.), *Illuminations: Essays and Reflections by Walter Benjamin* (New York, 1968).

7. Homi K. Bhabba (ed.), *Nation and Narration* (London, 1990).

8. Cf. Colm Tóibín, 'Martyrs and Metaphors' in Dermot Bolger (ed.), *Letters from the New Island* (Dublin, 1991), where Irish history is visualized as a series of short stories.

9. A process surveyed in Clare O'Halloran, 'Golden Ages and Barbarous Nations: Antiquarian Debate on the Celtic Past in Ireland and Scotland in the Eighteenth Century' (Ph.D., Cambridge, 1991).

10. See my 'History and the Irish Question' in *Paddy and Mr Punch* (London, 1993).

11. See J. A. Spence, 'The Philosophy of Irish Toryism 1813–52: A Study of Reactions to Liberal Reformism in the Generation between the First Reform Act and the Famine, with Especial Reference to Expressions of National Feeling among the Protestant Ascendancy' (Ph.D., London, 1991).

12. Other influential Mitchel titles include *The Last Conquest of Ireland (Perhaps)* (New York, 1860) and a two-volume *History of Ireland from the Treaty of Limerick to the Present Time* (Dublin, 1869).

13. Jameson does it for *La Chartreuse de Parme* in *The Political Unconscious*, pp. 119–21. Also see his discussion of Lévi-Strauss's critique of Propp on the grounds of 'empiricism' and his own criticism that the Propp approach is not sufficiently 'historicized'.

14. Cf. Propp: 'Just as cloth can be measured with a yardstick to determine

its length, tales may be measured by [my] scheme and thereby defined . . . the problem of kinship of tales, the problem of themes and variants, thanks to this, may receive a new solution.'

15. Quoted in R. Moran, 'Alexander Martin Sullivan (1829–1884) and Irish Cultural Nationalism' (M.A., Cork, 1993), p. 31.

16. *The Story of Ireland* (25th ed., London, 1888), p. 229.

17. ibid., p. 22.

18. This passage (p. 66) also provides a good example of Sullivan's storytelling style. 'Exile from Ireland! Did Columba hear the words aright? *Exile from Ireland!* What? See no more that land which he loved with such a wild and passionate love! Part from the brothers and kinsmen all, for whom he felt perhaps too strong and too deep an affection! Quit for aye the stirring scenes in which so great a part of his sympathies were engaged!'

19. p. 107.

20. p. 134.

21. p. 477.

22. p. 565.

23. Deliberately paralleled with the death of Brian Boru at Clontarf, or the Earl of Desmond's last resistance at Munster, in the manner of Sullivan's telling.

24. The last paragraph:

Victory must be with her. Already it is with her. Other nations have bowed to the yoke of conquest, and been wiped out from history. Other people have given up the faith of their fathers for a mess of pottage: as if there were nothing nobler in man's destiny than to feed, and sleep, and die. But Ireland, after centuries of suffering and sacrifice such as have tried no other nation in the world, has successfully, proudly, gloriously, defended and retained her life, her faith, her nationality. Well may her children, proclaiming aloud that 'there is a God in Israel', look forward to a serene and happy future, beyond the tearful clouds of this troubled present. Assuredly a people who have survived so much, resisted so much, retained so much, are destined to receive the rich reward of such devotion, such constancy, such heroism.

25. See the *Nation*, 27 April 1872 and 24 March 1868. T. D. Sullivan's *Story of England* enshrined this view. The Christian Brothers adopted this version of Irish history, explored by Barry Coldrey in *Faith and Fatherland: The Christian Brothers and the Development of Irish Nationalism 1838–1921* (Dublin, 1988) and brilliantly used by Conor Cruise O'Brien in *Ancestral Voices: Religion and Nationalism in Ireland* (Dublin, 1994).

26. De Certeau, op. cit., pp. 86–7. 'Far from being the reliquary or trash-can

of the past it sustains itself by *believing* in the existence of possibilities and by vigilantly awaiting them, constantly on the watch for their appearance.'

27. McCarthy, for instance, introduces Brian Boru thus: 'Then there came about an event so common in the history of nationalities that any intelligent reader might be able to anticipate it [any reader of Propp, at least]. The native Irish had been conquered and reduced to servitude, not because they were incapable of effective resistance, but because the man has not yet come who was destined to show them how to organize the means and secure the end. At the critical moment the man arose.' (*Ireland and Her Story*, London, 1903.)

28. See 'The Rediscovery of the Irish Past' in Vivian Mercier, *Modern Irish Literature: Sources and Founders* (Oxford, 1994). The *Revue Celtique* was founded in 1870. However, stories such as 'Deirdre' were in circulation, through Theophilus O'Flanagan in the *Transactions of the Gaelic Society*, as early as 1808. This was much used by Douglas Hyde in his *A Literary History of Ireland from Earliest Times to the Present Day* (London, 1899), which was more accessible to many of the popularists of the Revival.

29. 'The historian of the Conquest, and of the ages which have since elapsed, may have to regret the rough and tedious process of transition through which the country was now destined to begin its passage; but it will always be a satisfactory reflection that amongst its results has been our admission to a larger sphere of civilization, to a share in many peaceful as well as warlike glories, and to the general use of that noble language in which all the gains of science and all the highest utterances of modern poetry and philosophy have found a worthy expression' (p. 293).

30. *Nations and Nationalism* (Oxford, 1983) p. 57.

31. 'A Wet Day' in *Selected Essays and Passages* (Dublin, n.d.), p. 3.

32. Right down to explosive one-word chapter titles, and Old Testament excoriations.

33. See 'Dawn', the first chapter of his *History of Ireland: The Heroic Period* (Dublin, 1878).

There is not, perhaps, in existence a product of the mind so extraordinary as the Irish annals. From a time dating more than two thousand years before the birth of Christ, the stream of Milesian history flows down uninterrupted, copious and abounding, between accurately defined banks, with here and there picturesque meanderings, here and there flowers lolling upon those delusive waters, but never concealed in mists, or lost in a marsh. As the centuries wend their way, king succeeds king with a regularity most gratifying, and fights no battle, marries no wife, begets no children, does no doughty deed of which a contemporaneous note was not taken, and which has not been incorporated in the annals of his country. To think that this mighty fabric of recorded events, so stupendous in its dimensions, so clear and accurate in its details, so symmetrical and elegant, should be after all a mirage and a delusion, a gorgeous bubble, whose glowing rotundity, whose rich hues, azure, purple, amethyst and gold, vanish at a touch and are gone, leaving a sorry remnant over which the patriot disillusioned may grieve.

34. 'Its symbolism gleaming brighter and brighter against the waning light of Rome . . . it glitters like the morning star before the eye of the historians. That group of green mounds, palisaded and dyked, surrounded with painted wicker houses, is the central harmonizing point of the wild chaos which surges and bellows in the darkness and the haze – starlike now, it will itself be one day a sun.' (ibid., p. 47.)

35. Lord Morris, quoted in Hugh Art O'Grady, *Standish James O'Grady: The Man and the Writer* (Dublin, 1929), p. 36.

36. See Donnchadh Ó Corráin, 'Early Ireland: Directions and Re-directions' in *Bullán*, vol. i, no. 2 (Oxford, Autumn, 1994). Rudolph Thurneysen thinks *The Táin* was composed in the eighth century and written down in the ninth; Ó Corráin thinks it originated in the ninth.

37. p. 110.

38. 'I think I do not exaggerate when I say that the majority of educated Irishmen would feel grateful to the man who informed them that the history of their country was valueless and unworthy of study, that the pre-Christian history was a myth, the post-Christian mere annals, the medieval a scuffling of kites and crows, and the modern alone deserving of some slight consideration. That writer will be in Ireland most praised who sets latest the commencement of our history.' (*Cuculain and His Contemporaries*, London, 1880, pp. 33–4.)

39. Again, while avoiding the excesses of vol. 1; see ibid., p. 65. He even tried to construct a chronology, starting in 2379 BC, based on the 'mythological record of the bards', using Geoffrey Keating, and ending with Cuchulain's death in AD 9.

40. The hero becomes 'dejected when he looked upon the people, so small were they, and so pale and ignoble, both in appearance and behaviour; and also when he saw the extreme poverty of the poor and the hungry eager crowds seeking what he knew not'. (pp. 290–91.)

41. 'The account which a nation renders of itself must, and always does, stand at the head of every history.' (p. 119.)

42. For a contemporary version of this imbroglio, see 'The British Israelites at Tara' in Hubert Butler, *The Sub-Prefect Should Have Held His Tongue*, R. F. Foster (ed.) (London, 1990), pp. 68–72.

43. See also 'A General Introduction to my Work' in *Yeats on Yeats: The Last Introductions and the 'Dublin' Edition*, Edward Callan (ed.) (Dublin, 1981) and 'How I became a Writer' in *Listener*, 4 August 1938 and *Uncollected Prose by W. B. Yeats*, John P. Frayne and Colton Johnson (eds.) (2 vols., London, 1975), vol. 2. The emphasis is even stronger in these late writings, after O'Grady's death.

44. See Hubert Butler, op. cit.

45. 12 October 1901. Another exchange ran: ' "You have no sense of the responsibilities of editorship" (No. – Ed.)' (25 January 1902.) Scraps of Greek poetry which appealed to the editor were engagingly annotated: 'I hope the accents are right. I shook them out as from a pepper-castor.' (5 April 1902.)

46. AE, again: 'In O'Grady's writings the submerged voice of national culture rose up again, a shining torrent. It was he who made me conscious and proud of my country . . . He was the last champion of the Irish aristocracy and spoke to them of their duty to the nation as a fearless prophet might speak to a council of degenerate princes . . . When a man is in advance of his age, a generation, unborn when he speaks, is born in due time and finds in him its inspiration.' (Hugh O'Grady, op. cit., pp. 63–4.)

47. It was dated 1894, but copies were in circulation in December 1893.

48. p. 64.

49. They kept alive all the old traditions of pagan heroism, kept alive the remembrance and practice of the grand old pagan virtues of simple truth, courage, hospitality and magnanimity, and of heroic friendship and affection . . . They did more than this, they pointed the finger of ridicule at the comarbs, and at the whole bell-ringing fraternity, and the people laughed; the finger of scorn at their physical weakness and their fastings, their double-dealing, their quibblings, and general untruthfulness and unreliableness, and the people despised them while they feared. Through all the long period of the domination of the monasteries the bards kept alive the old secular spirit, and taught the people to look at things and men with their natural eyes and not through the stained glasses of the monks. (p. 67.)

O'Grady would not welcome current scholarly interpretations which see most bardic texts as heavily influenced by Providentialist Christian conditioning.

50. p. 78. They were probably well thonged too. 'A young, handsome Norseman, dressed in his gala attire for an assembly, and bearing the splendid weapons which they made in those lands, was as beautiful a spectacle as Europe anywhere produced at this time.' (p. 81.)

51. p. 98.

52. pp. 132–3. O'Grady claimed the victims at Drogheda were combatants,

given due warning; the Protector was ruthless but fair, and his soldiers (like good Protestants) 'paid for provisions and everything they got at market rates'. (p. 138.) He is compared vitriolically to Rinuccini, a 'jocose forger and ecclesiastical liar'.

53. In the style of a Carlylean wonder tale, with an Irish twist.

He ran past Dublin. Lady Tyrconnel, from the Castle battlements, cried out to him: 'Is that you, James? Where is your army from you? Wouldn't you turn in, James, and have some lunch?' But James only waved the back of his royal hand, as much as to say, 'No more now, dear lady, I'll tell you about it at Versailles, if I ever get there', and never stopped running . . . By day and by night, under the sun and under the moon and stars, without closing an eye or taking an honest meal, breaking the bridges behind him, placing guards at every defensible point along the way, through all Meath, through all Leinster, ran the last of the Stuarts. 'I am going to France for succours,' he said. 'No, I am going to France to make a plunge for England now that this dreadful Prince of Orange is out of it.'

Farewell for ever to King James. (pp. 158–9.)

54. p. 211. A similar analysis is given in Paul Bew, *Charles Stewart Parnell* (Dublin, 1980).

55. W. E. H. Lecky, at more or less the same time, had to execute a parallel manoeuvre; see Donal McCartney, *W. E. H. Lecky: Historian and Politician 1838–1903* (Dublin, 1994), Chapter 7.

56. p. 197. O'Grady also describes 1890s Ireland as 'like soft wax' waiting for an imprint (p. 163), an image repeatedly used by Yeats. The presentation copy to Lily has survived in his library. For references in public letters, see Frayne, op. cit., vol. 1, p. 308.

57. Such as *The Flight of the Eagle* and *The Coming of Cuculain*; he also warmly praised *The Bog of Stars*.

58. In a long article for the *Bookman*, August 1895, reprinted in Frayne, op. cit., vol. 1, pp. 368–9.

In Ireland we are accustomed to histories with great parade of facts and dates, or wrongs and precedents, for use in the controversies of the hour; and here was a man who let some all-important Act of Parliament (say) go by without a mention, or with perhaps inaccurate mention, and for no better reason than because it did not interest him, and who recorded with careful vividness some moment of abrupt passion, some fragment of legendary beauty, and for no better reason than because it did interest him profoundly. 'The effect' of his books, as Mill said of Michelet's History of France, 'is not to acquiescence, but stir and ferment'; and I disagree with his conclusions too constantly, and see the armed hand of nationality in too many places where he but sees the clash of ancient with modern institutions to believe that he has written altogether the true history of Ireland; but I am confident that, despite his breathless generalizations, his slipshod style, his ungovernable likings and dislikings, he is the first man who has tried to write it . . .

See also Frayne, op. cit., vol. 1, pp. 388–9, for WBY's interesting attack on 'the mystery play of devils and angels which we call our national history', and his praise of O'Grady for trying to puncture it.

59. It stayed in a revised list, including books 'of strong political feeling', and also in a subsequent list of one hundred best books. (ibid., vol. 1, pp. 356, 386.)

60. See *Autobiographies* (London, 1955), p. 220: 'All round us people talked or wrote for victory's sake, and were hated for their victories – but here was a man whose rage was a swan-song over all that he had held most dear, and to whom for that very reason every Irish imaginative writer owed a portion of his soul.'

61. In a tortured syntax which indicates extreme unsureness.

I do not find it difficult to follow Mr O'Grady, when he explains that the crown had so long been the most powerful of the clans, that its rule, and all the more because it was hitherto little but a nominal rule, was accepted, or half accepted, by the great chiefs, in place of that strong native rule which, but for it, would have come to silence their disorders; but I find it difficult to follow him when he says, or seems to say, that this loyalty was more than the cold and fitful loyalty born of expediency and necessity, and that Ireland, speaking a different language and having different traditions from England, had, I will not say no national antagonism, for nationality is a modern idea, but no racial antagonism to England. Mr O'Grady may be right, for I am no historian . . . (Frayne, op. cit., vol. 2, p. 49.)

Also see his letter to O'Grady reiterating the point.

62. Frayne, op. cit., vol. 2, p. 245.

63. R. J. Finneran, G. M. Harper, W. M. Murphy (eds.), *Letters to W. B. Yeats* (2 vols., London, 1977), vol. 1, pp. 76–7. Apologies soon followed, but the damage was done.

64. See J. W. Foster, *Fictions of the Irish Literary Revival: A Changeling Art* (Syracuse, NY, 1987), pp. 226–7, 239–40. *The Celtic Twilight* is a key text here, and should be related to Yeats's occult fiction of the period.

65. Finneran, Harper, Murphy, op. cit., p. 32; also A. Denson (ed.), *Letters from AE* (London, 1961), pp. 17–18.

66. To Lady Gregory, 5 August 1900, Berg Collection, New York Public Library.

67. At the very point (early December 1898) when he had foretold personal apotheosis, Gonne chose to reveal her past to him and explode all expectations of anything beyond a mystical marriage. See my *W. B. Yeats: A Life. Vol. 1: The Apprentice Mage 1865–1914* (Oxford, 1997), pp. 201–5.

68. To Lady Gregory, 31 January 1898, Berg Collection, New York Public Library.

69. See Paul Bew, *Ideology and the Irish Question: Unionism and Irish Nationalism 1912–1916* (Oxford, 1994).

70. [Stephen's diary] April 14. John Alphonsus Mulrennan has just returned from the west of Ireland. European and Asiatic papers please copy. He told us he met an old man there in a mountain cabin. Old man had red eyes and short pipe. Old man spoke Irish. Mulrennan spoke Irish. Then old man and Mulrennan spoke English. Mulrennan spoke to him about universe and stars. Old man sat, listened, smoked, spat. Then said:

– Ah, there must be terrible queer creatures at the latter end of the world.

I fear him. I fear his redrimmed horny eyes. It is with him I must struggle all through this night till day come, till he or I lie dead, gripping him by the sinewy throat till . . . Till what? Till he yield to me? No. I mean no harm. (*A Portrait of the Artist as a Young Man*, 1916; Everyman ed., London, 1991, p. 256.)

71. For a recent analysis of this process, see Colin Graham, ' "Liminal Spaces": Post-Colonial Theories and Irish Culture', *Irish Review*, no. 16 (Autumn/Winter 1994), pp. 29–43.

72. Thus Dr Alf O'Brien at the Desmond Greaves Summer School 1994, as quoted in the *Irish Times*, 29 August 1994: 'The central theme in modern Irish history was the fact of the conquest . . . Whatever the complexity of Anglo-Irish relations in the nineteenth century (a century particularly favoured by the "revisionist" school), or the problems of Irish landlords in that period, the fact of conquest still remained. He went on to examine the basic forces which brought about that conquest and its effects on both Ireland and England.'

73. For instance, the relationship of the Treaty to Partition; or land tenure reform to the eclipse of constitutional nationalism.

74. 'What is a Nation?', reprinted in Bhabha, op. cit., p. 11.

75. Some modern critics of 'revisionism', for instance, have resurrected D. P. Moran's self-revealing assertion that those who present a contingent, pluralist version are representing the Irish as 'mongrel'. (See his attacks on the cultural agenda of Yeats and Rolleston in the *Leader*, 5 January 1901.)

76. See J. W. Foster, op. cit., p. 283, for Padraic Colum's *The King of Ireland's Son* as a model of national narrative.

77. AE was for a time ambivalently attracted to it, writing a symposium-novel *The Interpreters* (1922) just after the event. It features a poet, Lavelle, who has created the revolution by 'ransacking the past and reviving the traditions of the nation' through the 'fairy tales of its infancy'. He speaks Blakean language, and obviously stands for Yeats. O'Grady appears as 'Brehon', an imaginative historian who has inspired the younger generation. Lavelle's poem about a sacrificial hero, 'Michael', is quoted from at the beginning of this essay. Both Lavelle and Brehon also turn up in a very late visionary novel, *The Avatars* (1935), in which AE tried to recapture the apocalyptic Celticism of his youthful expectations; but he was living in English exile by then.

78. 4 July [?] 1914, TS, p. 84; my thanks to Lord Dunsany for access to his grandmother's diary.

2 Theme-parks and Histories

1. 'Affirmations VIII: The Non-existence of Ireland', *New Age*, vol. xvi, no. 17, pp. 451–3 (25 February 1915).

2. Quoted by Fintan O'Toole in *Black Hole, Green Card: The Disappearance of Ireland* (Dublin, 1994), p. 33.

3. R. MacSearraigh Gordon, *Fáinne an Lae*, 24 September 1898.

4. 'Waiting for the Barbarians' in C. P. Cavafy, *Collected Poems* (translated by Edmund Keeley and Philip Sherrard and edited by George Savadis, London, 1990), pp. 14–15.

5. See my *Paddy and Mr Punch* (London, 1993), pp. 15–17, for a fuller consideration; also Francis T. Holohan, 'History Teaching in the Free State 1922–1935', *History Ireland*, vol. 2, no. 4 (Winter 1994), pp. 53–6.

6. See 'Yeats at War', below, pp. 58–9.

7. 'Symmetry and Repetition' in *Conflicts* (London, 1942); reprinted in John Gross (ed.), *The Oxford Book of Essays* (Oxford, 1991), p. 432.

8. Pierre Nora (ed.), *Les Lieux de mémoire* was published in seven volumes by Gallimard from 1984 to 1992; the English-language edition was edited by Lawrence D. Kritzman and translated by Arthur Goldhammer as *Realms of Memory: The Construction of the French Past*, published by Columbia University Press in three volumes, *Conflicts and Divisions* (1996), *Traditions* (1997) and *Symbols* (1998).

9. *Los Angeles Times Book Review*, 26 January 1999.

10. As sharply shown in an unpublished paper by Mary Daly, 'History à

la Carte: Historical Commemoration and Modern Ireland'. My thanks to Professor Daly for showing me this paper and providing a number of informative points.

11. Jim Jackson, 'Famine Diary: The Making of a Best Sellar', *Irish Review*, no. 11 (Winter 1991/2), pp. 1–8. This traces the history of Gerald Keegan's *Famine Diary: Journey to a New World*, published as an authentic first-hand account by Wolfhound Press in 1991, to a short story of 1895 written by Robert Sellar in Quebec.

12. Circular, from an organization called 'Irish Holocaust Graves', Chicago, 1996.

13. The main investor was the Irish Tourist Board, according to the *Irish Times*, 5 August 2000. Also see Fintan O'Toole, 'Strangers in Our Own Land' in op. cit.

14. 'Symmetry and Repetition' in op. cit., p. 431.

15. See my *W. B. Yeats: A Life. Vol. 1: The Apprentice Mage 1865–1914* (Oxford, 1997), pp. 418–20, 459–61.

16. A lecture on 'My Own Poetry' as reported in *Irish Times*, 25 February 1926.

17. By Edna Longley, *Belfast Telegraph*, 17 February 1998.

3 'Colliding Cultures': Leland Lyons and the Reinterpretation of Irish History

1. See, for instance, David Fitzpatrick, *Oceans of Consolation: Personal Accounts of Irish Migration to Australia* (Cork, 1994); Maria Luddy, *Women in Ireland: A Documentary History* (Cork, 1995); Hugh Dorian, *The Outer Edge of Ulster: A Memoir of Social Life in Nineteenth-Century Donegal*, Breandan Mac Suibhne and David Dickson (eds.) (Dublin, 2000).

2. F. S. L. Lyons, *Culture and Anarchy in Ireland 1890–1939* (Oxford, 1979), p. 177.

3. Reprinted in Ciaran Brady (ed.), *Interpreting Irish History: The Debate on Historical Revisionism 1938–1994* (Dublin, 1994), p. 19.

4. For this and other personal and biographical reflections, see my 'Francis Stewart Leland Lyons 1924–1983' in *Proceedings of the British Academy*, vol. lxx (1984).

5. Review of James W. Flannery, *W. B. Yeats and the Idea of a Theatre* in *Irish Times*, 10 December 1976.

6. Foster, 'Francis Stewart Leland Lyons', and personal recollections.

7. Francis T. Holohan, 'History Teaching in the Free State 1922–1935', *History Ireland*, vol. 2, no. 4 (Winter 1994).

8. Robert Tobin of Merton College, Oxford, is currently engaged on research into this area.

9. See my *Paddy and Mr Punch* (London, 1993), p. 15.

10. T. W. Moody, *Davitt and Irish Revolution 1846–1882* (Oxford, 1981).

11. Quoted in Brady, op. cit., pp. 36–7.

12. Famously in 'Nationalism and Historical Scholarship in Modern Ireland', *Irish Historical Studies*, vol. 26, no. 104 (1989), p. 349. Elsewhere he has stated his wish to reinstate 'the popular perception of Irish history as a struggle for the liberation of "faith-and-fatherland" from the oppression of the Protestant English': supplement to *Fortnight*, no. 297, Belfast.

13. Liz Curtis, *The Cause of Ireland: From the United Irishmen to Partition* (Belfast, 1994).

14. *Culture and Anarchy*, pp. 1–2.

15. 'T.W.M.' in F. S. L. Lyons and R. A. J. Hawkins (eds.), *Ireland under the Union: Varieties of Tension* (Oxford, 1980), p. 10.

16. 'J. M. Synge and the Ireland of his Time', reprinted in *Essays and Introductions* (London, 1961), p. 312.

17. Conor Cruise O'Brien, *To Katanga and Back: A UN Case History* (London, 1962), preface.

18. Edward Maurice, *A Sermon Preached ... On Thursday the 23rd of October, 1755* (Dublin, 1755), p. 7; quoted in Gerard McCoy, 'Local Political Culture in the Hanoverian Empire: The Case of Ireland 1714–1760', D.Phil. thesis (Oxford, 1994).

19. J. A. Spence, 'The Philosophy of Irish Toryism 1833–1852', Ph.D. thesis (London, 1991).

20. In 1892 only 9 per cent of undergraduates gave their father's profession as 'gentleman': R. B. McDowell and D. A. Webb, *Trinity College Dublin 1592–1952: An Academic History* (Cambridge, 1982), p. 324.

21. *London Review of Books*, 5–18 August 1982, reprinted in *We Irish: Essays on Irish Literature and Society* (London, 1986), pp. 169–75.

22. This address is reprinted as 'Varieties of Irishness' in *Paddy and Mr Punch*, pp. 21–39.

23. Sean O'Callaghan, *The Informer* (London, 1998).

24. Cf. comments in *Paddy and Mr Punch*, introduction.

25. 6 October 1982.

26. Brady, op. cit., pp. 93–4.

27. Richard Ellmann, *James Joyce* (revised ed., Oxford, 1982), p. 192.

28. Vintage, Random House US ed., 1961, pp. 331–3.

29. Speech in House of Commons, 30 June 1876, quoted in R. Moran,

'Alexander Martin Sullivan 1829–1884 and Irish Cultural Nationalism', M.A. thesis (University College, Cork, 1993).

4 Yeats at War: Poetic Strategies and Political Reconstruction

1. The doyen of the subject is Pierre Nora; see Chapter 2, note 8. Also see Patrick H. Hutton, *History as an Art of Memory* (London, 1993).

2. See, for instance, T. Dooley, *Irishmen or English Soldiers? The Times and World of a Southern Catholic Irish Man (1876–1916) Enlisting in the British Army during the First World War* (Liverpool, 1995); Terence Denman, *Ireland's Unknown Soldiers: The 16th (Irish) Division in the Great War* (Dublin, 1992); David Fitzpatrick (ed.), *Ireland and the First World War* (Dublin, 1992); Senia Paseta, *Before the Revolution: Nationalism, Social Change and Ireland's Catholic Elite 1879–1922* (Cork, 1999); Patrick Maume, *The Long Gestation: Irish Nationalist Life 1891–1918* (Dublin, 1999); Paul Bew, *Ideology and the Irish Question: Ulster Unionism and Irish Nationalism 1912–1916* (Oxford, 1994) and *John Redmond* (Dundalk, 1996).

3. See my *W. B. Yeats: A Life. Vol. 1: The Apprentice Mage 1865–1914* (Oxford, 1997), p. 128, for John Butler Yeats's expectations in 1893.

4. Quoted in ibid., p. 522.

5. See ibid., p. 448 (a comment he would have dared to make only in America).

6. ibid., p. 523.

7. A letter to his father, 12 September 1915: misdated in Allan Wade, *The Letters of W. B. Yeats* (London, 1954), p. 588.

8. For the Thomas Davis speech, see *Apprentice Mage*, pp. 523–5. 'Bloody frivolity' appears in a letter to Ernest Rhys, 31 May 1916, Kenneth Spencer Research Library, University of Kansas Libraries.

9. For this episode, and this exchange, see James Longenbach, *Stone Cottage: Pound, Yeats and Modernism* (Oxford, 1988), pp. 182–3.

10. This is the first completed version, in the Beinecke Rare Book and MS Library, Yale University. In *The Book of the Homeless* 'his youth' became 'youth', and was subsequently changed to 'her youth'. There is also a signed transcription in Yeats's hand in the National Library of Ireland, MS 30, 415. The charities in question were the American hostels for refugees and the Children of Flanders Rescue Committee.

11. For the Pound incident, see Longenbach, op. cit., pp. 260–63. The jeer about Kitchener is reported in a letter from Augusta Gregory to J. B. Yeats,

17 November 1917, National Library of Ireland, MS 18, 676, and the Bovril reflection is quoted in *Apprentice Mage*, p. 523.

12. This episode is explored by Christopher Blake, 'Ghosts in the Machine: W. B. Yeats and the Metallic Humunculus', *Yeats Annual*, forthcoming.

13. Pound to John Quinn, 1 May 1916, quoted in Longenbach, op. cit., p. 256.

14. *Nationality*, 29 January 1916.

15. To John Butler Yeats, 7 May 1916. My thanks to W. M. Murphy for this reference.

16. This series of letters, of mid May 1916, is in the Berg Collection, New York Public Library.

17. 8 November 1916. See Anna MacBride and A. Norman Jeffares (eds.), *Always Your Friend: The Gonne–Yeats Letters 1893–1938* (London, 1992), pp. 384–5.

18. Daniel J. Murphy (ed.), *Lady Gregory's Journals. Vol. 1: Books One to Twenty-nine, 10 October 1916–24 February 1925* (Gerrards Cross, 1978), p. 20.

19. See *Apprentice Mage*, pp. 417–21. The essay is to be found in W. B. Yeats, *Essays and Introductions* (London, 1961), pp. 311–42.

20. My thanks to David Gilmour.

21. See Yeats to John Quinn, 16 May 1917, Berg Collection, New York Public Library; also Murphy, op. cit., p. 20.

22. See Yeats to Gregory, 11 June 1917, Wade, op. cit., p. 629.

23. W. B. Yeats, *Autobiographies* (London, 1955), pp. 531–72.

24. W. B. Yeats to George Yeats, 18 May 1918 (private collection). The poem is interestingly analysed in D. Harris, *Yeats, Coole Park and Ballylee* (London, 1974), Chapter 5.

25. To Augusta Gregory, 31 May 1917, Berg Collection, New York Public Library.

26. W. B. Yeats to Clement Shorter, Wade, op. cit., p. 649.

27. W. B. Yeats to Augusta Gregory, 25 January 1918, Berg Collection, New York Public Library.

28. 10 October 1918, National Library of Scotland.

29. This is a strangely strident piece of intellectual autobiography, written in the summer of 1919 for AE's *Irish Statesman*, and deserves closer attention than it usually receives. It is reprinted in *Explorations* (London, 1962), pp. 263–80.

30. To John Butler Yeats, 7 June 1920. My thanks to W. M. Murphy for this reference.

31. W. B. Yeats to Augusta Gregory, 18 May 1920, Berg Collection, New

York Public Library; partially quoted in Murphy, op. cit. Yeats not only attended de Valera's public address on 11 May, but had a private audience with him at his hotel – requested by the Sinn Féin leader. The republicans hoped to enlist Yeats's public advocacy, but he avoided it.

32. *Toronto Evening Telegraph*, 3 February 1920, quoted in Karin Strand, 'W. B. Yeats's American Lecture Tours', Ph.D. thesis (Northwestern University, 1978), pp. 177–8.

33. ibid.

34. R. Fanning (ed.), *Documents of Irish Foreign Policy* (Dublin, Institute of Public Administration, 1998) vol. 1, no. 3, p. 5: a memo from Arthur Griffith to Dáil Éireann, issued from Gloucester Prison, 23 January 1919.

35. W. B. Yeats, *Autobiographies*, pp. 194–5.

36. 14 December 1920, Berg Collection, New York Public Library.

37. W. B. Yeats to Lennox Robinson, 29 October 1920, Morris Library, Southern Illinois University at Carbondale.

38. 3 December 1920, Berg Collection, New York Public Library.

39. TS by Joseph O'Reilly, 'W. B. Yeats and Undergraduate Oxford', Harry Ransom Humanities Research Center, University of Texas at Austin.

40. 12 January 1922, Berg Collection, New York Public Library.

41. *Dial*, February 1922.

42. 12 January 1922, Harry Ransom Humanities Research Center, University of Texas at Austin.

43. This celebrated exchange was published in the *Observer*, 3 June 1928, and subsequently the *Irish Statesman*. For a discussion of the issues, see Garry O'Connor, *Sean O'Casey: A Life* (London, 1988), pp. 246–50.

44. *Review of Reviews*, vol. 65, no. 317 (March 1922).

5 'When the Newspapers Have Forgotten Me': Yeats, Obituarists and Irishness

1. 30 January 1939.

2. Typed copy, National Library of Ireland, MS 30, 772.

3. National Library of Ireland, MS 30, 801.

4. 6 March 1939, Trinity College Dublin, 8104/77. She had already made detailed inquiries from shipping companies about transporting the remains from Marseilles to Sligo, and arrangements about the plot at Drumcliffe were in train by June.

5. In a letter to P. S. O'Hegarty, 11 February 1939, Kenneth Spencer Research Library, University of Kansas Libraries. 'He said to her [George Yeats] "If I

die out here bury me up in Roquebrune & then in a year or so when I am forgotten by the newspapers take me (rather his words were 'dig me up') to Drumcliffe . . ."' Also see George Yeats to W. Force Stead, 14 May 1939, Beinecke Rare Book and Manuscript Library, Yale University: 'WBY will be "planted" in Drumcliffe, Sligo, about the first week of October.'

6. E. C. Yeats to P. S. O'Hegarty, as above.

7. Masefield's initiative in the matter is recorded in a draft letter to George Yeats, Harry Ransom Humanities Research Center, University of Texas at Austin. 16 March 1939 was the hundredth anniversary of the birth of JBY. The music was the slow movement from Beethoven's Ninth; prayers and Psalm 23 were followed by V. C. Clinton Baddeley reading 'The Withering of the Boughs' and 'A Dialogue of Self and Soul'. The lesson came from Isaiah, Chapter 55. In between two hymns ('Praise to the Holiest in the Height' and 'The Day Thou Gavest, Lord, is Ended') Baddeley read 'Under Ben Bulben'. The service closed with the benediction, and the 'Dead March' from Saul. The family did not feel it was, overall, a success.

8. 31 January 1939.

9. 12 February 1939.

10. 30 January 1939.

11. 30 January 1939.

12. 4 February 1939.

13. 4 February 1939.

14. 30 January 1939.

15. 5 February 1939.

16. 30 January 1939.

17. 30 January 1939.

18. 5 February 1939.

19. ibid.

20. 7 February 1939.

21. vol. xiv, no. 3, July-September 1939.

22. 30 January 1939.

23. *Irish Times*, 30 January 1939.

24. See my *W. B. Yeats: A Life. Vol. 1: The Apprentice Mage 1865–1914*, pp. 435–6.

25. *Irish Press*, 30 January 1939.

26. 'An Irish Poet', *Arrow* (Summer 1939).

27. 'Poet and Artist', ibid. Similar opinions were expressed in Clarke's parallel piece in *Dublin Magazine*, vol. xiv, no. 2 (April–June 1939).

28. A. S. Forrest in *Today*, 27 April 1904.

29. 13 June 1935.

30. See below, pp. 105–6.

31. *Catholic Bulletin*, vol. xxix, no. 2 (February 1939).

32. ibid., vol. xxix, no. 3 (March 1939), p. 151.

33. In his Senate speech 'The Child and the State': See Donald R. Pearce (ed.), *The Senate Speeches of W. B. Yeats* (London, 1961), p. 168.

34. Perceptively discussed in Elizabeth Butler Cullingford, *Gender and History in Yeats's Love Poetry* (Cambridge, 1993), pp. 140–51; see also below, pp. 105–6, 192–3.

35. Particularly 'Some passages from the letters of W. B. Yeats to AE' in the *Dublin Magazine*, vol. xiv, no. 3 (July–September 1939).

36. 3 February 1939.

37. ibid., pp. 183ff.

38. 30 January 1939.

39. *Irish Times* and *Irish Press*, 30 January 1939.

40. There was, in fact, a certain contemporary effort to rehabilitate Moore's Irish credentials: see W. Stockley, 'Moore's Claim as Anglo-Irish Poet', *Dublin Magazine*, vol. xiv, no. 4 (October–December 1939).

41. *Catholic Bulletin*, vol. xxix, no. 4 (April 1939), pp. 241–4.

42. ibid., pp. 213ff. As the compiler of a valuable guide to Irish fiction in the English language, Brown had a position to defend.

43. See note 33, above.

44. *Studies*, vol. xxiii, no. 89 (March 1934), pp. 25–41, and no. 90 (June 1934), pp. 260–78.

45. *New Bearings in English Poetry* (London, 1932), p. 34.

46. *Studies*, vol. xxviii, no. 109 (March 1939), pp. 136–42.

47. ibid. Hogan later reviewed *Last Poems* and *Scattering Branches* in vol. xxix, no. 115 (December 1940), pp. 650–53, defining Yeats as 'this greatest of our poets', but the *Bulletin* was no longer around to be offended.

48. The d'Annunzio parallel was also made by David Garnett in the *New Statesman* (4 February 1939): 'but Yeats's spirit was the opposite of the filibustering Italian'.

49. This is the encounter described by Yeats in a letter to Ezra Pound, 3 February 1919 (see my *Paddy and Mr Punch*, London, 1993, p. 232). He had made a 'sensation' by publicly debating spiritism with a Catholic priest, and 'finished him off'.

50. Though Michael Tierney wrote on 'Nationalism and Revolution' in the June number (pp. 362–74), and covered general European politics from a mildly pro-Axis viewpoint from 1940.

51. 'Yeats and the Younger Generation', vol. v, no. 25 (January 1942).

52. 'The Future of Irish Literature', ibid.

53. *The Bell*, vol. i, no. 5 (February 1941).

54. *Catholic Bulletin*, vol. xxix, no. 7 (July 1939). This issue had been raised early on by M. J. MacManus (*Irish Press*, 1 February 1939): 'Today the poet's voice is more needed than ever, for of all writers and teachers he is the most individualistic. The world has seen the approaching menace of a new barbarism, in which that soulless thing, the State, is deified and in which the individual counts for nothing. The generous impulses of youth are being quenched and the slavery of mass thinking is being imposed. Germany has expunged the lyrics of her sweetest singer, Heine, from her school-books because a racial heresy is in the ascendant. That, to us, may seem abhorrent. But let us not take a smug pride in our own rectitude. Has Yeats ever reached the Irish school-books?'

55. vol. xxix, no. 12 (December 1939).

56. 'All Willy's books are out of print,' wrote Lily Yeats on 15 January 1945. 'The scarcity of paper prevents them being printed until after the war. George tells me that she only got £10 on the English editions. She doesn't know what the American is yet.' (To Ruth Lane-Poole; my thanks to W. M. Murphy for his transcription.) Also see Marion Witt to A. P. Watt, 15 June 1949 (Scribners' Archives, Princeton), making clear that Macmillan's had only *Collected Poems* (1933) available. 'All other volumes are out of print; most have been so for years.'

57. *Commonweal*, 31 March 1939.

58. *Yeats on Yeats: The Last Introductions and the 'Dublin' Edition*, Edward Callan (ed.) (Dublin, 1981), p. 63.

6. The Normal and the National: Yeats and the Boundaries of Irish Writing

1. My thanks to Peter Conradi for this quotation from his forthcoming biography.

2. 'The City' in *Collected Poems* (translated by Edmund Keeley and Philip Sherrard and edited by George Savidis, London, 1990), p. 22.

3. Quoted in John Wilson Foster, *Colonial Consequences: Essays in Irish Literature and Culture* (Dublin, 1991), p. 265.

4. See *Irish Emigration 1801–1921* (Dundalk, 1984), Part II, 'Determinants', and *Oceans of Consolation: Personal Accounts of Irish Migration to Australia* (Cork, 1994).

5. See Chapter 2, above, p. 33.

6. Martha Rove (ed.), *So Very English* (London, 1991).

7. *Women; or, Pour et Contre* (3 vols., London, 1818), vol. 3, p. 321.

8. See Chapter 1, above.

9. For the history of this contested site, see Jacqueline Hill, 'National Festivals, the State and "Protestant Ascendancy" in Ireland 1790–1829', *Irish Historical Studies*, vol. xxiv, no. 93 (May 1984) and 'Popery and Protestantism, Civil and Religious Liberty: The Disputed Lessons of Irish History 1690–1821', *Past and Present*, vol. 118 (1988).

10. *Leader*, 21 November 1908; quoted in Tom Garvin, *Nationalist Revolutionaries in Ireland 1858–1928* (Oxford, 1987), p. 64.

11. See my *W. B. Yeats: A Life. Vol. 1: The Apprentice Mage 1865–1914*, p. 382.

12. *The Last September* (1929; Penguin ed., 1942), p. 34.

13. *Synge and Anglo-Irish Literature* (Cork, 1931), Chapter 1, for the general argument; the reference to 'insolence' is on p. 26.

14. *United Irishman*, 24 October 1903; reprinted in John P. Frayne and Colton Johnson (eds.), *Uncollected Prose by W. B. Yeats* (2 vols., London, 1975), vol. 2, pp. 386–8.

15. *Apprentice Mage*, pp. 409–11.

16. ibid., p. 410.

17. A letter of 19 December 1921, Robert W. Woodruff Library, Emory University.

18. 8 November 1923; reported in *Irish Times*, 9 November 1923.

19. 14 June 1924, private collection.

20. *Catholic Bulletin*, vol. xiv, no. 9 (September 1924), pp. 746–7.

21. ibid., no. 10 (October 1924), pp. 836–7.

22. Daniel J. Murphy (ed.), *Lady Gregory's Journals* (2 vols., Gerrards Cross, 1978), vol. 1, p. 593.

23. Quoted ibid., p. 596. For a fuller quotation from this letter, see below, p. 193.

24. G. M. Harper and W. K. Hood (eds.), *A Critical Edition of W. B. Yeats's A Vision (1925)* (London, 1978), p. xi.

25. *Dial*, February 1926; reprinted in *Uncollected Prose*, vol. 2, p. 461.

26. 'The Irish Censorship', *Spectator*, 29 September 1928; reprinted in ibid., p. 480.

27. 13 November 1928, Beinecke Rare Book and MS Library, Yale University.

28. Elizabeth Butler Cullingford, *Gender and History in Yeats's Love Poetry* (Cambridge, 1993), Chapter 12.

29. Corkery, op. cit., pp. 3–4.

30. ibid.

31. This essay, 'The Big House', is discussed in my *Paddy and Mr Punch* (London, 1993), pp. 111–12.
32. 'The Young Writer' in *The Bell*, vol. xvii, no. 7 (October 1951).
33. Printed in *Death of a Chieftain* (London, 1964), pp. 61–87.
34. Postcard to K. H. Reid, Shaw Society of Canada, Toronto.

7 Square-built Power and Fiery Shorthand: Yeats, Carleton and the Irish Nineteenth Century

1. John Kelly and Eric Domville (eds.), *The Collected Letters of W. B. Yeats. Vol. 1: 1865–1895* (Oxford, 1986), p. 199.
2. ibid., pp. 171, 174–5, for Russell; pp. 205–7, for the *Nation's* attack.
3. See my *W. B. Yeats: A Life. Vol. 1: The Apprentice Mage 1865–1914*, p. 43.
4. ibid., pp. 97–8.
5. J. P. Frayne (ed.), *Uncollected Prose of W. B. Yeats* (2 vols., London, 1970), vol. 1, p. 395.
6. Robert Welch and Bruce Stewart (eds.), *The Oxford Companion to Irish Literature* (Oxford, 1996), p. 81.
7. *Stories from Carleton* (London, n.d., but 1889), p. xi.
8. In the *Observer*; see *Uncollected Prose*, vol. 1, pp. 141ff. He had the grace to include it with another book, O'Donoghue's edition of 'The Red-headed Man's Wife'.
9. ibid., p. 167, and *Collected Letters*, vol. 1, pp. 205–7.
10. *Stories from Carleton*, p. xvii.
11. *Uncollected Prose*, vol. 1, p. 364.
12. Two exceptions are Conor Cruise O'Brien and Vivian Mercier.
13. E. H. Mikhail, *W. B. Yeats: Interviews and Recollections* (2 vols., London, 1977), vol. 2, p. 300.
14. Introduction to *Sweeney Astray* (London, 1983).
15. *Essays and Introductions* (London, 1961), pp. 312–13.
16. *Apprentice Mage*, p. 524.
17. *New Ireland*, 17 July 1915, quoted in J. M. Hone, *W. B. Yeats: The Poet in Contemporary Ireland* (Dublin, n.d., but 1916), p. 41.
18. *Apprentice Mage*, p. 460.
19. W. B. Yeats, *Letters to the New Island: A New Edition*, George Bornstein and Hugh Witemayer (eds.) (London, 1989), p. xviii.
20. Allan Wade, *A Bibliography of the Writings of W. B. Yeats* (London, 1958), p. 220.

8 Stopping the Hunt: Trollope and
the Memory of Ireland

1. Details of Trollope's life in Ireland will be found in Victoria Glendinning, *Trollope* (London, 1992), Chapters 6–10; N. John Hall, *Trollope: A Biography* (Oxford, 1991), Chapters 8–11; and R. H. Super, *Trollope and the Post Office* (Ann Arbor, Mich., 1981).

2. See John Sutherland, 'Trollopiad', *London Review of Books*, 9 January 1992.

3. *An Autobiography* (London, 1883; references are to the 1946 edition), p. 77.

4. ibid., p. 68.

5. Andrew Sanders, *Anthony Trollope* (Plymouth, 1998), p. 10. For Freemasonry, see Derek Hawes, 'Was Trollope a Freemason?', *Trollopiana*, no. 47 (November 1999), pp. 14–22. This shows that he certainly was – in Ireland, if not actively in England, which carries its own significance.

6. These articles have been reprinted in the *Princeton University Library Chronicle*, vol. 26 (1964–5), pp. 71–101, edited by Helen Garlinghouse King, and are discussed in Glendinning, op. cit., pp. 184ff.

7. On the idealizing of social relations during the Famine in *Castle Richmond*, see Melissa Fegan's penetrating chapter in her Oxford D.Phil thesis, 'The Impact of the Famine in Literature 1845–1919' (1999).

8. Introduction to Oxford World's Classics edition (1989), pp. xii–xiii.

9. Glendinning, op. cit., pp. 385ff.

10. Owen Dudley Edwards, 'Anthony Trollope: The Irish Writer', *Nineteenth-Century Fiction*, vol. 38, no. 1 (1983–4), pp. 1–42, remains the most intensive treatment. There is also much of insight in Patrick Lonergan's M.A. thesis, 'The Representation of Phineas Finn in Anthony Trollope's Palliser Novels' (University College, Dublin, 1998).

11. *An Autobiography*, pp. 276–7.

12. *The Landleaguers* (Oxford World's Classics edition, 1993), p. 52.

13. ibid., pp. 256–7.

14. Introduction to ibid., p. xix.

15. Information from Dr Mary-Lou Legg.

16. *Ireland under the Land League* (London, 1892). Trollope's last Irish journeys are described in Glendinning, op. cit., pp. 494–6, and Hall, op. cit., pp. 502–4; for his contacts there, see N. John Hall, *The Letters of Anthony Trollope. Vol. 2: 1871–1882* (Stanford, Calif., 1983), pp. 962–7.

17. *The Landleaguers*, p. 270.

18. See L. P. Curtis, 'Stopping the Hunt' in C. H. E. Philpin (ed.), *Nationalism and Popular Protest in Ireland* (Cambridge, 1987), pp. 349–402.

19. *The Landleaguers*, pp. 255–6.

20. See my *Paddy and Mr Punch* (London, 1993), p. 292.

21. *The Landleaguers*, p. 101.

22. ibid., pp. 161–2.

23. A syndrome discussed in 'Marginal Men and Micks on the Make', *Paddy and Mr Punch*, pp. 281–305.

24. See Hall, *Trollope*, pp. 507–8.

9 Prints on the Scene: Elizabeth Bowen and the Landscape of Childhood

1. This curiosity was produced by the Aubane Historical Society, with an address in Millstreet, County Cork; the membership is allegedly in single figures. The same points were reiterated in the introduction to another of the Society's publications: Jack Lane and Brendan Clifford, *Elizabeth Bowen: 'Notes on Eire': Espionage Reports to Winston Churchill 1940–1942* (1999).

2. For a detailed discussion of this, see 'The Irishness of Elizabeth Bowen' in my *Paddy and Mr Punch* (London, 1993), pp. 102–21.

3. 'Places' in 'Pictures and Conversations', reprinted in Hermione Lee (ed.), *The Mulberry Tree: Writings of Elizabeth Bowen* (London, 1986), p. 282.

4. *Bowen's Court* (1942; references are to the 1984 Virago edition, published with *Seven Winters* and introduced by Hermione Lee), p. 453.

5. ibid., p. 248.

6. ibid., p. 278. For whingeing, see p. 187.

7. ibid., p. 452.

8. 'The Bend Back', reprinted in *The Mulberry Tree*, pp. 57–8.

9. *Bowen's Court*, p. 132.

10. 'The Big House', reprinted in *The Mulberry Tree*, pp. 25–30.

11. *Bowen's Court*, p. 78.

12. *The Mulberry Tree*, p. 28.

13. *Bowen's Court*, p. 451.

14. Preface to *Stories by Elizabeth Bowen* (London, 1959), reprinted in *The Mulberry Tree*, p. 128.

15. 'Autobiography', written for *Saturday Review of Literature* and reprinted in *Seven Winters and Afterthoughts* (New York, 1962), pp. 71–2.

16. 'Places' in 'Pictures and Conversations', reprinted in *The Mulberry Tree*, pp. 282–3.

17. *Seven Winters and Afterthoughts*, p. vii.

18. Reprinted in *The Mulberry Tree*, p. 149.

19. *Bowen's Court*, p. 444.

20. *Seven Winters*, p. 32.

21. There were scandals around tenement collapses in 1902, 1909 and 1911: see J. V. O'Brien, *Dear Dirty Dublin: A City in Distress 1899–1916* (London, 1982), p. 149.

22. See above, p. 3.

23. 'Autumn Journal', *Collected Poems*, E. R. Dodds (ed.) (London, 1960), p. 133.

24. *Bowen's Court*, pp. 433–4: 'throwing in what we have' is an image also used in 'The Big House'.

25. *Seven Winters and Afterthoughts*, p. 71.

26. *Seven Winters*, pp. 13–14.

27. ibid., p. 71.

28. *Bowen's Court*, p. 20.

29. Hermione Lee, *Reading in Bed: An Inaugural Lecture Delivered before the University of Oxford on 21 October 1999* (Oxford, 2000), pp. 7–10.

30. 'Pictures and Conversations', reprinted in *The Mulberry Tree*, p. 24.

31. Introduction to *The Demon Lover* (London, 1945).

32. *Seven Winters*, p. 52.

33. Reprinted in *The Mulberry Tree*, p. 111.

10 Selling Irish Childhoods: Frank McCourt and Gerry Adams

1. Mairead Dooley, 'The Crossover Apron' in *Thoughtlines: An Anthology of Research*, vol. 4 (2000).

2. References are to the Touchstone edition (New York, 1998).

3. New York, 1998.

4. *Angela's Ashes*, p. 11.

5. ibid., p. 92.

6. ibid., p. 177.

7. ibid., p. 125.

8. References are to the Flamingo edition (London, 1999).

9. *A Monk Swimming* (New York, 1998), p. 6.

10. ibid., pp. 168, 77, 80 – a small sample.

11. ibid., p. 160.

12. 15 October 1998; the following quotations also come from this report.

13. *A Monk Swimming*, p. 51.

14. Dingle, County Kerry, and New York, 1996.

15. See D. Sharrock and M. Davenport, *Man of War, Man of Peace: The Unauthorized Biography of Gerry Adams* (London, 1997).

16. 'Me and My Motor: Gerry Adams', *Guardian*, 13 December 1999.

17. *Before the Dawn*, p. 73.

18. ibid., p. 126.

19. Mark Urban, *Big Boys' Rules: The Struggle against the IRA* (London, 1992), pp. 26, 131; Patrick Bishop and Eamonn Mallie, *The Provisional IRA* (London, 1987), p. 267; J. Bowyer Bell, *The Irish Troubles: A Generation of Violence* (Dublin, 1993), pp. 357, 375, 538, etc.

20. *Before the Dawn*, p. 83.

21. ibid., pp. 100, 147.

22. *Big Boys' Rules*, p. 131; also Bowyer Bell, op. cit., p. 538.

23. *Before the Dawn*, pp. 205–6, 252.

24. *An Poblacht/Republican News*, 26 June 1979.

25. *Before the Dawn*, p. 317.

26. 'Shane', first published in *The Street*, reprinted in *Selected Writings* (Dingle, 1994), pp. 126–9.

27. ibid., p. 211.

28. *Irish News*, 13 February 1997.

29. *Selected Writings*, p. 116.

30. Fionnuala O'Connor, *In Search of a State: Catholics in Northern Ireland* (Belfast, 1993), pp. 246–7.

31. See R. W. Johnson, 'Why There is No Easy Way to Dispose of Painful History', *London Review of Books*, 14 October 1999 – an extended review essay on Anthea Jeffrey's *The Truth about the Truth Commission* (South Africa Institute of Race Relations, 1999).

32. See above, pp. 73–4.

11 The Salamander and the Slap: Hubert Butler and His Century

1. *Grandmother and Wolfe Tone* (Dublin, 1990), pp. 46–7. References to Butler's essays will be given to the volume in which they first appeared: but it should be noted that most of them also appear in two volumes of selections: *The Sub-Prefect Should Have Held His Tongue*, R. F. Foster (ed.) (London, 1990) and *Hubert Butler: Independent Spirit*, Elisabeth Sifton (ed.) (New York, 1996).

2. *Escape from the Anthill* (Mullingar, 1985), p. 1.

3. First published in the *Kilkenny Magazine*, 1962, reprinted as the title essay of *Grandmother and Wolfe Tone*, pp. 138–48.

4. *In The Land of Nod* (Dublin, 1996), pp. 235–6.

5. *Escape from the Anthill*, pp. 114–21.

6. *In the Land of Nod*, p. 233.

7. *Escape from the Anthill*, pp. 75–87, and *Grandmother and Wolfe Tone*, pp. 17–27.

8. See 'Illegitimate Aspirations', *Fortnight*, July–August 1991.

9. Donald R. Pearce (ed.), *The Senate Speeches of W. B. Yeats* (London, 1961), p. 95.

10. Chris Agee, 'Poteen in a Brandy-cask: The Ethical Imagination of Hubert Butler', *Yale Review* (Spring 1998), pp. 129–42.

11. See 'Divided Loyalties' in *Escape from the Anthill*, p. 98.

12. *The Children of Drancy* (Mullingar, 1988), pp. 211–21.

13. 'The County Libraries: Sex, Religion and Censorship', *Grandmother and Wolfe Tone*, pp. 50–63.

14. See above, pp. 105–6.

15. For this and other details, see Daniel J. Murphy (ed.), *Lady Gregory's Journals* (2 vols., Gerrards Cross, 1978), vol. 1, pp. 563–6. Gregory added tartly: 'Not very wise linking himself to three heretics, and they were not paid secretaries of an educational Board.'

16. *The Children of Drancy*, pp. 197–207.

17. ibid. The case for Yeats and his like as fathers of Auschwitz has been put even more crudely by John Carey in *The Intellectuals and the Masses* (London, 1992), pp. 13–15.

18. 'The Barriers' in *Grandmother and Wolfe Tone*, pp. 32–3.

19. See 'The Sub-Prefect Should Have Held His Tongue' and appendices in *Escape from the Anthill*.

20. Angela Bourke, *The Burning of Bridget Cleary* (London, 1998).

21. 'Editing the Master', a paper delivered at the Hubert Butler Centenary Symposium in Kilkenny, on 20 October 2000; my thanks to Antony Farrell for showing me the text and allowing me to quote from it.

22. For a report, see *Irish Times*, 24 October 2000, and Geoffrey Wheatcroft's 'Letter from Kilkenny', *The Times Literary Supplement*, 29 December 2000.

23. *Grandmother and Wolfe Tone*, p. 46.

24. *Escape from the Anthill*, pp. 311–12.

25. ibid., pp. 332–3.

26. This reflection about the march in the snow might be read against what he writes about the value of political demonstrations in 'Lament for Archaeol-

ogy', *Escape from the Anthill*, pp. 235–6. I subsequently tried to quote it at length in the review of *Escape to the Anthill* that I submitted to the *TLS*, a review that was cut down from immense length to a manageable quarter-page. But I had such a row with the editor that he took the book on holiday with him to see what the fuss was about – and was converted at once. Butler's next collection had the lead review, from John Bayley. A handsome acknowledgement, but no more than his due.

27. *Escape from the Anthill*, p. 338.

28. A letter to the author of 22 January 1990.

29. *Escape from the Anthill*, pp. 209–10.

30. *Nations and Nationalism since 1780: Programme, Myth, Reality* (Cambridge, 1990), pp. 182–3.

31. *Grandmother and Wolfe Tone*, pp. 17–18.

32. ibid., p. 140.

33. ibid., p. 142.

34. Quoted by Paul Arthur in *Political Quarterly*, vol. 79 (2000), p. 128.

35. *Grandmother and Wolfe Tone*, pp. 33–4.

36. ibid., p. 65.

37. ibid., pp. 67–8.

12 Remembering 1798

1. The claim that he tried to disown it is often made but, according to the author himself, is without foundation: see J. Kells Ingram, *Sonnets and Other Poems* (London, 1900), p. 6.

2. Patrick H. Hutton, *History as an Art of Memory* (Hanover, NH, 1993).

3. The best summation at the commemorative literature is Ian McBride, 'Reclaiming the Rebellion: 1798 in 1998', *Irish Historical Studies*, vol. xxxi, no. 123 (May 1999).

4. *The Irish* (Harmondsworth, 1947), p. 99.

5. PRO HO 100/82/160, quoted as Appendix D to Liam Kelly, *A Flame Now Quenched: Rebels and Frenchmen in Leitrim 1793–1798* (Dublin, 1998), p. 141. It seems likely that this influenced Robert Emmet's much more celebrated speech from the dock four years later.

6. Ian McBride, *Scripture Politics: Ulster Presbyterians and Irish Radicalism in Late Eighteenth-century Ireland* (Oxford, 1998), p. 231.

7. To T. P. O'Connor's *M.A.P.*, reprinted in *Sixteen Self Sketches* (London, 1949), p. 17.

8. McBride, *Scripture Politics*, p. 168.

9. See Louis Cullen's hostile remarks in 'The Internal Politics of the United Irishmen' and 'The Political Structure of the Defenders' in David Dickson, Daire Keogh and Kevin Whelan (eds.), *The United Irishmen: Republicanism, Radicalism and Rebellion* (Dublin, 1993); but see also Ian McBride's essay 'William Drennan and the Dissenting Tradition' in ibid., and the same author's extended consideration of Drennan's views in *Scripture Politics*. Perhaps a further shift in Drennan's favour may be seen in A. T. Q. Stewart, *A Deeper Silence: The Hidden Origins of the United Irishmen* (London, 1993) and Adrian Rice, 'No Lithe Interloper', *Causeway*, vol. i, no. 1 (September 1993).

10. *Partners in Revolution: The United Irishmen and France* (London, 1982); *Wolfe Tone: Prophet of Irish Independence* (London, 1989).

11. Pakenham defined what he found as a complete run of Irish newspapers, the confidential letters of protagonists such as Pitt, Camden, George III, Dundas and Wycombe, and the copious reports of Edward Cooke, whereas for the rebel side he had to rely on spy reports, early-nineteenth-century biographies, folk songs and local tradition. For an up-to-date analysis, see Deirdre Lindsay, 'The Rebellion Papers', *History Ireland*, vol. vi, no. 2 (Summer 1998), pp. 18–22.

12. Quoted and discussed in Anna Kinsella, 'The Nineteenth-century Interpretation of 1798', M.Litt. thesis (University of Dublin, 1992), p. 5. Madden was taken to task by the local historian Luke Cullen, who contradicted these statements, but they generally held the field – repeated, with careful argument, by Charles Dickson in *The Wexford Rising in 1798: Its Causes and Its Course* (Tralee, n.d., but 1953).

13. See Thomas Graham, 'Dublin in 1798: The Key to the Planned Insurrection' in Daire Keogh and Nicholas Furlong (eds.), *The Mighty Wave: The 1798 Rebellion in Wexford* (Dublin, 1996), pp. 65–78. The case there presented for the existence of a logical plan is more convincing than the rather excited assertion that the outcome was anything but a fiasco.

14. See Liam Kelly, op. cit., Chapter 2.

15. See Kinsella, op. cit., pp. 9ff, for the profuse references to '98 in the *Irish People* during the early 1860s. John O'Leary (the editor) later said that the inspiration of Wolfe Tone, relayed through Thomas Davis, did more to inspire the Fenian movement than 'famine or failure': *Recollections of Fenians and Fenianism* (London, 1896), p. 78.

16. Patrick F. Kavanagh, *A Popular History of the Insurrection of 1798* (Dublin 1870); A. M. Sullivan, *The Story of Ireland* (1867 and countless reprints); Patrick Pearse, 'Ghosts' in *Political Speeches and Writings* (Dublin, 1922), pp. 223–55.

17. See L. M. Cullen, *The Emergence of Modern Ireland 1600–1900* (London,

1981), pp. 210–33; 'The 1798 Rebellion in Its Eighteenth-century Context' in Patrick J. Corish (ed.), *Radicals, Rebels and Establishments* (Belfast, 1985), pp. 91–113; 'The 1798 Rebellion in Wexford' in Kevin Whelan and William Nolan (eds.), *Wexford: History and Society* (Dublin, 1987), pp. 248–95. Also see Kevin Whelan, 'Politicization in County Wexford and the Origins of the 1798 Rebellion' in Hugh Gough and David Dickson (eds.), *Ireland and the French Revolution* (Dublin, 1990).

18. Kevin Whelan, *The Tree of Liberty: Radicalism, Catholicism and the Construction of Irish Identity 1760–1830* (Cork, 1996), p. 159. But this idea was examined and scouted by Charles Dickson over forty years ago: *The Wexford Rising*, pp. 22, 180–81.

19. For how the Pakenham interpretation was received in Wexford, see Colm Tóibín, 'New Ways of Killing Your Father', *London Review of Books*, 18 November 1993.

20. Nancy Curtin, *The United Irishmen: Popular Politics in Ulster and Dublin 1791–1798* (Oxford, 1994). Her conclusion also chimes with McBride's in *Scripture Politics*.

21. *Theobald Wolfe Tone, Colonial Outside: An Analysis of His Political Philosophy* (Cork, 1982).

22. Kevin Whelan, 'The Republic in the Village: The United Irishmen, the Enlightenment and Popular Culture' in *Tree of Liberty*, pp. 59–68.

23. Arthur O'Connor, *The State of Ireland*, James Livesey (ed.) (Dublin, 1998).

24. Thus Kevin Whelan, *Tree of Liberty*, p. 95, stresses the distance of this group from popular culture; elsewhere he identifies the spread of the movement as intimately linked to pastimes such as hurling, *meitheal* and Maying. For a more detailed consideration of Whelan and 'popular culture', see T. C. Barnard, 'The Gentrification of Eighteenth-century Ireland', *Eighteenth-Century Ireland*, vol. 12 (1997), pp. 137–55.

25. Keogh and Furlong, op. cit., p. 10.

26. Alfred Webb to J. F. X. O'Brien, 21 September 1898 and 21 July 1898, National Library of Ireland, MS 13, 431(5).

27. *Personal Sketches*, vol. 1, p. 205, quoted in Dickson, *Wexford Rising*, pp. 215–16.

28. Quoted in J. Turpin, '1798, 1898 and the Political Implications of Sheppard's Monuments', *History Ireland*, vol. vi, no. 2 (Summer 1998), p. 45.

29. Revd Alexander Donovan, *The Irish Rebellion of 1898: A Chapter in Future History, from the Supplement to the Imperial History of England, AD 1900* (Dublin, 1893). Though Britain's Continental opponents are Russia and France, the conditions anticipated strangely predict Easter 1916. Irish MPs

set up a provisional assembly and government, civil war breaks out with 'loyal Volunteers' in Ulster, parts of Dublin are burned by the rebels. However, after General Wolseley brings pacification the insurrectionary leaders are exiled, while incendiary newspaper editors are hanged. 'McC—, who had been chosen President of the Irish republic because he had some shred of character, and was almost an imbecile, was placed in a lunatic asylum, where he amuses himself by writing novels.'

30. Senia Paseta, '1798 in 1898: The Politics of Commemoration' in *Irish Review*, no. 22 (Summer 1998), pp. 46–53; T. J. O'Keefe, 'The 1898 Efforts to Celebrate the United Irishmen: The '98 Centennial', *Éire-Ireland*, vol. xxiii (1988), pp. 51–73, and '"Who fears to speak of '98?" The Rhetoric and Rituals of the United Irishmen Centennial 1898', ibid., vol. xxviii (1992), pp. 67–91; Kinsella, op. cit., *passim*; L. Ó Broin, *Revolutionary Underground: The Story of the Irish Republican Brotherhood 1858–1924* (Dublin, 1976); Warwick Gould, John Kelly and Deirdre Toomey (eds.), *The Collected Letters of W. B. Yeats. Vol. 2: 1896–1900* (Oxford, 1997), pp. 695–707.

31. See my *W. B. Yeats: A Life. Vol. 1: The Apprentice Mage 1865–1914* (Oxford, 1997), pp. 179–97.

32. Ian McBride, 'Memory and Forgetting: Ulster Presbyterians and 1798' in *The 1798 Rebellion*, T. Bartlett, D. Keogh and K. Whelan (eds.) (Dublin, forthcoming); and O'Keefe, 'Rhetoric and Rituals', pp. 84ff.

33. News cutting in O'Leary Collection, UCD/SA. 'The remainder of the remarks did not reach the reporters,' which was a pity. He was speaking in response to Lord Mayor Tallon, a Parnellite who had surprisingly declared that Irishmen were best governed under English laws.

34. TS of 'Fuath na Gall' handout to members of the Paris Young Ireland Society, O'Leary Collection, UCD/SA.

35. Yeats to Gregory, 3 October 1897, *Collected Letters*, vol. 2, p. 135; *Tuam Herald*, 12 March 1898.

36. Fully described in *Irish Daily Independent*, 15 August 1898, and *Daily Express* (Dublin), 16 August 1898.

37. Cutting from *Workers' Republic* in O'Leary Collection, UCD/SA. He also claimed Mitchel and Tone were both direct ancestors of his own Irish Republican Socialist Party, rather than of any of the organizations represented on the platforms.

38. O'Keefe, 'Rhetoric and Rituals', p. 75. However, the intervention of the Spanish-American War short-circuited much planned transatlantic activity.

39. This detour was $75 extra. Booklet in O'Leary Collection, UCD/SA.

40. Whelan, p. 172.

41. See O'Keefe, '1898 Efforts', pp. 68ff.

42. Letter of 22 September 1897 to M. J. Quinn, O'Leary Collection, UCD/SA.

43. By the end of 1898 only £561 of the projected £14,000 had been found, most of it by Maud Gonne: see Ó Broin, op. cit., p. 91.

44. Turpin, '1798, 1898', p. 46.

45. 'Rhetoric and Rituals', pp. 73ff.

46. G. A. Lyons, *Some Recollections of Griffith and His Times* (Dublin, 1923).

47. Since 1995 the annual estimates of the Taoiseach's department have included a budget for commemorative programmes. My thanks to Mary Daly for this and other points.

48. James Livesey's edition of Arthur O'Connor, mentioned above, might also be instanced, and Tom Bartlett's collection of Wolfe Tone's autobiographical writings – though this is, regrettably, an assemblage rather than, as described, an 'edition'.

49. Kevin Whelan in the *Irish Times*, 24 March 1998.

50. ibid.

51. Cf. Brian Cleary in Keogh and Furlong, op. cit., p. 79: 'The nation's first republic was established . . . governed by a Committee or Directory of four Catholics and four Protestants.'

52. Daniel Gahan, *The People's Rising: Wexford 1798* (Dublin, 1995), p. 88; Tom Dunne, '1798: Memory, History, Commemoration' in *Journal of the Wexford Historical Society*, no. 16 (1996–7), pp. 115–16.

53. Brian Cleary in *Irish Times*, 28 January 1998.

54. *Irish Times*, 24 March 1998.

55. Emblematized by the handout in Wicklow Gaol claiming that 6 million died in the Famine: a significant confusion with the statistics of the Holocaust.

56. See for instance Kevin Whelan's views in Patrick O'Flanagan, Paul Ferguson and Kevin Whelan (eds.), *Rural Ireland 1600–1900: Modernization and Change* (Cork, 1987), pp. 62–85.

57. Tom Dunne, 'The Politics of Atrocity: Scullabogue, Representation and Reality', forthcoming; also article in *Irish Times*, 6 January 1998, and letters in *Irish Times*, 1 April, 15 April, 20 April, 24 April, 4 May 1998.

58. For 'Scullaboguery', see Brian Cleary in *Irish Times*, 23 March 1998.

59. Speech by Síle de Valera at the opening of the 1798 Exhibition in the National Museum, Collins Barracks, 25 May 1998. My thanks to Mary Daly for these references.

60. See Whelan, *Tree of Liberty*, pp. 134ff; P. Collins in *Irish Times*, 24 February 1998; and Kevin Whelan, 'The Origins of the Orange Order', *Bullán*, vol. 2, no. 2 (Winter/Spring 1996). For a countering view, McBride, 'Reclaiming the Rebellion', pp. 406–9.

61. 'Wexford's *Comóradh '98*: Politics, Heritage and History', *History Ireland*, vol. vi, no. 2 (Summer 1998), p. 53.

62. Keogh and Furlong, op. cit., p. 96.

63. O'Connor, op. cit., p. 24.

64. Quoted McBride, 'Memory and Forgetting'.

65. McBride, *Scripture Politics*, pp. 186–94; Curtin, op. cit., *passim*. Also see Allan T. Blackstock, '"A Dangerous Species of Ally": Orangeism and the Irish Yeomanry' in *Irish Historical Studies*, vol. xxx, no. 119 (May 1997), pp. 393–405.

66. Frank Wright, *Two Lands on One Soil: Ulster Politics before Home Rule* (Dublin, 1996), p. 42.

67. See McBride, 'Memory and Forgetting', for how 'New Light' rebels were identified with the '98 tradition as aberrations in the true Presbyterian tradition.

68. Neilson quote in Whelan, *Tree of Liberty*, p. 163; Dickson in epigraph to McBride, *Scripture Politics*.

69. O'Connor, op. cit., p. 6.

70. McBride, 'Memory and Forgetting'.

71. For attempts to play down informers, see Tom Bartlett, 'Informers, Informants and Information: The Secret History of the 1790s', *History Ireland*, vol. vi, no. 2 (Summer 1998), pp. 23–6, which does not really address the significance of their prevalence. Oliver Knox, *Rebels and Informers: Stirrings of Irish Independence* (London, 1997), though racy and written for a popular audience, contains much of insight.

72. See Henry Joy in McBride, 'Memory and Forgetting'.

73. 'Keeping Up the Flame: General Joseph Holt' in *History Ireland*, vol. vi, no. 2 (Summer 1998), p. 41.

74. Whelan, *Tree of Liberty*, p. 168.

75. *Escape from the Anthill* (Mullingar, 1985), p. 7.

Index

'Peter's Window' 193, 200–203,
  210
'Portrait of a Minority' 190
as a Protestant 190–91, 206–10
on religion 196
reputation 197, 199
'Riga Strand in 1930' 193
in St Petersburg 193, 200–202
on Shaw 189
*The Sub-Prefect Should Have
  Held His Tongue* 240n42,
  259n1
as translator 193
in Vienna 194
in Zagreb 193, 194
Butt, Isaac 48, 49, 180
Byrne, Miles 215, 217, 226, 232–3

Carbery, Mary:
  The Farm by Lough Gar 164
Carey, John:
  The Intellectuals and the Masses
  260n17
Carleton, William 98, 110, 111,
  132
  Autobiography 117
  The Black Prophet 118, 119, 120
  as a Catholic 113, 116, 117, 118
  Fardorougha the Miser 118, 120
  'The Hedge School' 117
  'The Lough Derg Pilgrim' 116,
    125
  'The Poor Scholar' 117, 119, 124
  as a Protestant 117–18, 119
  'Shane Fadh's Wedding' 117
  *Traits and Stories of the Irish
    Peasantry* 118, 119, 120
  'Tubber Derg; or, the Red Well'
    117, 119
  Valentine M'Clutchy 118, 124

'Wildgoose Lodge' 117
Yeats and 113–26
Carlyle, Thomas 4, 11
Carson, Edward 66
Cashel Heritage Society 29
Catholic Bulletin 26, 41–2, 43, 48,
  86, 87, 88, 90, 91–2, 93, 105,
  106
Catholic Committee 32
Catholic Truth Society 103
Catholic writers 90
  see also individual writers
Catholicism 7, 9, 13, 14, 15, 25–6,
  47–8, 49, 52, 86, 101, 125,
  144, 160, 196, 229–32
  Carleton as a Catholic 113, 116
  nationalism and 115
  Yeats and Catholicism 115
Cavafy, Constantine P. 26, 96, 100
  'Waiting for the Barbarians' 26
Cavendish, Lord Frederick 138
Celticism concept xv, xviii, 99
  see also folk lore
Celtword Mythology Centre,
  Tramore 33
censorship:
  Yeats on 101–2, 103–9
Chesney, George
  The Battle of Dorking 220
Chesterton, Gilbert Keith 62
Childers, Erskine 48, 234
childhood 164
  Adams on 165, 174–86
  Bowen on 148–63, 164
  Frank McCourt on 165–70, 172–4
Christian Brothers 9, 177, 238n25
Churchill, Lord Randolph 13
Cipriani, Amilcari 221
Clarke, Austin 85, 87
Cleary, Brian 230, 265n51